WE SAW LINCOLN SHOT

ONE HUNDRED EYEWITNESS ACCOUNTS

WE SAW LINCOLN SHOT

ONE HUNDRED EYEWITNESS ACCOUNTS

EDITED BY

TIMOTHY S. GOOD

UNIVERSITY PRESS OF MISSISSIPPI

JACKSON

Copyright 1995 by the University Press of Mississippi
All rights reserved
Manufactured in the United States of America

98 97 96 95   4 3 2 1

The paper in this book meets the guidelines for permanence
and durability of the Committee on Production Guidelines for
Book Longevity of the Council on Library Resources.

Library of Congress Cataloging-in-Publication Data

We saw Lincoln shot : one hundred eyewitness accounts / edited by
Timothy S. Good.
    p.   cm.
Includes bibliographical references.
ISBN 0-87805-778-1 (alk. paper). — ISBN 0-87805-779-X (pbk. :
alk. paper)
    1. Lincoln, Abraham, 1809–1865—Assassination.   I. Good,
Timothy S. (Timothy Sean)
E457.5.W4   1995
973.7'092—dc20   95-11094
                                                           CIP

British Library Cataloging-in-Publication data available

CONTENTS

W. H. Roberts • Henry W. Mason • Daniel H. Veader • George C. Maynard • Andrew Jackson Huntoon • Helen Truman • Annie P. Wright • John Davenport • W. H. Roberts • Edward Holy • Caleb Milligan • Charles Francis Byrne • W. J. Ferguson • John Lindsey • Mrs. Nelson Todd • Mrs. Nelson Todd • Thomas Sherman • Charles L. Willis • Jacob Soles • Jacob J. Soles • Samuel R. Ward • Kitty Brink • William H. Fallon • Joseph H. Hazelton • David Dorn • D. J. Richards • Samuel J. Seymour

PREFACE

Many books have been written about the assassination of Abraham Lincoln, but few have focused on the actual event of the assassination. Most writers have been attracted to the conspiracy that preceded the assassination or to the subsequent trial of the conspirators. Furthermore, among the books that have discussed the actual event in detail, such as Jim Bishop's *Day Lincoln Was Shot* (1955), few cite their sources and thus lack proper historical documentation. Other studies that discuss the actual assassination that are well documented, namely, George Bryan's *Great American Myth* (1940) and W. Emerson Reck's *A. Lincoln: His Last Twenty-Four Hours* (1987), do not make full use of eyewitness accounts.

Approximately one thousand patrons attended Ford's Theatre on the evening of April 14, 1865. I have collected one hundred eyewitness accounts of the event found in numerous depositories, including Ford's Theatre, the National Archives, the Library of Congress, the Lincoln Museum, and the Illinois State Historical Library, the Chicago Historical Society, the Clements Library at the University of Michigan, the State Historical Library of Wisconsin, and the Princeton University Archives. The accounts range from personal letters and diary entries to sworn legal testimony and also include many newspaper and magazine articles. The earliest ones were recorded immediately following the assassination in the boardinghouse where Lincoln lay dying; the most recent one is from the 1954 obituary of the last surviving witness. I have presented the accounts in chronological order, which shows some consensus in the earliest accounts that gradually deteriorates as time progresses.

Although other accounts exist, the one hundred presented in this book represent those I have deemed the most informative. In assessing the reliability of the various eyewitnesses, I have been guided by the work of Elizabeth Loftus, whose studies have shown that human memory recalls events with substantially less accuracy over time, incorporating different details and picturing an event differently each time it is recalled. This is especially true when people recall events they witnessed years or decades before. Thus the accounts of the Lincoln assassination that were recorded in 1865 should be considered more reliable than those recorded decades after the event. Nevertheless, previous writers on the assassination have placed no greater confidence in those accounts recorded in 1865 than those recorded later. As a result, major parts of the mythology concerning the Lincoln assassination are erroneous, and inaccuracies have been perpetuated by writers because they have misused the testimony of many of the eyewitnesses.

Although other accounts do exist, the one hundred accounts presented in this book represent the largest number ever collected in one place. Several eyewitnesses gave more than one account during their lifetimes; in most cases I have included only the earliest one or the one containing the most information. Of the accounts recorded in the twentieth century, I have selected only those that provide substantial information.

To help the reader make sense of the many facts presented in the accounts and to provide background information for the complicated events that occurred simultaneously or in rapid succession on that evening, I have reconstructed from the eyewitnesses' statements an overview of events and my own analysis of the sometimes contradictory statements. In some instances my conclusions differ from the accepted theories. I invite readers to study the eyewitness accounts as I have done and form their own conclusions.

ACKNOWLEDGMENTS

I wish to thank those people who helped me complete this project. Frank Hebblethwaite, former museum curator for Ford's Theatre National Historic Site, first introduced me to the eyewitness account file and provided guidance on numerous occasions. Meredith Berg, history professor of Valparaiso University, time and time again helped with the editing of my undergraduate thesis. Ed Bearss reviewed the text, offered suggestions, and provided encouragement throughout the project. Mike Kaufman, Lincoln assassination expert, in a lecture at Ford's Theatre suggested questioning the existing beliefs about the assassination and provided evidence contradicting the belief that Booth broke his leg in the theater. In addition, Jody Esper, psychology professor at Valparaiso University and eyewitness expert, offered advice on the reliability of eyewitness accounts. Bruce Berner, associate dean of Valparaiso University School of Law, offered advice on the reliability of courtroom testimony. Keith Schoppa, history professor at Valparaiso University, read and commented on my undergraduate thesis. The late Willis Boyd, former history professor at Valparaiso University, allowed me to share my findings with his Civil War history class and also read and commented on my undergraduate thesis. Tom Schwarz, historian at Illinois State Historical Library, freely gave of his time to help find some eyewitness accounts. Bill Hanchett, Lincoln assassination expert, discussed the finer points of the story with me. Ruth Cooke, of Louis A. Warren Lincoln Library, provided numerous eyewitness accounts. Dorothy Wodrich of the Moellering Library staff at Valparaiso University made numerous searches for interlibrary loan requests. Trudie Calvert spent a great deal of time polishing the text. JoAnne Prichard saw this manuscript to publication. Jeff Sandlin first made me believe that this material might be publishable. And finally, my friends in the Park Service and my family have been a great help.

WE SAW LINCOLN SHOT

One Hundred Eyewitness Accounts

THE LINCOLN ASSASSINATION
AN OVERVIEW

THE SETTING

On April 9, 1865, at Appomattox Court House, Virginia, a war that had cost the nation six hundred thousand American lives came to an end. Yet some Confederates were unwilling to accept the loss of their cause, as would be vividly displayed at Ford's Theatre just five days later. Abraham Lincoln, who had recently advised a policy of "malice toward none, charity for all," would be assassinated on Good Friday, April 14, 1865, four years to the day that the Civil War had begun with the lowering of the Stars and Stripes over Fort Sumter.

"Some people find me wrong to attend the theatre, but it serves me well to have a good laugh with a crowd of people," Lincoln once commented.[1] Lincoln expected to enjoy a relaxing evening on April 14. According to court testimony provided by the Ford brothers a month after the assassination, a messenger arrived from the White House early that day requesting four seats for the evening's performance.[2] These seats were to be reserved for the president, the first lady, General Ulysses S. Grant, and Mrs. Grant. The Fords reserved the box the Lincolns had used in the past. These seats—actually the worst in the house from which to view events on stage—were angled toward the audience rather than the stage. The placement was no accident because the Fords wanted their audiences to have a good view of the well-known occupants of the boxes.

Good Friday was not a popular night for theatergoers so the Fords were pleased to be able to embellish their advertisements of the play, *Our*

View from stage of presidential box and general arrangements

American Cousin, with the announcement that President Lincoln and General Grant would be in attendance that night.

One man who came to Ford's Theatre that evening for another reason than to view the play was the twenty-six-year-old actor John Wilkes Booth. Booth, who had operated as a Confederate spy during the later years of the Civil War, had made at least one attempt to kidnap Lincoln. This time his plans called for murder. He gathered his co-conspirators— David Herold, George Atzerodt, and Lewis Powell—to assist in the execution of his plan, which was to assassinate three federal officials that evening: President Lincoln, Vice-President Andrew Johnson, and Secretary of State William Seward. Booth himself took on the most important task, the assassination of Lincoln, while Atzerodt and Powell were assigned to assassinate Johnson and Seward respectively.

While these plans were being laid, the management of Ford's Theatre prepared for its honored guests. In the 1860s Ford's Theatre and Grover Theatre (today the National Theatre) were the capital's premier theaters and thus keen competitors. The Lincolns had attended both theaters during their years in the White House, an act of impartiality that probably intensified the rivalry between the two. To take the greatest advantage of the presence of the Lincolns and the Grants, the Fords had the front of the presidential box decorated with four American flags, two on poles at either side of the box and two draped over the front edge. American flags were in short supply because of postwar celebrations so the Fords decorated the middle column of the box with a blue Treasury Guards flag. Finally, an engraving of George Washington was placed directly below the Treasury Guards flag. The theater was ready; the stage was set.

THE ENTRANCE OF THE PRESIDENT

Many of the events that took place from the moment Ford's Theatre opened its doors on April 14 to the moment Lincoln died are difficult to pinpoint with certainty. The best available evidence suggests that the play began at 8:00 P.M. and that the presidential party, consisting of the Lincolns and the last-minute substitutes for the Grants, Major Henry R. Rathbone and his fiancée, Clara Harris, entered the theater about thirty minutes later.

More than a thousand Washingtonians prepared to attend the theater on 10th Street that evening. They would make their way to Ford's Theatre either by foot or by horse-drawn coach over the capital's unpaved streets, timing their departures to coincide with the raising of the curtain on Act 1.

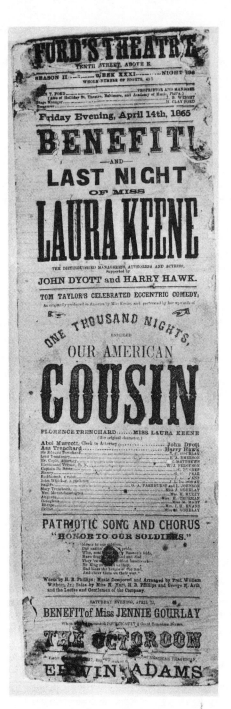

Final playbill prepared for Lincoln's attendance at Ford's Theatre, April 14, 1865

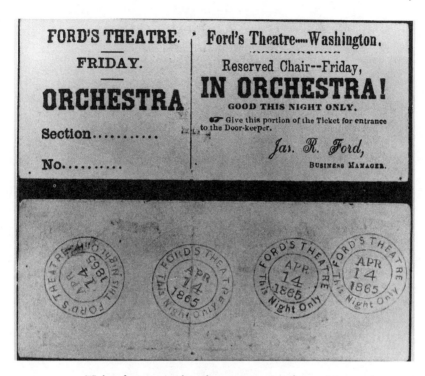

Ticket for reserved orchestra seat, April 14, 1865

Unfortunately, eyewitness accounts, tickets, playbills, and newspapers fail to disclose the curtain time. Of the published works on the assassination, only George S. Bryan's *Great American Myth* states that the performance began at 7:45 P.M., although Bryan provides no documentation for this claim.[3] An assessment of the primary sources shows that this peculiar omission of the curtain time was not exclusive to Ford's Theatre. Curtain times for Grover's Theatre, Ford's rival, were not advertised either. Both the *Evening Star* and the *National Intelligencer*, the most widely read newspapers in Washington during the Civil War, provide only the time at which the doors opened: 7:00 P.M. The city's only theaters that listed their curtain times in advertisements were those that were less prestigious than Ford's or Grover's. Usually, an hour elapsed between the time these less-renowned theaters opened their doors and raised the curtains. If this practice held true for Ford's Theatre as well, we may infer that the play *Our American Cousin* commenced at or about 8:00 P.M.

After the doors opened, people began filing into the gaslit theater and

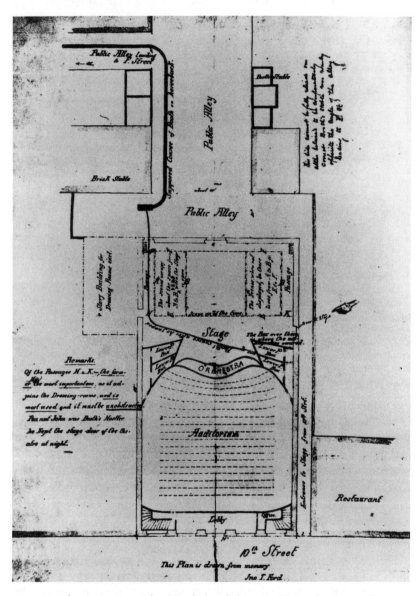

Draftsman's copy of original sketch by Jno. T. Ford, May 1865

scattered themselves among the four sections: the orchestra level, the dress circle, the parquet, and the family circle. The one dollar seats at the orchestra level were, with the exception of the eight boxes, the most expensive as well as the best seats in the house. The seats at the rear of the orchestra level (the parquet section) and the front rows of the first balcony (the dress circle) were considered the next best seats and sold for seventy-five cents. The seats in the rear of the first balcony were known simply as the balcony seats and were priced at fifty cents. The worst seats in the house were in the second balcony, the section known as the family circle, and seats there cost only twenty-five cents. Wicker-bottomed wood frame chairs were used elsewhere, but the family circle had simple wooden benches. The most expensive seats, the eight boxes, were on the flanks of the stage, four to a side. The bottom four boxes were at stage level; the other four boxes were at the first balcony level. The presidential box, as it was called when reserved for the chief executive, was on the level of the first balcony.[4]

As the curtain rose and the gaslights were dimmed, the small orchestra in the pit and the actors on the stage began their performances. But on this night, the guests of honor, who were the main attraction for many of the patrons, were nowhere to be seen. The overwhelming majority of the patrons that night who subsequently recorded their impressions stated that the president arrived rather late, at or about 8:30 P.M.[5] George Bryan and Jim Bishop, who have written extensively about the circumstances surrounding the assassination, agree with this estimate, while the most recent author on the subject, W. Emerson Reck, confesses uncertainty.[6] The reasons for Reck's uncertainty are puzzling in view of the many eyewitnesses who support the 8:30 estimate. Jason S. Knox (April 15, 1865; dates in parentheses are those of the eyewitnesses' accounts) and Spencer H. Bronson (April 17, 1865) both claim that President Lincoln and his guests entered the theater at 8:30.[7] Only two much later recollections, those of Mrs. Nelson Todd (1935) and Joseph H. Hazelton (post-1900), challenge this generally agreed-upon conclusion.[8] Mrs. Todd estimated the time of the presidential entrance at 9:30 P.M., while Hazelton placed Lincoln's arrival at some time during the second act. In light of all this evidence, there seems little reason to believe that the Lincolns and their guests did not enter Ford's Theatre during the first act at about 8:30 P.M.

After the members of the presidential party had left their carriage and entered the theater lobby, John Buckingham (April 14, 1903), the doorkeeper, "passed them within." The presidential party then ascended the main spiral staircase at the north side of the theater and continued along the rear of the balcony.[9] The presidential party was soon noticed and welcomed warmly. The majority of the eighteen accounts that describe the audience's reaction to the Lincolns and their guests recall that the patrons rose to their feet.[10] Many of these accounts describe the greeting as "enthusiastic," even "vociferous," not an unexpected response from a pro-Lincoln and pro-Union audience.[11] The orchestra even joined in the tribute. Major Henry Rathbone (May 1865), who at the time was walking along the rear of the balcony; Harry Hawk (1894), who was acting on the stage; Daniel D. Beekman (1911), who was seated in his second row orchestra seat; and W. H. Taylor (1908), who viewed the events from his dress circle seat, all state that the ensemble began playing "Hail to the Chief" in honor of the president.[12]

The president's reaction to this generous welcome is noted in four accounts. Dr. Leale (1867) wrote that the president responded with a "smile and a bow," although he appeared "expressively mournful and sad."[13] Henry Williams (early twentieth century) and Oliver Gatch (1908) said Lincoln bowed several times to the audience. Hazelton (early twentieth century) recalled him waving to the audience from the front of the box.[14]

From his seat on the same side of the dress circle as the presidential box, Leale (1867) remembered seeing an "usher" accompanying the presidential party as it approached the box.[15] The "usher" opened the door, allowed the presidential party to enter, closed the door, and seated himself nearby. Helen Dubarry (April 16, 1865) noted that two "gentlemen" accompanied the presidential party and added that these "two gentlemen were watchmen in citizens dress who have always accompanied the President since the war commenced."[16] Unfortunately, while these reliable accounts clearly establish the presence of at least one person with the president who was functioning in an official capacity, the identity or position of the individual remains uncertain.

After this interruption, the play resumed while the audience and the four late guests took their seats. Meanwhile, John Wilkes Booth, in the saloon adjacent to Ford's, prepared to make a less conspicuous entrance into the theater.

THE ENTRANCE OF THE ASSASSIN

Historians have long debated two issues in connection with the events that occurred in the interval between the time of Booth's entrance into the theater and Lincoln's assassination: the presence of a presidential "guard" and the identity of that guard if, in fact, there was one. The eyewitness accounts confirm that someone acting in an official capacity was stationed outside the presidential box, although that person's identity cannot be determined.

As the play moved through the first three acts, the audience's attention was naturally drawn to the stage, although some probably were distracted by the honored guests. Few, however, seemed to notice the entrance of a man clad in black. John Buckingham (May 1865), the doorkeeper, immediately recognized the man as John Wilkes Booth. According to Buckingham, Booth entered the theater twice that evening after the presidential party had arrived. The doorkeeper believed that Booth, a famous Shakespearean actor who had performed frequently at Ford's Theatre, was spending most of his time that evening at the saloon next door. Buckingham recalled that when Booth made his final entrance into the theater, the two men shook hands and conversed briefly. The unsuspecting doorkeeper noticed nothing unusual in the actor's demeanor or appearance. Both the .44 caliber derringer and the nine-inch dagger that Booth carried were easily concealed. After this brief exchange, Booth entered the door that led to the parquet and the dress circle. After spending some time watching the play that he would soon bring to a premature and tragic conclusion, Booth, again according to Buckingham, returned through the parquet door and immediately ascended the staircase to the first balcony, which was located on the same level as the presidential box.[17]

No eyewitness noted the time when Booth made his final entrance into the theater. Based on the determination of the time of the assassination—10:30 P.M.—which will be addressed later, Booth's fifth entrance probably occurred about fifteen minutes earlier.

After ascending the south staircase, Booth proceeded along the rear of the dress circle. He encountered Captain Theodore McGowan (May 1865) of the United States Army occupying a seat. As he approached the captain, Booth indicated his desire to pass. McGowan lifted his head and, although annoyed, leaned back, complying with Booth's unspoken request. The dark figure then passed in front of the captain, temporarily blocking his view of the play before slipping behind A. M. Crawford (April 14, 1865), who was seated directly to McGowan's right.[18] Booth had aroused the suspicion of both men, and they watched carefully as he slowly descended into the darkness toward the box seats.

Others seated in the dress circle also noticed the man who was now approaching the presidential box. Some of these eyewitnesses also re-

PLAN OF THE DRESS CIRCLE OF Ford's New Theatre, 10th Street WASHINGTON, D.C.

Erected A.D. 1865 by John T. Ford.

Private Box No. 7.

Private Box No. 8.

Private Box No. 5.

Private Box No. 6.

Note: The seats are registered by the rule of decimals.

membered seeing a second individual stationed outside the presidential box. One of these, Dr. Todd (April 30, 1865), at "10:25" observed "a man walking along side of [the] Presidential box." Ferguson (April 14, 1865) watched "Booth go to the door leading to the passage of the private box." Both recalled that the black-clad stranger removed an object, possibly a pack of calling cards, from his coat and offered a card to the man who was seated outside the box.[19] Todd identified the recipient of the card as an "usher," while McGowan concluded that he was the president's messenger. According to Todd, the "usher" took the card into the box, presumably to obtain Lincoln's permission to admit Booth. A short time later, the door opened and Booth entered the box.[20] McGowan recalled that after offering his calling card, Booth entered the small antechamber to the presidential box.[21] Leale, a fourth witness to this sequence, like Todd, described the person posted outside the box as an "usher." Leale also noted that a man, presumably Booth, was "speaking with another near the door and endeavoring to enter." Leale further wrote that when "he [Booth] at last succeeded" in entering the box, "the door was closed."[22]

The remaining accounts that comment on Booth's movements are more general. Ferguson (May 15, 1865), Gatch (1908), and Troutner (1915) simply recall that Booth moved into the presidential box but mention no person outside the box.[23] In their studies of the event, both Bryan and Reck determined that there was a person outside the box, but Bishop concluded that no one was outside the box.[24] The most reliable eyewitness accounts however, clearly support the conclusion that someone in an official capacity was outside the box, looked at the calling card John Wilkes Booth presented, and allowed him entrance into the presidential box.

The identity of the man outside the box is impossible to establish. John Parker was the guard assigned to accompany President Lincoln to the theater that evening.[25] Yet Parker may not have been the man stationed outside the box. It could have been the president's messenger or someone else. Historians Bryan and Reck have speculated that the individual in question was Charles Forbes, the presidential messenger, although there is no reliable evidence to support this claim.[26] Neither Forbes nor Parker ever made any reliable claims concerning his role on the night of the assassination.

THE ASSASSINATION

The theater patrons, attentive to the drama that was unfolding on stage, had no inkling of the tragedy that was about to take place. When the

Presidential box showing rocker in which Lincoln was shot, sofa, chairs, partition, wallpaper and door to box 7 through which Booth entered

sound of the gunshot erupted from the presidential box, which an over-whelming majority claimed to have heard, most thought first to determine the source and the meaning of the noise, not to check the time. None of the eyewitnesses would attempt to determine the moment of the assassination until hours or days later. Therefore, the estimates concerning the timing of Booth's attack vary considerably. The weight of the evidence, however, supports the conclusion that the assassination occurred about 10:30 P.M.

As Booth entered the darkness of the anteroom, he could hear on the stage below the actor Harry Hawk reciting his soliloquy. Booth opened the door to the box and found himself standing behind its four occupants, whose attention was surely on the stage.[27] Booth raised the one-shot pistol to within point-blank range of Lincoln's head. He pulled the trigger. Lincoln's head was apparently turned slightly to the left, for the bullet crashed into his skull behind the left ear and proceeded diagonally across the brain before lodging behind his right eye. He never regained consciousness.

Booth then attempted to escape from the box to the stage below. Major Rathbone (May 1865), who had been alerted by the shot, peered through the smoke attempting to catch a glimpse of the intruder. The smoke from the black powder explosion provided Booth with a temporary advantage. A violent struggle then ensued between the major and the assassin. As Booth fought to free himself from the major's clutches, Rathbone made one final lunge. Booth (April 1865) thrust a nine-inch dagger at his attacker. Instinctively, Rathbone raised his arm and parried the blow. The knife cut him to the bone from the shoulder to the elbow, leaving a bloody gash.[28]

Most of the eyewitnesses determined the moment of the assassination on the basis of their recollections of the point at which the play was interrupted. Basset (April 15, 1865), Beekman (1911), Rathbone (May 1865), and Schwarz (1916) all claim that the shooting occurred during Act 3, scene 2.[29] The most reliable account, Harry Hawk's (April 14, 1865), supports this conclusion.[30] His account is credible not only because of the time at which it was recorded but also because of the author's position on the stage. Hawk wrote to his parents: "I was playing Asa Trenchard in 'The American Cousin.' [sic] The old lady of the theatre (Mrs. Muzzy) had just gone off stage, and I was answering her exit speech, when I heard the shot fired."[31] This point in the play occurs in Act 3, scene 2. Twenty-nine years after the tragedy, Hawk elaborated on this explanation by providing the last lines that he spoke before the shot was fired: "Well, I guess I know enough to turn you inside out, old woman, you damned old sockdologizing mantrap." He heard the shot after he uttered those words.[32] Except for the expletive, these lines are identical to those scripted for Asa Trenchard in Act 3, scene 2. Additional, although less explicit, support for this conclusion is provided by Roeliff Brinkerhoff (1900), Ferguson (April 14, 1865), Emerson (1913), and Fallon (1928), all of whom place the shot in the midst of Act 3, which had a total of seven scenes.[33]

Of all the contemporary eyewitness accounts, only that of Knox (April 15, 1865) recalled the assassination as occurring as late as the end of the third act. Crawford (April 14, 1865) recollected that the shot occurred during Act 3, scene 3, and Shepherd (April 14, 1865) vaguely recalled waiting for a scene change when she heard the shot.[34]

Some of the eyewitnesses gave a precise time for the shot. William T. Kent, a government clerk, in a affidavit given on April 15, testified that the shot occurred at 10:30, the same time given in Maynard's account (1910) and roughly the time of Act 3 of the performance. Some later accounts, notably those of Kitty Brink (1935) and Captain Isaac Hull (1906), placed the shot at 10:00 P.M.[35] Hence on the basis of the testimony of the most reliable eyewitnesses, it can be concluded with some confidence that Lincoln was shot during Act 3, scene 2, at approximately 10:30 P.M.

THE ESCAPE

Booth surely knew that the audience would be horrified by his act and that his chances of fleeing through the angry crowd were slim. Therefore, he chose an escape route which he believed would be safer than his route of entry; he planned to jump from the presidential box to the stage below, then dash off backstage to the alley where his horse was waiting. Booth, of course, could not foresee that he would catch his boot on a flag that decorated the box and would land awkwardly upon the stage. The reliable eyewitness accounts provide strong evidence that Booth's leg was not broken in the course of his jump from the box to the stage.

Although most of the audience had heard a gunshot, these people were considerably less certain about the events that followed. The sudden appearance of a strange man in riding attire upon the stage added to this confusion. Although more than forty of the eyewitnesses remembered that a man jumped to the stage from the presidential box, the manner in which he jumped is a matter of disagreement. The actor "fell," "slid," "leaped," or "vaulted," according to different eyewitness accounts.[36] No eyewitnesses suggested that the assassin exited the box by any other route.

The distance that Booth covered in this leap is also controversial. Estimates range from nine to fifteen feet. Unfortunately, the theater was gutted in 1866, destroying any physical evidence to verify the distance. Thus the best evidence is not the eyewitness accounts, but rather drawings of the theater that were completed by Alfred Waud within a week of the assassination. In one of these drawings, the distance from the box to the stage was given as approximately ten feet six inches.[37] Although it may seem risky to jump this distance, Booth was an experienced stuntman and had made leaps without incident from even greater heights in Shakespearean plays.[38]

Some of the accounts note that Booth caught his boot on a flag as he jumped. All of the following accounts agree on this detail: Daniel Beekman (1911), Spencer Bronson (April 17, 1865), William Fallon (1928), James Ferguson (1930), William Flood (1911), Oliver Gatch (1908), Jason Knox (April 15, 1865), W. H. Robert (1917), W. Taylor (1908), Mrs. Todd (1935), and Henry Williams (date unknown).[39] Unfortunately, only two of these, Bronson's and Knox's, were recorded in 1865. Even more unfortunate, Bronson's location within the theater has never been determined. Yet it is known that Knox was seated in the second row of the orchestra, a location that allowed an excellent vantage of both the leap and the landing. Because Knox's account is highly reliable in other particulars and there are no contradictory versions of this incident, it can be concluded that Booth did pull down a flag or a piece of a flag, most likely with the spur of his riding boot.

After ripping the flag in midair, the assassin fell onto the wooden stage. From their orchestra seats, Edwin Bates (April 15, 1865), Spencer Bronson (April 17, 1865), Frederick Sawyer (April 15, 1865), and Dr. Taft (April 16, 1865) all agreed that Booth concluded his jump ungracefully.[40] In the dress circle, Will T. Kent (April 15, 1865) observed Booth "staggering" momentarily, while Police Chief A. C. Richards (April 17, 1885) saw him drop "on one knee when he reached the floor." Actor Harry Hawk (April 16, 1865), by far the best eyewitness to this event because of his location on stage at the time, confirmed the other accounts by noting that the assassin "slipped when he gained the stage."[41]

Many later accounts nurtured the widespread belief that Booth broke his left leg when he hit the stage. Gatch (1909) claimed that Booth was "obviously injured by [the] fall," and Troutner (1915), along with Mrs. Todd (1925), stated that he had clearly broken his leg. Further support for this conjecture comes from other twentieth-century accounts, such as those of Byrne, Truman, Dorn, Schwarz, and Williams.[42]

Published works have also perpetuated this belief. Jim Bishop asserted that Booth's "leg snapped, just above the instep." Although he provided no supporting evidence, Bishop further concluded that Booth "limped" off the stage. In *A. Lincoln: His Last Twenty-Four Hours*, Reck also concluded that Booth fractured the "fibula of his left leg just above the ankle."[43] This conclusion rests on the dubious testimony of two twentieth-century eyewitness accounts.

Booth was the only contemporary eyewitness who claimed that he broke his leg while jumping from the box. This evidence was taken from his diary account, which was dated April 14, although probably not recorded until several days after the event. Since much of the available evidence points to the conclusion that Booth's diary entries are not credible on other issues, there is reason to doubt his testimony on this issue. Booth claimed in his diary that he was "stopped, but pushed on" while attempting to enter the presidential box when he was actually freely allowed to enter. The former Confederate spy also claimed that there was a colonel by Lincoln's side whereas Rathbone's uniform clearly indicated that he was a major. The eyewitness accounts also take issue with Booth's description of the words he spoke at the time of the assassination. His claim that he broke his leg in his leap to the stage must be considered unreliable in light of these other inaccuracies. An explanation for Booth's broken leg that makes Booth appear far less dashing is provided by David Herold, Booth's companion in his escape, and Dr. Samuel Mudd, who set Booth's broken leg. Both testified that Booth informed them that he had broken his leg when his horse fell on him.[44]

The eyewitness accounts that were recorded in 1865 do not even hint that Booth fractured his leg while he was in the theater. He is described as running across the stage with no mention of a limp, much less a broken leg. From their orchestra seats, Bates (April 15, 1865), Flood (1911), Knox (April 15, 1865), Sawyer (April 15, 1865), and Dr. Taft (April 15, 1865) all described the assassin's movement as "rush[ed]" or indicate that he "ran" across the stage.[45] From the parquette view of Daggett (April 15, 1865), the dress circle view of Ferguson (1930), and the stage view of Hawk (April 16, 1865), Booth "ran" after his fall.[46] Evans (1915), Gourlay

(1924), Matthews (1881), and Withers (May 1865) all noted that the assassin was running without any indication of an impairment.[47] Hence the conclusion that Booth escaped injury in his leap to the stage seems congruent with the reliable eyewitness testimony and that of Herold and Dr. Mudd.

Many of the eyewitnesses saw a dagger in Booth's hands after he recovered from the fall. Bates, Daggett, DuBarry (April 16, 1865), Hawk, Kent, Sawyer, Captain McGowan (May 1865), McIntyre (May 5, 1865), Richards, Simms (May 1865), and Dr. Todd are among the most reliable of the more than a dozen people who commented on the appearance of a knife.[48]

Backstage, William Withers (May 1865), the orchestra director, and Gourlay (1924), an actress in the play, had the misfortune to be caught standing directly in the assassin's path of escape.[49] Both claimed that as he ran across the stage Booth cut Withers, causing superficial wounds on the leg and in the neck. Charging out of the theater's rear door, Booth then mounted his horse and galloped into the night. After he met with David Herold, the two fugitives would be pursued for twelve days by Union troops before being surrounded in a tobacco shed near Port Royal, Virginia. Herold would leave the shed and surrender to the soldiers while Booth, after refusing to surrender, would be shot and killed.

BOOTH'S FINAL LINES

During John Wilkes Booth's escape from the theater, many of the patrons claimed that he had spoken a word or a phrase either from the presidential box or from the stage below. The differences in the patrons' recollections have led to a variety of conclusions concerning Booth's final declaration. W. Emerson Reck is unable to reach a conclusion concerning Booth's spoken words, and George Bryan avoids the issue entirely.[50] Despite this uncertainty, the evidence suggests that Booth uttered the words "Sic Semper Tyrannis" and that he spoke this Latin phrase not from the box but from the stage where he had performed so many times before.

Five different sources allege that Booth spoke from the box before his leap to the stage: Major Henry Rathbone (May 1865) and Booth (April 15, 1865) himself, who were both in the box, Harry Hawk (April 16, 1865), who was on the stage, and John Devenay (May 12, 1865) and John Downing, Jr. (April 24, 1865), who were in the audience. The veracity of these witnesses is difficult to assess, for there is little agreement among them. Hawk, whose soliloquy had been interrupted by the gunshot, recalled having heard the phrases "Sic Semper Tyrannis" and "The South shall be free" shouted from the box.[51] Devenay, in court testimony on May 12, and Downing, in his letter, recalled hearing "Sic Semper Tyrannis" from the box, although Downing admitted that "the excitement was very great at the time," which might have been responsible for the disparity among the accounts.[52] Rathbone, in court testimony one month after the event, claimed to have heard something that sounded like the word "Freedom." Booth himself in a diary entry, probably written a few days after the assassination, claimed to have said only "Sic Semper."[53] Although all five of these eyewitnesses seem credible, none of their assertions is supported by any other eyewitness. It can only be assumed that insofar as three of the four men—Booth, Hawk, and Rathbone—were directly involved in the events as they transpired, their attention may have been distracted, resulting in an inaccurate account of what must have seemed to be a matter of slight importance at the time.

There is substantial evidence that Booth shouted only "Sic Semper Tyrannis" and did so from the stage. Ten reliable eyewitnesses recalled having heard Booth proclaim "Sic Semper Tyrannis," the state motto of Virginia, to the stunned audience from the stage.[54] The phrase, which means "thus always to tyrants," had been used as a rallying cry by the colonists against King George III during the American Revolution. Among the more reliable eyewitnesses who recalled this exclamation are Basset (April 15, 1865), Bates (April 15, 1865), Bronson (April 17, 1865), Buckingham (May 1865), Daggett (April 15, 1865), J. Ferguson (April 14, 1865), Kent (April 15, 1865), Knox (April 15, 1865), Richards (April 17, 1865), Dr. Taft (April 16, 1865), and Dr. Todd (April 20, 1865). Most of the witnesses were well situated to observe events occurring on stage. Bates, Knox, and Taft were in the front row of the orchestra level. Ferguson, Kent, Richards, and Todd were all seated toward the front of the dress circle. This evidence is overwhelming.

Alternative viewpoints are therefore of only passing interest. Basset and McIntyre (May 5, 1865) are the only two eyewitnesses to have heard "Revenge for the South." In a slightly altered version Miss Shepherd recalled hearing "The South is avenged!" Ferguson (1930) and Daggett (April 15, 1865) credit Booth with saying, "I have done it!" Lindsey (1930) and Maynard (1910) simply remember the actor shouting incoherently as he crossed the stage, while Daniel Ballauf (April 14, 1895) believed that Booth said nothing.[55]

On this issue, the reliable majority of eyewitnesses suggest a common conclusion: Booth, after leaping to the stage, shouted "Sic Semper Tyrannis" to the surprised and startled audience. After this, his last performance, he exited not to applause but to silence, a silence that soon exploded into cries of anguish.

PANDEMONIUM

Although many of the theater patrons were too disoriented to react immediately to the assassination, the eyewitness accounts indicate that three physicians—Dr. Charles Leale, Dr. Charles Taft, and Dr. Albert King—immediately entered the box to attend to the president and that it was Leale who discovered Lincoln's fatal wound.

Theater patrons who heard the shot that killed Lincoln differed in their assessments of its meaning. Emerson (1917), backstage, thought that the shot was fired outside the theater in a postwar celebration.[56] Ennis (date unknown), in the orchestra section, believed that the shot was part of the play.[57] Sanford (April 17, 1865) dismissed the shot as an accidental discharge.[58] These reactions were surely mirrored by the audience as a whole, which partly explains why the patrons did not immediately pursue the assassin.

By the time Booth began to cross the stage, however, both Mrs. Lincoln and Major Rathbone attempted to alert others. Bronson (April 17, 1865), Knox (April 15, 1865), and Taylor (1908) specifically remembered Mrs. Lincoln screaming incoherently from the box.[59] Captain Bedee (date unknown) in the auditorium and Mrs. Brink (1935) from backstage agree that Mrs. Lincoln screamed, "My husband is shot!"[60] Major Rathbone (May 1865), in his vain attempt to alert the patrons, yelled, "Stop that man!" as the assassin escaped.[61] Evans (1915) also recalled Rathbone shouting these words to the confused audience.[62]

Fully alerted to the significance of events, three men now sought to stop Booth. Knox (April 15, 1865) and J. B. Stewart (May 20, 1865), from their second row orchestra seats, leaped over the footlights to the stage. They ran backstage but were too late.[63] Booth had disappeared. Meanwhile, Captain Pren Metham (1881) had elbowed his way through the crowd, crossed the stage, and thrust open a door he hoped would lead to the alley into which the assassin had fled.[64] Unfortunately, it led to the ladies' dressing room.

Several witnesses recalled that after the assassin had escaped, the audience was informed, most likely by Laura Keene, that the president had been shot. Basset (April 15, 1865), Coyel (date unknown), and Hazelton (date unknown) concur in this view and also contend that she attempted to quiet the crowd.[65] Others, such as Beekman (1911), Gourlay (1924), Greer (1914), Sherman (1930), Soles (1931), and Veader (1926), remembered hearing someone announce, "The President has been shot!" or words to that effect, although they did not identify the speaker.[66] At that point, pandemonium erupted throughout the theater as cries for revenge and medical assistance filled the auditorium.

In the presidential box, meanwhile, the injured Rathbone dashed to the door to limit entry to those who might offer medical assistance to the injured president. He discovered that the door had been blocked by a brace, presumably placed there by the assassin to deter his pursuers. After removing the brace, Rathbone let Dr. Charles Leale, a military surgeon, enter the box. A few minutes later, Rathbone, after allowing one additional surgeon (probably Dr. Albert King) to enter the box, instructed Colonel Crawford (April 14, 1865), to prohibit further entry.[67]

Evidence suggests that a third doctor, military surgeon Charles Taft (April 16, 1865), successfully gained entry to the presidential box directly from the stage below.[68] Several accounts mention that a person entered the box from the outside by being pushed up from the stage. Included in this listing are the generally reliable accounts of Bates (April 15, 1865), Bronson (April 17, 1865), and Shepherd (April 14, 1865).[69] Bedee (date unknown), who claimed to have been the man responsible for providing a boost, Maynard (1910), and Taylor (1908) all agree that the man who entered from the outside of the box was in military uniform.[70] Finally, Dr. Taft (April 16, 1865) testified that it was he who was lifted to the box from the stage.[71]

Looking back on events as they transpired inside the box, four different people claimed to have located the bullet wound. None of these claims is corroborated by another witness. Circumstances indicate, however, that Dr. Leale's claim is the most credible.[72] First, Dr. Leale was the only one who claimed to have reached the box first. This is probably true because his seat was located on the south side of the dress circle, close to the presidential box. According to Leale's account, upon entering the box, he saw his beloved president sitting in a high backed armchair with his head turned slightly to the right. While she desperately attempted to hold her mortally wounded husband, Mrs. Lincoln pleaded with Leale to save him, and the young doctor responded that he would do all he could. His initial diagnosis, though, was not promising. He felt Lincoln's cold wrist and failed to discover a pulse. The breathing was irregular and weak. With the help of those in the box, the president was placed on the floor for closer examination. Since Rathbone was now bleeding profusely from a knife wound, Leale cut open the president's coat and shirt on the assumption that the murder weapon had been a knife. Meanwhile, Miss Keene, who had made her way from the stage to the box presumably via the south staircase, held the president's head in her lap. Leale proceeded to lift his eyelids and discovered evidence of brain damage. Then, while searching for injury to the rear of Lincoln's head, he found the president's mortal wound. Bedee (date unknown), Flood (1911), and Dr. Gatch (1908) all make similar claims for themselves.[73] Yet Leale's proximity to the presidential box, the certainty of his identification as a doctor upon entering the box, and the timing of his recollection of events indicate that it was most likely he who discovered Lincoln's fatal wound.

Leale then performed artificial respiration, which restored the president's breathing. This quick action temporarily stabilized Lincoln's vital signs. Collectively, the three doctors, Leale, King, and Taft, would now decide whether the president should be removed from the theater.

LINCOLN'S FINAL HOURS
Who carried Lincoln from the theater to his deathbed? This is indeed one of the most perplexing questions surrounding the assassination. Over a dozen eyewitnesses claimed to have assisted in removing the president from the theater. This number is clearly too high.

As the doctors began their examination of Lincoln, the theater was cleared of its patrons. Buckingham, the doorkeeper, stated in his trial testimony that Harry Ford requested that Mayor Richard Walch of Washington, D.C., attempt to calm the audience and request that the patrons leave the premises.[74] Walch complied with Ford's request whereupon the theater was emptied and Lincoln was carried from the theater. Although Bates (April 15, 1865) remembered this sequence somewhat differently, Knox's (April 15, 1865) recollection completely supports Buckingham's testimony on this point.[75]

The circumstances surrounding Lincoln's removal from the theater to his deathbed across the street are suffused with controversy. First, there is disagreement concerning the manner in which Lincoln was carried. Reck has speculated that he was carried on the box partition, while Bishop claims that Lincoln was carried directly by his bearers.[76] Among the eyewitnesses, Evans (1915) and Troutner remembered that a shutter was pressed into service as a makeshift stretcher.[77] Flood (1911), Greer (1914), and Taylor (1908) simply recalled a stretcher or an "improvised" stretcher.[78] Neither Dr. Leale (1867) nor Dr. Taft (April 15, 1865), by far the most reliable eyewitnesses in this case, mentioned how Lincoln was carried.[79] From these accounts, it is reasonable to conclude that the president was placed on a flat board of some kind. Most likely, he was not carried in anyone's arms.

The entourage removing the president probably followed the same route that Lincoln himself had taken upon entering the theater two hours before. It proceeded around the rear of the dress circle to the semicircular stairs and descended to the lobby. Both Emerson (1913) and McIntyre (May 5, 1865), who were standing in the lobby during the president's removal, observed that Lincoln had been practically denuded of garments as a result of the doctor's search for a stab wound.[80]

From the lobby, Lincoln's bearers proceeded slowly across the crowded street as Union soldiers formed a narrow path through the chaotic mass of onlookers. Finally, the entourage arrived at the home of William Petersen, where it ascended the spiral staircase that led to the entrance of the boardinghouse.

Dr. Leale claims in both his 1867 and 1909 accounts that he joined the litterbearers and was assisted by Drs. Taft and King.[81] His account and Albert Daggett's (May 15, 1865) are the only ones from the nineteenth century that mention by name those who carried the stricken president to his deathbed. All the other accounts that comment on this episode were recorded in the twentieth century. This limitation of evidence is reflected in the popular accounts of the Lincoln assassination. Bryan, for example, sidestepped the issue of numbers and names of litterbearers by not making any claims on this issue.[82]

Jacob Soles and his three friends, John Corey, Jacob Griffiths, William Sample, are often mentioned in accounts of the assassination as the bearers of Lincoln's body.[83] All were members of the same Union army regiment and had attended the theater together. Reck and Bishop both accept Soles's claim in this regard.[84] Yet the earliest account known that perpetuates Soles's claim was recorded in 1931, over sixty years after the fact.[85] Furthermore, Soles was the only one of his group to assert that he had helped carry the president's body. Bedee, Flood, Greer, and Hazelton are others who claimed to have carried the president, but all of their accounts were given in the same time period as Soles's and are therefore equally suspect.[86] Thus although Dr. Leale, Dr. King, Dr. Taft, and Albert Daggett certainly assisted in carrying Lincoln from the theater to the

Petersen house, none of the other members of the entourage can be identified with certainty.

Throughout the long night that followed Booth's attack on Lincoln, the Petersen house was the scene of mournful activity. Leale, King, and Taft, the doctors who originally attended Lincoln, together with Surgeon General Joseph K. Barnes and Assistant Surgeon General Charles H. Crane, both of whom arrived later, maintained their hopeless vigil. Upon his arrival at the Petersen house, Secretary of War Edwin Stanton immediately seized control of the situation and began interviewing eyewitnesses from the theater. The dying president was in the back bedroom and the devastated Mrs. Lincoln in the front parlor while Stanton conducted the first interviews in the middle bedroom. A young injured veteran, Charles Tanner, served as Stanton's recording secretary. It was soon evident that John Wilkes Booth was the assassin.

Throughout the somber evening, many of Lincoln's friends and cabinet officials came to pay their last respects. Most did not linger. They knew he would not live very long.

As his life gradually slipped away, Lincoln's breathing became irregular. His right eye, behind which lay the .44 caliber bullet, began to swell. His lower extremities had become cold from poor circulation and the doctors added several blankets to those already covering the body. Meanwhile, Lincoln's grieving eldest son, Captain Robert Todd, was comforted by Senator Charles Sumner in the back bedroom.[87]

By morning Lincoln's condition had worsened, and at 7:22 A.M. he died. One of the doctors placed coins on his eyes and stepped back from the deathbed. The silence that followed was finally broken by Stanton's immortal epitaph: "Now, he belongs to the ages."[88]

ONE

THE FIRST ACCOUNTS
APRIL–MAY 1865

Twelve of the eyewitnesses' accounts are particularly significant because of their locations within the theater on the night of the assassination and the time frame within which they recorded their descriptions of the events they observed. Four of these crucial eyewitnesses were located on the orchestra level, six in the dress circle, one in the presidential box, and one on stage.

Of the four eyewitnesses seated on the orchestra level, Dr. Charles Sabin Taft sat in the front row and witnessed not only the assassination but Lincoln's death and autopsy as well. His recollections were recorded in personal notes written on April 16, 1865. Jason S. Knox, who sat just one row behind Taft, broke a promise he had previously made to his father never to attend the theater so he could see President Lincoln and General Grant on the night of April 14. His seat was located on the south side of the auditorium almost directly under the presidential box, so he could not actually see the events that transpired in the presidential box, but he had an excellent view of the stage. His recollections were recorded in a letter to his father on April 15. Frederick A. Sawyer and Edwin Bates both obtained seats on the orchestra level of the theater, just three or four rows from the stage. Not only were these witnesses close to the stage, but they wrote their impressions within hours of the event. Sawyer recorded his account in a letter written at one o'clock in the morning of April 15, while Bates described the assassination in a letter to his parents the next day.

Six crucial eyewitnesses were located in the dress circle. James P. Ferguson, like Knox, deliberately procured seats at the opposite side of the dress circle to ensure an excellent view of General Grant, whom he described as a "favorite." His account was recorded twice: first in an interview with Secretary of War Edwin Stanton on April 14 and again during the Lincoln conspirators' trial on May 15, 1865. William T. Kent, a clerk in the office of the paymaster general, also sat on the north side of the dress circle almost directly opposite the presidential box. He provided an affidavit on April 15 and court testimony on May 16. Dr. Charles Leale, who was stationed at the United States Army General Hospital at Armory Square in Washington, D.C., was another patron who had purchased his ticket so he could see President Lincoln, whom he adored. Leale arrived late and was unable to secure a seat on the orchestra level, but he did find a vacant seat on the dress circle's south side within forty feet of the presidential box. He was thus able to reach the president shortly after he had been wounded. On April 15 Leale recorded his invaluable account in the form of personal notes. Another doctor in the audience that evening, George B. Todd, was most likely seated in the dress circle on the north side. His account took the form of a letter to his brother dated April 15. Captain Theodore McGowan and A. M. Crawford procured their seats in the extreme rear of the dress circle, which placed them directly in the path that Booth would later use to reach the presidential box. McGowan's description of the events surrounding the assassination was provided in court testimony taken on May 15, while Crawford was interviewed at the Petersen house by Secretary of War Edwin Stanton in the hours following the assassination.

Two other key eyewitnesses observed the assassination from significantly different vantage points. Major Henry R. Rathbone, an occupant of the presidential box, recorded his account within weeks of the tragic event. Rathbone provided his information in an affidavit dated April 17 and again in court testimony taken on May 15. Actor Harry Hawk, a star in the play that evening, was on stage at the time of the assassination. His account was recorded both in an interview with Stanton on April 14 and in a letter written to his parents two days later.

John Wilkes Booth is included here with considerable reservation. He wrote his brief account of the assassination in a notebook sometime between the assassination and his own death twelve days later. As perpetrator of events that others could only react to in stunned horror, Booth was in the best position to assess his own actions. Unfortunately, as this account will attempt to demonstrate, Booth's notebook entries seem to have been written principally to justify his actions and actually provide few facts about the assassination itself, some of which are debatable.

Thus these thirteen eyewitnesses (including Booth) provide the core of the evidence for this reconstruction of Lincoln's assassination. Others are cited only to demonstrate the diversity among the accounts and the failings of the human memory in recalling events of years past. The accounts are presented chronologically, divided into four sections—those of April 1865, testimony given at the conspiracy trial in May 1865, those written between 1877 and 1909, and a large number of reminiscences that appeared between 1909 and 1954. I have provided the name of the witness, his or her location in the theater if known, and the date and source of the account when available. Some newspaper and magazine clippings do not give full information, but I have provided the names of the depositories where they may be found. I have made few attempts to identify the witnesses or to check the veracity of the account because I have focused on the accounts and not on the lives of those who provided them.

The April 1865 accounts are by far the most reliable. They were recorded by individuals for a variety of reasons: to assist in the assassination investigation, to share with others what they had seen, or as a way they sought to come to terms with the tragedy they had witnessed.

The first three accounts, which were recorded within hours of the assassination, were the product of the investigation. While in the Petersen house, Secretary of War Edwin Stanton, after visiting the unconscious president, questioned three men who attended Ford's Theatre that evening to determine the assassin's identity. A young Union soldier, Charles Tanner, who had had both legs amputated because of war injuries, recorded the answers that A. M. S. Crawford, Harry Hawk, and James Ferguson provided. These are the first and probably the most reliable accounts.

A. M. S. Crawford
Location: Dress circle, south side
Tanner testimony, Union League of Philadelphia
April 14, 1865

> *Crawford was probably a member of the Veterans' Reserve, soldiers who were not fit for active duty and were used for guard duty or other less strenuous activities.*

Crawford's seat was close to the presidential box, and he was prob-
ably the first person to enter it after the assassination. Following Ma-
jor Rathbone's orders, he played a crucial role that night by allowing
only certain individuals to enter the presidential box.

Because Crawford was seated directly along the assassin's path, his
account provides the most vivid detail concerning both Booth's physi-
cal appearance and his approach to the presidential box.

Stanton's foremost goal in questioning Crawford was to determine
the assassin's identity. Charles Tanner recorded Crawford's answers.

I was sitting in the dress circle of Ford's Theatre, not on the upper row of
seats but on the upper floor. I suppose about five feet from the door of the
box. My chair was close to the row of chairs in front. Captain McGowan
who was with me was at my right and against the wall. This murderer came
around about the middle of the first scene of the 3rd act of the play of "Our
American Cousin." To pass us he had to come around me and then to pass
in front of the Captain. I looked up at him four or five times. He attracted
my attention. I thought first that he was intoxicated. There was a glare in
(his) eye and he was a little over middling [height]. He had a dark slouch
hat, a dark coat, jet black hair, dark eyes, a heavy black [mustache], no
whiskers, and no beard. It was just at the close of the third scene as all the
attention was directed to the stage. He left very suddenly and stepped into
the box where the President was. I turned to Capt. McGowan intending to
say something to him in reference to this man's manner. The next instant
the shot was fired. I said at once that it was in the President's box and
jumped to the door. I passed through the door and into the box. A
gentleman whom I afterwards ascertained to be Major Rathbone who
asked me not to allow anyone to enter the box and I sent for a surgeon.

STANTON: Can you describe the man that jumped from the box?

Yes, sir. I saw him as he ran across the stage. I saw him as he passed
across two thirds of the stage and out between the scenes. He had a knife
in his right hand. As he went through the scene he threw his hand behind
him and the knife was in sight. I think his face was familiar. The side of his
face was towards me. It was the left side of his face. No immediate pursuit
was made on the stage, not for a moment or two. He was dressed in
ordinary business suit. He very strongly resembled the Booths. What
attracted my attention particularly was the glare in his eye. He did not say
a word that I heard. I think he shot the President with the left hand. There
was a dispatch brought to the President about 20 minutes before this
occurred. I think the name of the bearer was [S. P.] Hanscomb. He asked
me where the President was. I showed him and he went in and gave it to

him. He was a rather good looking, short necked fellow about five feet
eight inches high with grayish pants I think. I could identify him among a
thousand if I could see him in the same position. My residence is at No.
136 Penn. Ave. I am a Lieutenant in the V.R. Corps.

Harry Hawk
Location: Stage
Tanner testimony, Union League of Philadelphia
April 14, 1865

> *Harry Hawk was playing the leading role in the play* Our Ameri-
> can Cousin *on April 14, 1865. During Act 3, scene 2, alone on the
> stage, he delivered one of the more humorous lines of the play. Those
> were probably the last words Lincoln heard.*
>   *In his interview with Stanton, Hawk was the first person to identi-
> fy John Wilkes Booth as the assassin.*

I was on the stage at the time of the firing and heard the report of the
pistol. My back was towards the President's box at the time. I heard
something tear and somebody fell and as I looked towards him he came in
the direction in which I was standing and I believe to the best of my
knowledge that it was John Wilkes Booth. Still I am not positive that it
was him. I only had one glance at him as he was rushing towards me with
a dagger and I turned and run and after I ran up a flight of stairs I turned
and exclaimed "My God thats John Booth." I am acquainted with Booth.
I met him the first time a year ago. I saw him today about one o'clock.
Said I, "How do you do Mr. Booth" and he says "how are you Hawk."
He was sitting on the steps of Ford's Theatre reading a letter. He had the
appearance of being sober at the time. I was never intimate with him. He
had no hat on when I saw him on the stage. In my own mind I do not
have any doubt but that it was Booth. He made some expression when he
came on the stage but I did not understand what.

James P. Ferguson
Location: Dress circle, left
Tanner testimony, Union League of Philadelphia
April 14, 1865

> *Ferguson owned a restaurant directly to the north of Ford's Theatre.
> He procured seats on the north side of the dress circle so that he could*

view General Ulysses S. Grant, who was expected to attend with the president.

Ferguson's account is the first one to mention the words Booth spoke as he crossed the stage.

Mr. Ford came to me today about 1 or 2 o'clock and told me that my favorite, Gen. Grant was going to be present at the theatre tonight and had secured a box. I went in the theatre and engaged seats 58 and 59 on the opposite side from the Presidential box. When the President came in I saw that Gen. Grant was not with him but I still kept watch of the box expecting Gen. Grant to come in knowing that if he came in he would go in the same box with the President. After curtain went up for the 3rd act I saw Mr. Booth go to the door leading to the passage of the private box which the President occupied and by the door. In a moment afterwards I was looking with an opera glass to see which the citizen was that was with the President. I then heard the report of the pistol and saw Mrs. Lincoln catch him around the neck. I saw him throw up his right arm at the same time I saw Booth with his hand in his side and pull a knife and move between Mrs. Lincoln and a lady in the same box. He put his hands in the cushion of the box and threw his feet right over. As he jumped over he pulled part of a state flag off and had part of it under his feet when he fell on the stage. The very moment he struck he exclaimed "Sic Semper Tyrannis." As he came across the stage facing me he looked me right up in the face and it alarmed me and I pulled the lady who was with me down behind the bannister. I looked right down at him and he stopped as he said, "I have done it" and shook the knife. All I know of Mr. Booth is this. I never saw him in my life until about two or three months ago. I have often heard of Wilkes Booth. He himself told me that he was born and raised in Baltimore. He is a theatrical man by profession. I heard him say a few weeks ago that he had an estate left him in the oil regions of Penn. He played here some five or six weeks ago at the benefit of Mr. John McCollum. He came today near one or two o'clock in front of my house. I think the President was shot just about 10 o'clock, just as the curtain went up for the 3rd act. I do not know what became of Booth after he left the stage. There was great excitement. I think there were many persons in the orchestra who might have caught him if they had immediately pursued him. I do not know the color of the horse. I think it was a little small bay horse. He told me when he bought the horse but I do not know [remember] for now. He says he's a very nice horse, he can gallop, and can almost kick me in the back. It was not a pacing horse. He started off on a hop. I went down to Mayor Wallach and stated these things to him. Mr. Harry Hawk was on the stage at the time. The same hat which Wilkes Booth had on when I saw him today is now in charge of the police at the station house. They say they found it in the box which the President occupied.

Basset
Location: Unknown
Diary, Library of Congress
April 15, 1865

Basset's first name is unknown. He is the only one who stated that Booth said both "Sic Semper Tyrannis" and "Revenge for the South" as he crossed the stage.

At half past ten o'clock on the night of the 14—in the front upper left hand private box in Ford's Theatre, while the second scene of the third act of "Our American Cousin" was being played, a pistol was fired and Abraham Lincoln shot through the neck and lower part of the head. A second after the shot was fired a man vaulted over the ballister of the box saying Sic Semper Tyrannis and adding revenge for the South, ran across the stage with a knife in his right hand. The man was of middle stature, well built, that he wore a black moustache. His hair and eyes were black. The crowd ascended the stage. The actresses, pale, ran wildly about. Miss Keene, whose benefit night it was, came forward endeavoring to quiet the audience. Several gentleman climbed to the box, and finally the audience was ordered out.

Mrs. Lincoln, Miss Harris and Major Pathburn [sic] were in the box with the President. The assassin left behind him his hat, a spur and a horror and gloom never equaled in this country. The hat was picked up in the President's box.

The President was removed to the house of Mr. Peterson [sic], opposite the theater. Every measure of precaution was taken to preserve order in the city and every street was patrolled, every road out of Washington was picketed, and every avenue of escape guarded. It was the conclusion that the murderer of President Lincoln was John Wilkes Booth. His hat was found and identified by several persons who had seen him within the last two days, and the spur which he dropped by accident after he jumped to the stage was identified as one of those which he obtained from the stable when he hired his horse. The President died at the house of Mr. Peterson, opposite to the theater, at seven o'clock and two minutes on the morning of the 15—

Edwin Bates
Location: Orchestra level, front
Letter to his parents, Library of Congress
April 15, 1865

> *Bates's account is especially useful for the detail it provides of Booth's escape from the box and across the stage. He was concerned with how the North would respond to the South in the wake of the assassination.*

I went to the theatre last night & saw him for the first time—& soon after an event did occur—not happy as I had predicted in my letter, but one the most horrible & atrocious that as ever been recorded in the annals of history—the assassination of Mr. Lincoln. I was accompanied by Mr. Sawyer the gentleman that wrote you about me last fall & was seated in the orchestra chairs next to the stage & nearly underneath the box occupied by Mr. Lincoln & friends. I first heard the report of a pistol & immediately after a man jumped from Mr. Lincolns box a distance of 10 or 15 feet upon the stage right before & not more than 10 feet from me. He fell partly upon his side but instantly rose & with a long dagger in hand rushed rapidly across the stage & disappeared before any in the vast house full of people could realise what had occurred. He was a fine looking man dressed in a full suit of black & it was my impression at the first instant that some body had fired a pistol at him & he had jumped down upon the stage for safety or had been knocked down. I rec [received] this impression from the fact that a pistol had been fired & he had no pistol in his hand but his dagger I saw & before he had got half way across the stage I comprehended that the man was an assassin & that some deadly attack had been made upon Mr. Lincoln. The audience generally seemed about the same time to comprehend the whole matter & began to cry catch him, kill him, but before any could get upon the stage he had disappeared from view behind the scenes. It was in the midst of a play, "Our American Cousin" in which the "yankee" is represented to be a Vermonter hailing from Brattleboro & is on a visit to England to see his English relatives, the piece is amusing & it was between two of the acts of this play while a few of the actors were just coming on the stage that it occurred. The actors seemed no more to comprehend the matter than the audience or they might perhaps have stopped the man as he ran right past them if they had not been intimidated by his dagger. As it was he rushed out at the rear of the theatre mounted a horse & disappeared & has not yet been caught although recognised by a dozen different people in the theatre. His name is John Wilkes Booth an actor & who has frequently played in this theatre & conversant with the different places of egress from it. He had not until last night ever succeeded in attaining any reputation in his profession as an actor but now he has acquired a reputation in tragedy which will render him famous & infamous in history in all time. In the box with Mr. Lincoln was Mrs. Lincoln & also another gentleman & lady. This gentleman I hear was also stabed by the man. Those who got first to Mr. Lincoln were those seated in the part of the house I was, who jumped upon the stage & by the assistance of each other & climbing up the posts they could get up to near the box & the lady I mentioned as being in the party & apparently 25 or 30 years of age assisted them in, there was immediately a call for water & stimulants from those who first reached the box & the whole of the vast audience was under the wildest excitement & indignation when it became known the [sic] Mr. Lincoln was mortally wounded. They were all soon requested to leave the theatre but before all had done so Mr. Lincoln was carried out insensible to a house opposite in which condition he remained until he expired this morning. I forgot to mention that as the man rose as he partially fell upon his knees as he touched the stage he raised his dagger & as he ran across the stage uttered the words "Sic semper tyrannis." As Mr. S & myself walked slowly to the hotel we agreed that the probability was that the man when found would be discovered to be some insane person, that the lowest depths of human depravity even in a rebel of the worst type would not permit to commit such a horrible deed in so bold a manner before thousands of people & where there could be so little chance of escape. But soon after we got to the hotel news came that Mr. Seward & all his household had been assassinated, that it was a grand conspiracy, that the other members of the Cabinet were safe but that suspicious persons had been seen about the residence of Mr. Stanton & C, also that Gen Grant who left on the evening train for Philadelphia had been shot in the cars. This morning this is contradicted & to day the General has returned here. It appears from letters found in Booths room that this murder had been premeditated for some time & it was the intention to have it come off at the inaugural on 4th March but opportunity did not offer, that all the Cabinet & other leading men were to be included is now supposed, that

Gen Grant was to be included last night was very probable—as it was reported in the papers of yesterday morning that he would accompany the President to the theatre in the evening.

Booth is a native of Baltimore, & before it was known with any certainty that it was him I heard a gentleman state (who knew him well, he said), that he could not be the man—for he had long known him & had never known him to be a secessionist that he had taken no part in the rebellion—had been out West, "acting" for last year or two & latter had been in the petrolium business. It is certain that two & probably more are in the plot that it was got up in Baltimore, some think also it was known to the Confederate authorities at Richmond. Even if they had succeeded in accomplishing all they desired & destroyed all—President Cabinet & Generals—what good could result to the southern cause at this stage of the war? Once such a blow might have staggered the north but now that time is past.

The excitement here is terrific, the street-corners & hotels are crowded with people swearing deep & deadly vengance to all rebels & the whole south—& so it will be over the north & what the results will be none can tell. Mr. Lincoln was certainly a "Saul among the people" & the early peace & prosperity that I had hoped under his hand would soon return to the country I am afraid now is far distant. His conciliatory policy I am satisfied although distasteful to the radicals & perhaps a majority of the people was the surest & quickest road to peace. The rebel armies dispersed soon peace & prosperity would have been restored to the South. That policy may now be changed. Mr. Johnson who is now President is more vindictive. I heard him say in a speech last week that the leaders in the rebellion he would hang as high as Haman.

No event except those of family history has ever filled me with such profound sadness as this. I have no heart to prosecute further the business upon which I came here & which I had reason to hope I would soon successfully accomplish. I think now I shall leave here in a day or two & return South on the next steamer. I hope for the sake of the Union men of the South & the south generally that it will be found when the assassins are caught & examined that no part of this plot was concocted at the South or was known to Southern leaders.

I will write you from N York before starting for C

> Affectionately yours
> Edwin

Frederick A. Sawyer
Location: Orchestra level, second row
Letter, "An Eyewitness Account of Abraham Lincoln's Assassination."
Civil War History, Ford's Theatre National Historic Site
April 15, 1865

> *Sawyer accompanied Bates to the theater that evening. That they changed their seats several times indicates that the theater was not filled to capacity. Although Sawyer and Bates had almost the same view of the assassination, their accounts include different details. Sawyer does not mention Booth's utterances on the stage. The doctor whom he saw climb into the box was probably Dr. Taft and the "ticket-taker" who identified Booth was probably John Buckingham, the doorkeeper.*

April 15, 1865
Willard's Hotel, Room 128
Washington, D.C.
April 15th 1865
1 o'clock A.M.
I cannot sleep. My mind is so excited by what has occurred tonight that only horrid dreams await my slumbers should I chance to have them. Last night at about 8 o'clock Mr. Edwin Bates & myself went to the Theatre on 10th St. called "Ford's Theatre—we took orchestra chairs near the front of the house three or four rows from the Stage; a few moments elapsed when we were requested to move as those seats were "reserved." We moved forward to the 2d row of chairs from the Stage about one third the way from the stage "left" toward the "right"—Before we had moved however, cheers from the whole house indicated that some distinguished person had entered the house: it soon became known that Mr Lincoln & his wife & some two or three other persons had entered the private box (the second one upward from the stage) which was draped with the American flag.

The play was "Our American Cousin," with Laura Keene as Florence Trenchard. After sitting through the first act Mr. Bates & myself left the lower part of the house & went up in to the "dress circle," on the opposite side of the house in order that we might get a better view of the President & his party. We staid there some time, when we returned to the seats below & this time I took the chair on the end of the second row from the

Stage & as near Mr. Lincoln's box as possible in that row. Mr Bates sat next me—After sitting there a few minutes a report of a pistol was heard and a man of about 5 ft. 9 inches dressed in a black suit of clothes leaped onto the Stage apparently from the President's box. He held in his right hand a dagger whose blade appeared about 10 inches long—He did not strike the stage fairly on his feet, but appeared to stumble slightly. Quickly recovering himself he ran with lightning speed across the Stage & disappeared beyond the scenes on the Stage "right" our "left"—The whole occurrence, the shot, the leap, the escape—was done while you could count eight. The excitement in the house was intense. Every one leaped to his feet, and the cry of "the President is assassinated" was heard getting where I could see into the President's box, I saw Mrs. Lincoln, or a lady who had been pointed out to me as she, waving her hands to & fro in apparent anguish. Several parties climbed up into the box, & soon there was an inquiry if there "was a surgeon in the house" The call not being heard I repeated it in a loud voice & one answered that he was coming. He ran forward & climbed into the box—What occurred there I do not know. Mr. Bates & myself moved with the crowd toward the door as there was a request to that effect made by some one on the Stage—whether by Laura Keene or by a man, I do not remember. I think by a man, however. I do remember Laura Keene's coming forward & imploring people to be seated, within a minute or two after the shot & the escape. When we got to the door we heard the ticket-taker say that John Wilkes Booth was the man who had done this atrocious act, that Booth had entered the house a short time before; that he knew him well, & that he was the man who had run across the Stage. Others said that as he passed across the Stage he cried "Sic Semper Tyrannis," the motto of the State of Virginia. I cannot say I heard this. The confusion was great the moment the pistol was fired, & my first thought was that there was a side scene of the play; instantly I remembered that there was nothing of this sort in the play, but by the time I had recovered my thoughts sufficiently to realize that such was not the case, the man had disappeared. We left the Theatre and came up To Willard's—When we got to the corner of 14th St & Pa. Av. we met a group of men & heard the Secretary Seward had just had his throat cut, & Mr. Fredk. Seward had also been badly cut. Later we heard that Mr. Seward was alive & might possibly recover & that Mr. F. Seward would also probably recover. But we heard soon the sad news that the assassin had made sure of his aim with the President & that he was dead.

The report is that a man with a light coat had called at Mr Seward's house & insisted upon seeing him as he had a note from his physician & must have an immediate audience that no sooner was he in the room than he attacked Mr. S, & succeeded in cutting his throat badly, but did not sever any considerable artery.

Mr. J. B. Stewart told me this night at Willard's that on seeing the man jump from the box to the Stage he himself leaped to the Stage, (having been sitting very near the Stage on the other end of the same row of chairs in which I was sitting) & cried out to the actors in the side scenes to "stop that man." But they did not succeed in doing so, & Mr. Stewart himself rushed after him & heard the door of the theatre "slam"—He essayed to open it, but did not get hold of the right place at once which caused a slight delay—not however enough to prevent Mr. Stewart's seeing the man mount a horse which stood about 10 or 15 feet from the door. The horse made apparently a misstep, & then galloped up the alley. Mr. Stewart is sure that he can identify the assassin.

The excitement in the city is intense. Every man feels horror or expresses it, at this atrocious murder of the first citizen of the Republic & the attempt to murder the Premier. What would have been the fate of either of these men it is hardly doubtful. A strong cord & short shrift. Strong men have wept tonight & the nation will mourn tomorrow.

It is such a tragedy as I never hoped to witness, & one which will chill the blood of all true men every where.

The exact time when this murder occurred it is hard to state, but as nearly as I can calculate, it was not far from 1/2 past 10 o'clock, on the 14th day of April: on the same day which has witnessed the raising of the glorious flag of the Republic over the walls of Ft. Sumter, the assassin's hand has cut off in the very highest point his usefulness & honor that man who felt no desire but to bless & serve his country & civilization. To God belongs the punishment of this great crime. But to unsanctified man it is hard to forgive such a terrible retribution upon those to whom any part of the guilt belongs—May God in his mercy prevent our people from becoming as bloodthirsty as the enemies of this Govt. seem to be.

[Saturday, 15th April. The death of Mr. Lincoln did not occur till this morning at 7.22]

It is reported that the telegraph wires have been cut between Baltimore & Washington.

It was given out yesterday that the President & General Grant would be at Ford's Theatre last night. But Gen. G. left for Phila. at 6 o'clock P.M.

Apr. 13th or he might have shared the same dreadful fate. How many more martyrs to slavery!

Jason S. Knox
Location: Orchestra level, second row
Letter to his father, Princeton University Archives
April 15, 1865

> *Knox's differs from the other reliable accounts only in his conten-*
> *tion that Booth said, "Revenge for the South," as he crossed the stage.*

Dear Father: It is with sad feelings that I take up my pen to address you. Last Friday night at 10 o'clock, I witnessed the saddest tragedy ever enacted in this country. Notwithstanding my promise to you not to visit the theater, I could not resist the temptation to see General Grant and the President, and when the curtain at Ford's rose on the play of Our American Cousin my roomate and I were seated on the second row of orchestra seats, just beneath the President's box.

The President entered the theater at 8 1/2 amid deafening cheers and the rising of all. Everything was cheerful, and never was our magistrate more enthusiastically welcomed or more happy. Many pleasant allusions were made to him in the play, to which the audience gave deafening responses, while Mr. Lincoln laughed heartily and bowed frequently to the gratified people. Just after the 3rd act, and before the scenes were shifted, a muffled pistol shot was heard, and a man sprang wildly from the national box, partially tearing down the flag, then shouting "sic semper tyrannus, the south is avenged" with brandished dagger rushed across the stage and disappeared. The whole theater was paralyzed.

But two men sprang for the stage, a Mr. Stewart and myself. Both of us were familiar with the play, and suspected the fearful tragedy. We rushed after the murderer, and Mr. Stewart being familiar with the passages, reached the rear door in time to see him spring on his horse and ride off— I became lost amid the scenery and was obliged to return.

The shrill cry of murder from Mrs. Lincoln first roused the horrified audience, and in an instant the uproar was terrible. The silence of death was broken by shouts of "kill him" and strong men wept, and cursed, and tore the seats in the impotence of their anger.

Finally the theater was cleared and the President removed. Still greater was the excitement in the city. Rumors of the murder of Secy Seward and

OSBORN
PRINTING CO.

3055 Biglerville Road • P.O. Box 547 • Biglerville, PA 17307 • Phone 717 677-8111

his son reached us as we gained the street. Mounted patrols dashed every where, bells tolled the alarm, and excited crowds rushed about the avenues. Despair was on every countenance, and black horror brooded over the city—dark clouds had gathered in the heavens, and soldiers sternly paced their patrol.

Yesterday morning the President died. At 8 o'clock, the kindest, noblest, truest heart ceased to beat, and Abraham Lincoln was dead. Bitter, bitter will be the tears of repentance.

Andrew Johnson has been sworn. His speech was simple. "The duties now are mine, the results are God's." I trust he may perform his task faithfully, but oh, for the confidence, and the hope that we had in Lincoln. Like a ship without a rudder is the nation tossed.

Outwardly are we quiet, but in each heart, what despair.

But I must cease—Lotta and Will R left here Friday night. I presume by this time they are with you. From them you can learn of me better than I can write. Love to all.

Your affec. son
Jas. S. Knox

Major Henry R. Rathbone
Location: Presidential box
Affidavit, National Archives
April 15, 1865

> *Major Henry R. Rathbone, and his fiancée, Clara Harris, were last-minute substitutes because the Lincolns had apparently requested the company of several individuals, including General Grant and his wife, who did not accept the presidential invitation.*
>
> *Rathbone received a severe knife wound in his arm from Booth. Despite the injury, he remained conscious and escorted Mrs. Lincoln from Ford's Theatre to the Petersen house, where he collapsed from loss of blood. Physically he recovered from his wound, but apparently the assassination left deep emotional scars. In 1867 he married Clara Harris, but years later, on Christmas Day, he stabbed himself in the arm and shot and killed his wife. Rathbone spent the rest of his life in a mental institution, where he died in 1911.*
>
> *The following account contains rich detail concerning the presidential box and the events that occurred there.*

—on the 14th day of April Instant, at about 20 minutes past eight o'clock in the evening he, with Miss Clara H. Harris left his residence at the corner of 15th and H Streets and joined the President and Mrs. Lincoln and went with them in their carriage to Fords Theatre in Tenth Street. The box assigned to the President is in the second tier, on the right hand side of the audience and was occupied by the President and Mrs. Lincoln, Miss Harris and this deponent and by no other person. The box is entered by passing from the front of the building in the rear of the dress circle to a small entry or passageway about eight feet in length and four feet in width. This passageway is entered by a door which opens on the inner side. The door is placed as to make an acute angle between it and the wall behind it on the inner side. At the inner end of this passageway is another door standing squarely across and opening into the box. On the left hand side of the passageway and very near the inner end is a third door which also opens into the box. This latter door was closed. The party entered the box through the door at the end of the passageway. The box is so constructed that it may be divided into two by a movable partition, one of the doors described opening into each. The front of the box is about ten or twelve feet in length and in the centre of the railing is a small pillar overhung with a curtain. The depth of the box from front to rear is about nine feet. The elevation of the box above the stage including the railing is about ten or twelve feet.

When the party entered the box a cushioned arm chair was standing at the end of the box furthest from the stage and nearest the audience. This was also the nearest point to the door by which the box is entered. The President seated himself in this chair and, except that he once left the chair for the purpose of putting on his overcoat, remained so seated until he was shot. Mrs. Lincoln was seated in a chair between the President and the pillar in the centre, above described. At the opposite end of the box— that nearest the stage—were two chairs. In one of these, standing in the corner, Miss Harris was seated. At her left hand and along the wall running from that end of the box to the rear stood a small sofa. At the end of this sofa next to Miss Harris this deponent was seated, and the President, as they were sitting, was about seven or eight feet and the distance between this deponent and the door was about the same. The distance between the President as he sat and the door was about four or five feet. The door, according to the recollection of this deponent, was not closed during the evening.

When the second scene of the third act was being performed and while this deponent was intently observing the proceedings upon the stage with his back towards the door he heard the discharge of a pistol behind him and looking round saw through the smoke, a man between the door and the President. At the same time deponent heard him shout some word which deponent thinks was "Freedom." This deponent instantly sprang towards him and seized him. He wrested himself from the grasp and made a violent thrust at the breast of this deponent with a large knife. Deponent parried the blow by striking it up and received a wound several inches deep in his left arm between the elbow and the shoulder. The orifice of the wound is about an inch and a half in length and extends upwards towards the shoulder several inches. The man rushed to the front of the box and deponent endeavored to seize him again but only caught his clothes as he was leaping over the railing of the box. The clothes, as this deponent believes, were torn in this attempt to seize him. As he went over upon the stage, deponent cried out with a loud voice "Stop that man." Deponent then turned to the President. His position was not changed. His head was slightly bent forward and his eyes were closed. Deponent saw that he was unconscious and, supposing him mortally wounded, rushed to the door for the purpose of calling medical aid. On reaching the outer door of the passage way as above described, deponent found it barred by a heavy piece of plank, one end of which secured in the wall and the other resting against the door. It had been so securely fastened that it required considerable force to remove it. This wedge or bar was about four feet from the floor. Persons upon the outside were beating against the door for the purpose of entering. Deponent removed the bar and the door was opened. Several persons who represented themselves to be surgeons were allowed to enter. Deponent saw there Colonel Crawford and requested him to prevent other persons from entering the box. Deponent then returned to the box and found the surgeon examining the Presidents person. They had not yet discovered the wound. As soon as it was discovered, it was determined to remove him from the Theatre. He was carried out this deponent then proceeded to assist Mrs. Lincoln, who was intensely excited, to leave the Theatre. On reaching the head of the stairs, deponent requested Major Potter to aid him in assisting Mrs. Lincoln across the street to the house which the President was being conveyed. The wound which deponent had received had been bleeding very profusely and on reaching the house, feeling very faint from the loss of blood, he seated himself in the hall and soon after fainted away and was laid upon the floor. Upon the return of consciousness deponent was taken in the carriage to his residence.

In the review of the transaction it is the confident belief of this deponent that the time which elapsed between the discharge of the pistol and the time when the assassin leaped from the box did not exceed thirty seconds. Neither Mrs. Lincoln nor Miss Harris had left their seats.

> H. R. Rathbone
> Subscribed and sworn before me this
> 17th day of April, 1856 [sic]
> A B Ollie
> Justice (indecipherable) D.C.

Will T. Kent
Location: Dress circle, north
Affidavit, National Archives
April 15, 1865

> *This affidavit was sworn testimony given under oath to Justice Abram Olin, one of the Justices of the Supreme Court of the District of Columbia. Because of the date on which his account was recorded and his seat location Kent's account is one of the most reliable.*
>
> *It is rather surprising that Kent was able to enter the presidential box, find the murder weapon, and remove it.*

My name is Will T. Kent. I am clerk in the office of the Paymaster General. I was at Ford's Theatre last night, seated in the left hand side nearly opposite the President's box. About half past ten I heard a shot I thought it was in the play. A man appeared in front of the President's box and got upon the stage swinging himself down partly by the curtains and partly jumping. I noticed he had a large dagger in his left hand I think. He appeared to stagger but recovered himself. He held the dagger up just as he got upon the stage and said in a tragical tone very clearly and distinctly sic semper tyrannis. I immediately left my seat and went around behind the audience and went into the President's box. Some persons had reached the box before me and were placing the President on the floor. The President was insensible. I went out and away from the theater but missing my keys I went back to the theater and went back into the box the President had occupied. In moving about to find my keys, my foot struck against something and staring down I picked up a pistol the same that is now shown me, and in the possession of the Property Clerk of the Metropolitan Police.

Albert Daggett
Location: Parquette (rear of orchestra level)
Letter to friend Julie, Louis A. Warren Lincoln Library
April 15, 1865

*Although Daggett's account is rather lean on the events inside
Ford's Theatre, he provides an excellent personal view of the Civil
War and the effect of President Lincoln's death on the country. His
imagery of the nation as a "Ship of State" that will survive this storm
is not unlike that used by Daggett's contemporary, Walt Whitman.*

Within the last 12 hours this city has been the scene of the most terrible
tragedies that can be found upon the records of history. Abraham Lincoln, our noble, self sacrificing and patriotic President has fallen by the
hand of an accursed, traitorous assassin.

The fearful act was committed last evening at 10 o'clock at Ford's
theatre in 10th Street. I was almost an eyewitness of the melancholy occurrence occupying a front seat in the "Parquette" not more than twenty
feet from the President's box. I had been out and was just entering the
inner door when I heard the report of a pistol and turned just in time to
see the hell hound of treason leap from the box upon the stage and with
glittering dagger flourishing above his head disappear behind the scenes.
As he leaped from the box he exclaimed "Sic Semper Tyrannis"! and just
before he disappeared from the stage he cried out "I have done it—the
South is avenged" It is impossible to describe the intense excitement that
prevailed in the theatre. The audience arose as one person and horror was
stamped upon every face. I helped carry the President out and we bore
our precious burden into the house of Mr Peterson next door to my
boarding house where he remained until his death which melancholy
event took place at precisely twenty two minutes past seven this morning.
The mind cannot contemplate the results. Mr. Lincoln to see and to know
whoever was to honor and to love him has relaxed his hold from the
"Ship of State" to which he has clung with such heroic and noble daring,
during the past 4 years of a fratricidal war unknowing and unparalleled.
The good old ship is now at the mercy of the winds. God grant that she
may survive the storm, and anchor in safety in some good harbor, in the
harbor of peace and prosperity. But Tuesday evening last I listened to his
voice, a voice from Richmond and the defeated army of General Lee. As it
rung out clear and loud from the historic corridor of the executive man-

sion at his last speech, the last he shall ever made cheer upon cheer greeted him last night as he entered the theatre. I looked plainly into his face and I assure you it was a smiling one, as he stooped in his last bow, the last one ever to be made to an enthusiastic audience, as he entered the door of his private box which was so appropriately decorated with union flags. It is difficult to realize the fearful [indecipherable] though I have seen the brain, motionless from its place which but a few hours ago directed the affairs of this great Republic and the rattle of the wheels of the hearse upon the pavement has not yet died away, up the avenue, as the earthly remains of Abraham Lincoln was being [brought] home to the Executive Mansion for a last brief residence there, prepatory of their being deposited in the vault of death.

But I have not yet completed this dreadful chapter of horror. At the same hour of the attack upon Mr. Lincoln a murderer entered the house of Secretary Stanton with designs upon the life of that good and patriotic statesman. After forcing his way into the house he was stopped by Mr. Frederich [sic] W. Seward the assistant Secretary whose head he crushed in with the but end of a pistol and otherwise wounded, he then pushed his way to the chamber of the Secretary who was still suffering from his recent accident, the fracture of an [indecipherable] and jaw, and dragging him from his bed attempted to cut his throat. This he partially succeeded in doing and would undoubtedly have accomplished it had it not been for the interference of the nurse, a disabled soldier who recovered from stabs while dragging him from the prostrate body of Mr. Seward. Major Seward was also badly cut supposing his work accomplished he started to leave the room at the door of which he met Mr. Hansell the chief messenger of this Department. In endeavoring to prevent the escape of the [indecipherable] Mr. Hansell was severely wounded. It is possible that the Secretary will recover, but the assistant Secretary is said to be beyond the influence of human skill and probably his soul has [indecipherable] this passed that headful [indecipherable] from which no [indecipherable] ever returned the 14 of April, 1861. When fort Sumpter was first fired into nothing has [indecipherable] so calculated to take the loyal millions of the country and cause then to [indecipherable] upon the authors of this unholy rebellion [indecipherable] lost its champion when Abraham Lincoln ceased to breath and now deeds must take the place of words. Andrew Johnson is now President of the United States. Let us hope that his misconduct during the inauguration ceremonies resulting from too free use, on account of sickness. Of spirits will be Abraham Lincoln, but, supported by the people of the country he will mash this hydra of treason and rebellion North and South so deep into the soil as which it germinated that the [indecipherable] knew the [indecipherable] of Gabriel will fail to call it forth on the morning of the resurrections, the crimson blood of a Lincoln of a Seward and of a hundred thousand fallen patriot's and master calls loudly for revenge and it calls not in vain. The news has just reached me that one traitor at last in this city had met his deserts. He dared to say in company that he was glad President Lincoln was dead, the words had hardly left his mouth before the bullet from the pistol of a union soldier went crashing through his brain and his soul was summoned to the aweful presence of his maker with those horrible words upon his lips. The same fate awaits others if treason does not hold its infamous tongue. The greatest . . . the city. Everywhere and . . . from the highest to the lowest is drapped in mourning. The faces of the persons by are stamped with the most grief woe. The sun is hidden by black clouds and even the skies cries great tear of rain. Thus has a nation passed through such an ordeal as this. It has been practically ascertained that the murderer of President Lincoln was John Wilkes Booth an actor who appeared in Fords on several occasions. The officers of justice are at his heels and it is impossible for him to escape. A reward of 50,000 has already been offered for the apprehension Write soon

Yours forever,

Dag

Charles A. Sanford
Location: Unknown
Letter to Goodrich, Clements Library, University of Michigan
April 16, 1865

> *Sanford's confusion concerning the pistol shot was probably the norm for the theater patrons and helps to explain why there was minimal pursuit of Booth. His assertion that Secretary of State William Seward and Assistant Secretary of State Frederick Seward were assassinated was mistaken. Although William Seward was stabbed several times in the face and Frederick Seward received a mild concussion from Lewis Powell's attack, both survived. Lewis Powell, also known as Lewis Paine, was found guilty in the conspiracy trial and executed by hanging.*
>
> *The last paragraph of Sanford's account is especially insightful in indicating how some Northerners reacted to the assassination.*

Dear Goodrich,

Washington is in mourning to-day. We think it no shame to weep here to-day. Of course you know at this moment that our President died a few hours ago. As I was going to dinner last night and passing Ford's Theatre, I saw by a poster that Laura Keene was to make her last appearance that night and she and her supporters were to render "Our American Cousin" I had been studying hard all day and was weary and I stopped and procured a ticket The play was going on Just about half past ten o'clock when I heard the report of a pistol. I at first thought it was accidently discharged by some soldier or drunken man and looked around but saw no one stir or excitement + [indecipherable] something was wrong + as I turned my face to the stage I saw a man thrust aside the flags that decorated the box which the President and General occupied and leap out of the box down upon the stage which at that time was empty with Ivory knife in hand and, if I mistake not a revolver in the other. He wisked across the stage shouting out something which I did catch but which other officers was Virginia's motto "Sic Semper tyrannis." Many with myself at first took it to be a part of the play. Everybody was confounded and paralyzed. Nothing was announced from the President's box and no one comprehended the moment. We could not persuade ourselves that the President had been assassinated. At first we sat still till the murderer escaped from among the scenery. Then all rose up trying to recover themselves—inquiring anxiously what is meant and if the President had been assassinated. It was an awful moment. Could we believe our own eyes? Had the great-hearted President of the United States—the idol of the people—the genius of the times been assassinated and that too so openly and boldly? Alas we could not avert the facts! It was too times! I will send you a paper which will describe the excitement and [indecipherable] too and for which was kept up all night. We are all sad. The President's remains were removed to the White House this morning. "Folds in the stars and stripes" The streets are full today and the very heavens weep bitterly because of our grave calamity. Secretary Seward and son were also assassinated. I have just received a letter from you describing the joy in the [indecipherable] over the late successes. Washington has been intensely enthusiastic of late. Thursday night she gave the greatest celebration I ever witnessed. I cannot describe it. It baffled all description. . . . [Sanford continues with a vivid description of the celebration and then provides additional information on the assassination.]

   It is reported that Boothe is arrested. It was a widely laid conspiracy. It doubtless was intended to include Stanton + Grant + others. The Rebs will suffer now. Mrs. Lincoln was frantic. She passed right by my side in the front of me in charge of two officers. She was throwing her hands + [indecipherable] about in terrible agony. I am in a poor mood to write you today. Please write soon.

Ever yours,
Charles A. Sanford

John Wilkes Booth
Location: Presidential box
Datebook, Ford's Theatre National Historic Site
April 1865

> *Booth's diary was actually an 1864 datebook which contains calendar entry pages ending on Saturday, June 11, 1864. A few unidentified pages at the book's end were removed, most likely by Booth. The datebook was retrieved by Union soldiers at the Garrett farm in Virginia where Booth was shot and killed.*
>
> *Booth apparently did not record his daily activities but used the diary to record a justification for his actions. The book's primary value lay in providing Booth's motives for assassinating Abraham Lincoln.*
>
> *All four details Booth recorded concerning the assassination are contradicted by the reliable eyewitness accounts. Booth claimed that Lincoln had a "colonel" at his side whereas Rathbone held the rank of major. Booth maintained that he "pushed" his way into the box although others indicate he was actually allowed to enter. He also claimed that he shouted "Sic semper" from the box before he shot Lincoln while the evidence overwhelmingly supports the conclusion that he shouted "Sic Semper Tyrannis" on stage after he had shot the president. And finally, Booth recorded that he broke his leg in "jumping" although the 1865 eyewitnesses claimed that he did not appear to limp as he crossed the stage. He may actually have injured his leg when his horse fell on him during his escape through Maryland. These four inaccuracies are consistent with Booth's personality. He craved a reputation as a dashing actor and subsequently as a daring patriot who was striking a blow for his country by assassinating Lincoln. Hence in recording his version of the assassination, Booth altered the story in his favor. His deed would have been far more impressive if he had had to force his way into the box, if a colonel rather than a major had been at Lincoln's side, if he had shouted to his victim before firing, and if he had injured himself during the deed rather than when fall-*

ing from a horse. Booth had a personal interest in how history would
tell his tale and therefore may not be the best eyewitness.

Ti amo
the Ides
   Until to day nothing was ever thought of sacrificing to our country's
wrongs. For six months we had worked to capture. But our cause, being
almost lost, something decisive & great must be done. But it's failure was
owing to others, who did not strike for their country with a heart. I
struck boldly and not as the papers say. I walked with a fine step through
a thousand of his friends, was stopped, but pushed on. A colonel was at
his side. I shouted Sic semper before I fired. In jumping broke my leg. I
passed all his pickets, rode sixty miles that night, with the bone of my leg
tearing the flesh at every jump. I can never repent it, though we hated to
kill. Our country owed all her trouble to him, and God simply made me
the instrument of his punishment. The country is not—April 1865 what it
was. This forced union is not what I have loved. I care not what becomes
of me. I have no desire to out-live my country. This night (before the
deed), I wrote a long article and left it for one of the Editors of the
National Intelligencer, in which I fully set forth our reasons for our
proceedings. He or the Govmt—After being hunted like a dog through
swamps, woods, and last night being chased by gun boats till I was forced
to return wet cold and starving, with every man's hand against me, I am
here in despair. And why? For doing what Brutus was honored for. What
made Tell a Hero. And yet I for striking down a greater tyrant than—
they ever knew am looked upon as a common cutthroat. My action was
purer than either of theirs. One hoped to be great himself The other had
not only his country's but his own wrongs to avenge. I hoped for no gain.
I knew no private wrong. I struck for my country and that alone. A
country groaned beneath this tyranny and prayed for this end, and yet
now behold the cold hand they extend to me. God cannot pardon me if I
have done wrong. Yet I cannot see any wrong except in serving a degener-
ate people. The little,—the very little I left behind to clear my name, the
Govmt will not allow to be printed. So ends all. For my country I have
given up all that makes life sweet and Holy, brought misery upon my
family and am sure there is no pardon—in the Heaven for me since man
condemns me so. I have only heard of what has been done (except what I
did myself) and it fills me with horror. God try and forgive me, and bless
my mother. To night I will once more try the river with the intent to

cross; though I have a greater desire and almost a mind to return to Washington and in a measure clear my name, which I feel I can do. I do not repent the blow I struck. I may before my God but not to man.—I think I have done well, though I am abandoned, with the curse of Cain upon me, when if the world knew my heart, that one blow would have made me great, though I did desire no greatness. To night I try to escape these blood hounds once more. Who, who can read his fate God's will be done. I have too great a soul to die like a criminal. O may he, may he spare me that and let me die bravely. I bless the entire world Have never hated or wronged anyone. This last was not a wrong, unless God deems it—so. And its with him to damn or bless me. And for this brave boy with me who often prays (yes, before and since) with a true and sincere heart. Was it crime in him, if so, why can he pray the same I do not wish to shed a drop of blood, but "I must fight the course." 'Tis all that's left me.

Harry Hawk
Location: Stage
Letter to his parents, reprinted in *Boston Herald,* April 11, 1897, Ford's Theatre National Historic Site
April 16, 1865

> *Hawk provided more detail in this letter to his parents than he gave to Stanton. The key difference lay in the exclamations attributed to Booth. In his testimony, Hawk did not say anything about Booth's utterances. In this letter, Hawk wrote that Booth said both "Sic Semper Tyrannis" and "The South shall be free."*

My Dear Parents:
This is the first opportunity I have had to write to you since the assassination of our dear president on Friday night, as I have been in custody ever since. I was one of the principal witnesses of the sad affair, having been on the stage at the time of the fatal shot. I was playing Asa Trenchard in "The American Cousin." The old lady of the theater (Mrs. Muzzey) had just gone off the stage, and I was answering her exit speech, when I heard the shot fired. I turned, looked up at the president's box, heard the man exclaim "Sic semper tyrannis," saw him jump from the staff and drop to the stage. He slipped when he gained the stage, but got upon his feet in a moment, brandished a large knife, saying "The South shall be free," turned his face in the direction I stood, and I recognized him as Wilkes Booth. He ran toward me, and I seeing the knife, thought I was the one he

was after, ran off the stage and up a flight of stairs. He made his escape out of a door in the rear of the theater, mounted a horse and rode away. The above all occurred in the space of a few seconds, and at the time I did not know the president was shot, although if I had tried to stop him he (Booth) would have stabbed me. I am now under $1,000 bail to appear as a witness when Booth is tried, if caught. All the above I have sworn to. You may imagine the excitement in the theater, which was crowded, with cries of "hang him," "who is he," from every one present. It was the saddest thing I ever knew. The city only the night before was illuminated, and everybody was happy. Now all is sadness. Everybody looks gloomy and sad. Mrs. Lincoln was laughing at my speech when the shot was fired.

Helen DuBarry
Location: Unknown
Letter to her mother, Illinois State Historical Library
April 16, 1865

> *DuBarry's account is unusual in contending that two "watchmen" accompanied the Lincolns that evening. They may have been John Parker, the president's guard, and Charles Forbes, his messenger. Unfortunately, she did not identify them individually nor did she say which one allowed Booth to enter.*

My Dear Mother

Beck has not come from the Office yet and I have not received your letter but as I have a good deal to write I will begin now. I suppose by tomorrow the mail will go out from Washin. No trains left yesterday. What I have to write is with reference to the great Tragedy which has caused a Nation to mourn. I had the misfortune to be at Ford's Theatre on Friday evening and to hear the shot which deprived us of a President.

It was given out during the day that Mrs. Lincoln had engaged a "Box" for the President and Genl. Grant and having a desire not only to see them but to see the "American cousin" performed, we determined to go. Before we went Beck knew that the Genl. would not be there as he was to leave for his home in the evening. We went a few moments before the time and waited some time for the President to arrive and as he did not come until late the performances commenced and we thought we were to be disappointed in not seeing him. In the midst of the 2nd scene there was a great applause and cheering and our attention was directed from the stage to

the Dress circle—close to the wall walked Miss Harris—Mrs. Lincoln—
Major Rathbun—a gentleman the President & another gentleman behind
him. These two gentlemen were watchmen in citizens dress who have
always accompanied the President since the War commenced. We followed him with our eyes until he entered the Box little thinking we were
looking for the last time at him. He sat looking on the stage his back to us
and out of our sight behind the flags except occasionally when he would
lean forward. Mrs. Lincoln was in front of him and we only saw her
occasionally. We saw her smile & turn towards him several times. It was
while every one's attention was fastened upon the stage that a pistol shot
was heard causing every one to jump (as an unexpected shot will) & look
up at the President's Box merely because that was the direction of the
sound and supposing it to be part of the performance we all looked again
on the stage—when a man suddenly vaulted over the railing—turned
back & then leaped to the stage—striking on his heels & falling backward
but recovered himself in an instant and started across the stage to behind
the scenes flourishing a knife—the blade of which appeared in the reflection of the bright lights to be half as long as man's arm—and making use
of the expressions you have seen in the Papers. He had nearly disappeared
before we could understand what it was or what had happened. We first
thought it was a crazy man—when he jumped on to the stage we jumped
to our feet & stood spell bound—as he crossed the stage some few started
towards the stage crying—our President! our President is shot! catch
him—hang him! Miss Harris was seen to lean over the railing for water &
that was all that broke the stillness in that box. If those watch had called
out soon as the man jumped to give us an idea of what had happened he
could have been caught—& said "take out the ladies & hang him here on
the spot." Beck fearing a mob hurried me out—leaving the audience still
standing awed & speechless. We waited outside until a young man came
out and said "He is dead—no doubt about it!"

Before we got out of the door some one said "It was J. Wilkes Booth"
and before I got out, the idea that our Chief was gone—almost our sole
dependence—overcome me & I could not control myself & sobbed aloud
We met several outside the door just coming in asking "For God's sake
tell me is it true?" as if they had heard already rumors of the great tragedy.
The reason that we could not suddenly realize what had occurred was
because we could not anticipate that an assassin could be in the Box with
the President. His only danger seemed to be from a shot fired by one of
the audience.

Booth entered the front door and asked some one there if Genl. Grant was there that night—then went along to the door of the Box—just where we had seen the President enter knocked at the door & to the watch who opened it, said he wished to speak to the President, that he had a communication for him showing an Official envelope & giving him a card with the name of a Senator written on it. The watch stepped aside & the assassin entered & fired immediately while Mr. Lincoln was looking on the stage.

The excitement that night was intense & a mob of about 2000 went to the Old Capitol Prison to burn it & they called upon the people to come out & see the rebels burn. The Police & troops were out & put a stop to it or it would have been done. The assassin at Sewards first stabbed the nurse through the lungs & killed him I believe—knocked the skull of Fred Seward with a butt of a pistol & stabbed another son—all had opposed his entrance and the old man hearing the scuffle at the door & thinking it was some one after him, rolled out of bed to stab him so he only had two cuts—on his neck & face—which will not prove serious if he has strength after his former sickness. There is no doubt that it was Booth who killed the President. Laura Keene says she can testify that it was him.

The secessionists here have all draped their houses in crape—and acknowledge that it was the worst thing for the South that ever happened—their best friend is gone & Andy J.—will be more severe than ever Lincoln was—Andy Johnson joined the Temperance Society after the Inauguration and every one who saw him at his own Inauguration were much pleased with his manner as he seemed impressed with the responsibility before him.

There are rumored changes to be made in the Cabinet already There was a strange coincidence at the Theatre Friday evening. In the play the American Cousin won the prize at Archery and on receiving the medal was congratulated. He said he hadn't done nothing—all it required was a steady hand a clear eye—to pull the trigger & the mark was hit as he said it he looked right up at the President.

That was in the play & he looked there merely because he was the principal person present but afterwards it struck every one as a strange coincidence.

On Friday Beck received a letter from Duane who is a prisoner at Point Lookout begging him to forget the Past & to find out for him if he would be allowed to take the oath of allegiance to the U.S. that he was sick enough of the Confederacy and very sorry he had ever had any thing to do with it. That afternoon Beck went to the Comm. Genl. of prisoners but he was out—and of course after the awful tragedy Beck did not feel like interceding for a rebel I do not know what he will do now—he may go to Genl. Grant—if Hoffman won't do anything. Don't say anything about it.

I suppose you have read all I have told you, in the Papers but being there myself I supposed you would like to hear it over just as I saw it. The Authorities think that there is no chance for the assassins to escape but I think it is like hunting for a needle in a haystack. . . .

> your aff dau
> Helen DuB

Julia Adeline Shepherd
Location: Dress circle
Letter to her father, Illinois State Historical Library
April 16, 1865

> *Shepherd's engaging account provides a minute-by-minute descrip-*
> *tion of the events. Although her account is in the present tense, she*
> *probably wrote it after the assassination.*

Dear Father:—It is Friday night and we are at the theatre. Cousin Julia has just told me that the President is in yonder upper right private box so handsomely decked with silken flags festooned over a picture of Washington. The young and lovely daughter of Senator Harris is the only one of the party we can see, as the flags hide the rest. But we know that "Father Abraham" is there; like a father watching what interests his children, for their pleasure rather than his own. It has been announced in the papers he would be there. How sociable it seems, like one family sitting around their parlor fire. How different this from the pomp and show of monarchial Europe. Every one has been so jubilant for days, since the surrender of Lee, that they laugh and shout at every clowning witticism. One of the actresses, whose part is that of a very delicate young lady talks of wishing to avoid the draft, when her lover tells her, "not to be alarmed for there is no more draft," at which the applause is long and loud. The American cousin has just been making love to a young lady, who says she will never marry but for love, yet when her mother and herself find he has lost his property they retreat in disgust at the left of the stage, while the American cousin goes out at the right. We are waiting for the next scene.

The report of a pistol is heard. . . . Is it all in the play? A man leaps from the President's box, some ten feet, on to the stage. The truth flashes upon me. Brandishing a dagger he shrieks out "The South is avenged," and rushes through the scenery. No one stirs. "Did you hear what he said, Julia? I believe he has killed the President." Miss Harris is wringing her hands and calling for water. Another instant and the stage is crowded— officers, policemen, actors, and citizens. "Is there a surgeon in the house?" they say. "Several rush forward and with superhuman efforts climb up to the box. Minutes are hours, but see! they are bringing him out. A score of strong arms bear Lincoln's loved form along. . . . Major Rathbone, who was of their party, springs forward to support [Mrs. Lincoln], but cannot. What is it? Yes, he too has been stabbed. Somebody says "Clear the house," so every one else repeats "Yes, clear the house." So slowly one party after another steals out. There is no need to hurry. On the stairs we stop aghast and with shuddering lips—"Yes, see, it is our President's blood" all down the stairs and out upon the pavement. It seemed sacrilege to step near. We are in the street now. They have taken the President into the house opposite. He is alive, but mortally wounded. What are those people saying. "Secretary Seward and his son have had their throats cut in their own house." Is it so? Yes, and the murderer of our President has escaped through a back alley where a swift horse stood awaiting him. Cavalry come dashing up the street and stand with drawn swords before yon house. Too late! too late! What mockery armed men are now. Weary with the weight of woe the moments drag along and for hours delicate women stand clinging to the arms of their protectors, and strong men throw their arms around each other's necks and cry like children, and passing up and down enquire in low agonized voices "Can he live? Is there no hope?" They are putting out the street lamps now. "What a shame! not now! not to-night!" There they are lit again. Now the guard with drawn swords forces the crowd backward. Great, strong Cousin Ed says "This unnerves me; let's go up to Cousin Joe's." We leave Julia and her escort there and at brother Joe's gather together in an upper room and talk and talk with Dr. Webb and his wife who were at the theatre. Dr. W. was one of the surgeons who answered the call. He says "I asked Dr. —— when I went in what it was, and putting his hand on mine he said, 'There!' I looked and it was 'brains'. . . .

Last Thursday evening we drove to the city, and all along our route the city was one blaze of glorious light. From the humble cabin of the contraband to the brilliant White House light answered light down the broad avenue. The sky was ablaze with bursting rockets. Calcium lights shone from afar on the public buildings. Bonfires blazed in the streets and every device that human Yankee ingenuity could suggest in the way of mottoes and decoration made noon of midnight. Then as the candles burned low and the rockets ceased, we drove home through the balmy air and it seemed as though Heaven smiled upon the rejoicings, and Nature took up the illumination with a glory of moonlight that transcended all art.

To-day I have been to church through the same streets and the suburbs with the humble cottages that were so bright that night shone through the murky morning, heavy with black hangings, and on and on, down the streets only the blackness of darkness. The show of mourning was as universal as the glorying had been, and when we were surrounded by the solemn and awe-stricken congregation in the church, it seemed as though my heart had stopped beating. I feel like a frightened child. I wish I could go home and have good cry. I can't bear to be alone. You will hear all this from the papers, but I can't help writing it for things seen hard to write now. I dare not speak of our great loss. Sleeping or waking, that terrible scene is before me. . . .

Spencer Bronson
Location: Unknown
Letter to his sister, Louis A. Warren Lincoln Library
April 16, 1865

> *Bronson's account is one of the few that translated Booth's phrase.*
> *His language indicates that Bronson was a strong Lincoln supporter.*
> *Bronson's punctuation is poor but, for the most part, I have left the*
> *letter in its original form.*

Dear Sister

Your last letter was received in due time was pleased to hear that Edward had been heard from even if it was almost one month ago. The rejoicing over our victories has been turned into mourning President Lincoln has been struck down in the midst of his usefulness, the pride of his age, the benefactor of his race, the liberator of a nation & the friend of suffering humanity everywhere has been murdered by a demon in human form & all because he was the Chief Magistrate of the nation.

I was present & saw this scene enacted & such an act that has no parallel since the days of Roman greatness when Caesar was struck down in the Roman senate by an idle mob. But I will tell a little of what I saw their although I presume you have read the full account of this dastardly murder. As I was reading the morning papers on the 14 inst I saw a statement that the President & Gen Grant would visit Fords Theatre that evening. I had been gaining that week & resolved that I would make an attempt to be present not so much for the attraction of the play but for the sake of seeing Mr Lincoln & most of all Gen Grant who I have heard but seen once At an early hour. I was at the Theatre which is but three squares from this hospital. 800 came & the private box where the two greatest in the age was to set was still unoccupied The curtains arose & the play commenced entitled "Our American Cousin" the star performer being Miss Laura Keene About 8 1/200 [sic] Mr Lincoln & lady accompanied by a single couple entered the house being received by enthusiastic cheers as they took their seats The play went on & all went smoothly every one being interested in the play. Then suddenly a pistol shot is heard—No one is alarmed for it is believed to be part of the play. A clang takes place a dark form is seen to fall from the private box his spurs catching in the flag as he descends. A second & he recovered & irising [sic] in a tragical attitude he draws a dagger & with his white face towards the crowd he repeated in latin "So be it ever to tyrants" & rapid left the stage making his exit by a back door mounted a horse rode away The intire crowd started in pursuit but were halted by an exclamation that he had been caut [sic] & loud cries resounded from all parts of the house "Hang him" "shoot him" But it was but a game of some encomplisher [sic] for to draw off the scent so that the murderer might escape In the mean time Mrs Lincoln came to the front of the box with loud cries & screems know to the horror struck audience that Mr Lincoln had been assassinated Help was called for & men was hoisted up with water & spirits Miss Keene [mostly?] regain her presence of mind & went around into the box holding the President head while an examination was being made Enclosed is one of the handbills of the Theatre that evening

I will also send you a paper with the full account of the affair & also a good portrait of the murderer who I am shure is J Wilkes Booth who I have seen before I will write again before long the city is mad with excitement at the act. three men has been shot dead by soldiers for saying they were glad the President was dead

Thus far the murderer has not been caught. Save the hand bill

Dr. Charles A. Leale
Location: Dress circle, right
Letter to General Benjamin Butler, Library of Congress
July 20, 1867

> *Leale's account is one of the most detailed. He provides an invaluable description of the medical attention given to Lincoln inside the theater. Although it was written in 1867, it is included with the April 1865 accounts because Leale based the letter on notes written within days of the assassination.*

My dear General,

Yours of the 15th inst. has been received and heard of the assassination of our late President Abraham Lincoln, and in answer to which I herewith forward to you an account in brief of what transpired from the time that the President entered the theatre until the time of his death on the following morning, which account is principally copied from (a never published) one written by me a few hours after leaving his death bed in which I noted the events in connection with what transpired on that most memorable and never-to be forgotten night that are so indeniably impressed upon my mind. More especially on account of the grave responsibilities that rested upon me. As I was the first person to arrive to his assistance was requested by Mrs. Lincoln to do what I could for him, discovered where he had been wounded by the ball of the assassin, removed the coagula from the opening through the cranium and had charge of him until Dr. Stone his family physician arrived which was about twenty minutes after we had placed him comfortably in bed in the house of Mr. Petersen and as I alas remained with him until his death, the following account of what transpired is respectfully transmitted.

Very Respectfully Your Obedient Servant
Charles A. Leale, M.D.
Brevet-Captain and Late A. Surgeon United States Volunteers

Major General B. F. Butler
Member of United States Congress and
Chairman of Assassination Investigating Committee

On the evening of the 14th April 1865 while engaged with the execution duties of the United States Army General Hospital "Armory Square" Washington I was requested to visit Ford's Theatre, being told that the President Lincoln, General Grant and Staff were to be there.

I arrived at the theatre about 8 1/4 PM and endeavored to procure a seat in the orchestra but it being so densely crowded I left it for the dress circle where I found a vacant seat on the same side and within 40 feet of the President's box, the play was then progressing and in a few minutes I saw the President, Mrs. Lincoln, Major Rathbone, and Miss Harris enter, the play ceased for a short time and as soon as they were seen by the audience they were cheered which was responded by the President with a smile and a bow. The President as he proceeded to the box looked expressively mournful and sad.

The door of the box was opened by an usher who proceeded them but who after they had all entered closed the door then took a seat near by for himself. All parts of the theatre were well filled and the play of Our American Cousin was progressing very pleasantly until about 5 minutes past 10 when on looking towards the box I saw a man speaking with another near the door and endeavoring to enter, which he at last succeeded in doing after which the door was closed.

I again looked toward the stage and was pleased with the amusing part then being performed, but soon heard the report of a pistol, and about a minute or two after I saw a man with dark hair and bright black eyes, leap from the box to the stage below, while descending he threw himself a little forward and raised his shining dagger in the air, which reflected the light as though it had been a diamond, when he struck the stage he stumbled a little forward but with a bound regained the use of his limbs and ran to the opposite side of the stage soon disappearing behind the scenes.

I then heard cries that the President had been murdered which were followed by those of "Kill the murderer" "Shoot him" etc which came from different parts of the audience.

I remained in my seat believing it until I saw some one open the door of the box, and heard him call for a Surgeon and help.

I arrived at the door of the box, and upon saying that I was a Surgeon was immediately admitted.

When I entered the box, Mr. Lincoln was sitting in a high backed armchair with his head leaning towards his right-side and which was supported by Mrs. Lincoln who was weeping bitterly. Miss Harris was at her left-side behind the President, Major Rathbone was at the door of the box.

While approaching the President I was told that he had been murdered, and I sent for some Brandy and water.

Upon Mrs. Lincoln being told that I was a Surgeon she said, "Oh Doctor do what you can for my dear husband" "do what you can for him and for Dr. Stone."

I told her that I would do all which was in my power to do.

When I reached the President he was almost dead, his eyes were closed he was parallel. I placed my finger on his right radial pulse, but could feel no movement of the artery. His breathing was exceedingly stertorous there being long intervals between each inspiration and he was in a most profoundly comatosed condition.

With the assistance of two gentlemen I immediately placed him in a recumbent position while doing this and holding his head and shoulders my hand came in contact with blood on his left-shoulder, the thought of the dagger then recuffed to me, and supposed that he might have been stabbed in the subelavical artery or some of its branches. I asked a gentleman near by to cut his coat and shirt off that shoulder to enable me if possible to check the supposed hemorrhage, as soon as his arm was bared to a distance below the shoulder, and I saw that there was no wound there, I lifted his eyelids and examined his eyes, the pupil of which was dilated. I then examined his head and soon discovered a large firm clot of blood situated about one inch below the superior curved line and an inch and a half to the left of the median line of the occipital bone.

The coagnin which was firmly matted with the hair, [was] removed [I] passed the little finger of my left hand directly through the perfectly smooth opening made by the ball, he was then apparently dead.

When I removed my finger which I used as a knife an oozing of blood followed and he commenced, to show signs of improvement.

I believe that he would not have lived five minutes longer if the pressure on the brain had not been relieved and if he had been left that much longer in the sitting posture.

The Brandy and water, now arrived and I put a small quantity into his mouth which was the only thing that passed into his stomach from his assassination until his death.

Dr. C. S. Taft and Dr. A. F. A. King now arrived, and after a moments consultation we agreed to remove him.

While in the theatre, I was several times asked the nature of the wound and said that the ball had lodged in the encephalens and that it was a mortal wound.

We now commenced to remove him carefully descending the steps first while supporting his head and shoulders as soon as we arrived at the door of the box, I saw that the passage was densely crowded by those coming towards that part of the theatre.

I called out twice "Guards clear the passage" which was so rapidly done that we proceeded without a moments delay towards the stairs leading to the hall which is entered from the street, when we arrived at the head of the stairs we turned around those holding his lower extremities descending first.

There was an officer present who rendered great assistance in making the passage through the crowd.

When we arrived to the street I was asked to place him in a carriage and remove him to the White House this I refused to do being fearful that he would die as soon as he would be placed in an upright position. I said that I wished to take him to the nearest house and place him comfortably in bed.

We slowly crossed the street there being a barrier of men on each side of an open passage towards the house. Those who went ahead of us reported that the house directly opposite was closed.

I saw a man standing at the door of Mr. Peterson's [sic] house and beckoning us to enter which we did and immediately placed him in bed, all of which was done in less than twenty minutes from the time that he had been assassinated we not having been in the slightest interrupted while removing him. . . .

Dr. Charles Sabin Taft
Location: Orchestra level, first row
Article in *Century Magazine*, February 1893, Library of Congress
April 1865

> *Like Leale's account, Dr. Charles Sabin Taft's provides an excellent description of the medical care provided for the president.*

The notes from which this article is written were made the day succeeding Mr. Lincoln's death, and immediately after the official examination of the body. They were made, by direction of Secretary Stanton for the purpose of preserving an official account of the circumstances attending the assassination, in connection with the medical aspects of the case.

On the fourth anniversary of the fall of Fort Sumter, the beloved President, his great heart filled with peaceful thoughts and charity for all,

entered Ford's Theater amid the acclamations of the loyal multitude as-
sembled to greet him. Mr. Lincoln sat in a high-backed upholstered chair
in the corner of the box nearest the audience, and only his left profile was
visible to most of the audience from where I sat, almost under the box, in
the front row of orchestra chairs, I plainly saw that Mrs. Lincoln rested
her hand on his knee much of the time, and often called his attention to
some humorous situation on the stage. She seemed to take great pleasure
witnessing his enjoyment.

All went on pleasantly until half-past ten o'clock when during the
second scene of the third act, the sharp report of a pistol rang through the
house. The report seemed to proceed from behind the President's box.
While it startled every one in the audience, it was evidently accepted by all
as an introductory effect preceding some new situation in the play, several
of which had been introduced in the earlier part of the performance. A
moment afterward a hatless and white-faced man leaped from the front of
the President's box down twelve feet to the stage. As he jumped, one
of the spurs on his riding-boots caught in the folds of the flag dropped
over the front, and caused him to fall partly on his hands and knees as he
struck the stage. Springing quickly to his feet with the suppleness of an
athlete, he faced the audience for a moment as he brandished in his right
hand a long knife, and shouted "Sic Semper Tyrannis!" Then, with a rapid
stage stride, he crossed the stage, and disappeared from view. A piercing
shriek from the President's box, a repeated call for "Water! water!" and
"A surgeon!" in quick succession, conveyed the truth to the almost paralyzed audience. A most terrible scene of excitement followed. With loud
shouts of "Kill him!" "Lynch him!" part of the audience stampeded toward the entrance and some to the stage.

I leaped from the top of the orchestra railing in front of me upon the
stage, and, announcing myself as an army surgeon, was immediately lifted
up to the President's box by several gentleman who had collected beneath.
I happened to be in uniform, having passed the entire day in attending to
my duties at the Signal Camp of Instruction in Georgetown, and not
having had an opportunity to change my dress. The cape of a military
overcoat fastened around my neck became detached in clambering into
the box, and fell upon the stage. It was taken to police headquarters,
together with the assassin's cap, spur, and deringer, which had also been
picked up, under the supposition that it belonged to him. It was recovered, weeks afterward, with much difficulty.

When I entered the box, the President was lying upon the floor surrounded by his wailing wife and several gentlemen who had entered from the private stairway and dress circle. Assistant Surgeon Charles A. Leale, U.S.V., was in the box, and had caused the coat and waistcoat to be cut off in searching for the wound. Dr. A. F. A. King of Washington was also present, and assisted in the examination. The carriage had been ordered to remove the President to the White House, but the surgeons counter-manded the order, and he was removed to a bed in a house opposite the theater. . . .

Samuel Koontz
Location: Unknown
Letter to a friend, Louis A. Warren Lincoln Library
April 24, 1865

> Koontz described the gentleman outside the box as "Lincoln's ser-
> vant," indicating that the gentleman's attire or actions did not cause
> Koontz to consider him a guard. Koontz's description of the activities
> in the Petersen house were probably learned from newspapers.

My Dear Friend,
It may not be uninteresting to you to get a letter from Washington just at this time. I presume you have heard all manner of stories in relation to the murder of our beloved President, so I write for the purpose of letting you know the truth about this terrible tragedy. I was present at the Theater and saw it all, in fact I was only about 15 ft. from the President when he was shot, although he was in a private box in the Theater. . . . Lincoln when he came in, had a pleasant smile for all, they cheered him, and the band struck up "Hail Columbia" little did I think that when I would next behold him he would be cold in the arms of death. Lincoln & his wife, Miss Harris & Major Rathbone, were all who were in the box. Booth went through the door of the box, told the man who was Lincolns servant at the door, that Lincoln had sent for him. A number of persons saw him go in to kill the President. In less than a minute after he went in, I heard the report of the pistol & saw him jump out of the front of the box, down upon the stage, which was at least 12 ft., brandishing a knife, and running across the stage exclaiming, 'sic semper tyrannis', this is the latin motto of the state of Virginia, and means, 'thus always to tyrants'. Just as he leapt from the box, all was quiet, no one knew at first what was the matter, then at the second thought, the whole audience sprung upon their feet &

shouted 'Kill him, kill him, kill him!' Miss Harris exclaimed—'the President's shot'. One man I believe run after Booth but he had no pistol—he saw him jump on a horse which he had ready behind the theater. Major Rathbone had a tussle with him in the box, but he stabbed Rathbone with his big knife and got loose. I immediately rushed into the box, when Miss Harris exclaimed, 'for God's sake go for a Surgeon' I immediately run up the street got Dr. Lieberrman up who was soon present, together with other distinguished surgeons, but alas! the assassin had done his crime too well and all the highest medical skill could not save the life of the patriot, the statesman, the Christian, the martyr,—Abraham Lincoln. . . . Booth I am sorry to say, has not yet been caught. . . . In about 20 minutes after Lincoln was shot, they carried him across the street into a private house where he died the next morning at precisely 22 minutes past 7 o'clock. He never spoke a word after he was shot; but laid perfectly unconscious until he died. . . . I write to give you the truth, I know how likely you are to be imposed upon in the country. . . . Yes I will tell you a little more. Booth shot the President with a single barrel pistol, the ball entered the head about 2 inches behind the left ear, and it lodged about three inches deep in the head towards the forehead. The pistol was found in the box. . . .

S. J. Koontz

John Downing, Jr.
Location: Dress circle
Letter to a friend, Louis A. Warren Lincoln Library
April 26, 1865

> *Although Downing was unique in asserting that Booth spoke from the box, his account provides insight into a contemporary individual's view of the assassination, Lincoln, and the Civil War.*

At my light, near the great unfinished Washington monument, is an encampment of soldiers from which comes the sad funeral strains of a band playing a dirge over the bier of a dead hero. It awakend sad thoughts, but still in consenance with the dreamy, hazy quiet that over the landscape. And then how consoling the thought that he died not in vain. If anything will touch a man's better nature it is such a sound as this. The very thought of it almost brings tears to the eye, and awakens holier resolves. Numerous little negro children—whose parents were probably slaves a few months ago—are constantly passing, and turn their great white eyes

up to me with an expression of mirth and satisfaction which is unde-
scribably ludicrous. Poor things—they are happy enough now, but when
they grow older, how sad it would be, that lesson of inferiority which the
white people will impress upon them so deeply. With our aspirations and
hopes, their life could be intolerable miserable. No matter how intelligent,
how amiable or how noble, one of this race may be he is only a "nigger,"
after all. Such is to be the fate of every one of these little children. They
are so bright and intelligent too. O, it is too bad, and almost enough to
make one question the goodness of our creator. I can reconcile myself to
this decree, only by thinking and believing that in the next world—or this
world purified and beatiful, which?—all will be made right to our comprehension. I thank God, my friend, that I have faith enough for this.
Some of these little creatures are almost white too. But it makes no
difference. One drop of negro blood is enough to damn them in the eyes
of this community. I lose all patience with these semi-barbarous whites
who argue that the "nigger" is not good as a white man, in the old
stereotyped fashion and my northern abolitionism often displays itself
very decidedly in my arguments with them. The negro, as a rule is as good
in every respect, except of course in education and "refinement," as most
of my opponents, or I either, for that matter. So much—and too much for
ethnology. My heart sinks when I try to speak or write of Abraham
Lincoln. I cannot yet realize that he is indeed dead, and the troubled
events of the past two weeks seem like the phantasius [sic] a dream. I was
present at the theatre and saw the terrible crime committed which re-
moves from us a second Washington. That evening about 7 o'clock I saw
the Rebel generals Ewell, and five others, who were captured before
Petersburg a few days before, and just after looking at them, my companion, who had never seen Gen. Grant proposed that we should go to Ford's
Theatre, as it had been announced in the evening papers that he would be
there together with the President and Mrs. Lincoln. Although I had seen
the Lieutenant General, I was willing and anxious to see him again and so
we went, and chose seats in the dress circle, just opposite the private
box—or boxes, for there were two of them, merged in one, and called the
state box, which by the way was highly decorated with flags and a picture
of Washington—in which the presidential party would sit. I had often
seen the President and his wife there, and knew very well where they
would sit. Shortly after eight, the President, Mrs. Lincoln, Miss Harris—
the daughter of Senator Harris of New York—and her foster brother,
Maj. Rathbone, arrived and took their positions where we could get an

excellent view of each one. The main object of our presence was disappointed, Gen. Grant was not there, but had gone to New Jersey to see his family. We soon got over our disappointment however, observing the play, which, as you know, was "Our American Cousin." The acting was excellent as of course, it would be with Laura Keene's company.—and the President and Mrs. Lincoln seemed to enjoy it highly—the latter, in particular laughing often and very heartily. I could detect a broad smile on Uncle Abraham's face very often, while, at other times, he rested his face in both of his hands, bending forward, and seemingly buried in deep thought. At the end of the second scene of the third act, while Asa Trenchard, "Our American Cousin" was on the stage alone, I was startled by the sudden report of a pistol, which rang loud and clear throughout the theater. I thought that it sounded on the stage near the farther end, and looked in that direction, but seeing nothing unusual, the thought struck me, "perhaps the President has been assassinated" for I had often thought of the probability of such an event on some such occasion. As I looked towards the President's—box I saw some commotion, and heard a slight disturbance, when in a second, the form of a man appeared on the balustrade standing perfectly erect hatless, with a knife in his right hand, shouted in a clear sonorous voice "Sic Semper Tyrannus" [sic] leaped to the stage below—a distance of ten or twelve feet—and striding across the stage, disappear before the audience could recover from the shock. Then arose loud cries of "Kill him," "kill him," for they knew intuitively what had happened. Mrs. Lincoln screamed, the audience rushed onto the stage, the actresses turned pale—even through their rouge and "lily-white," and confusion reigned generally—Soon after, the President already dying—was carried across the street and the audience left the house. The streets were immediately filled, and I then heard that the Secretary of State, and his two sons and nurse had been killed in Philadelphia, and in a short time they had everybody of any consequence in the city assassinated, until I almost began to doubt the fact of my own existence. It was a night of horror such as I hope never to witness again. Towards morning I retired—"but not to sleep." Visions of murder and death floated through my brain and before my eyes and I arose at 9 the next forenoon, thoroughly worn out. Of course there was no work. Everybody arrayed his house in mourning—and men, women and children and negroes wore an expression of horror and grief such as I never witnessed before.

The next Sunday I went to the church where Mr. Lincoln had attended.

His pew was draped in mourning, but every other was crowded and hundreds were unable to enter the house at all. The performances were very solemn and interesting. I also went to my regular place of worship (Rev. Dr. Hall's "Church of the Epiphany" Episcopal), and heard a beautiful tribute to the lamented dead. Appropriate allusion was to the event in every church except one, which is known to be of "Secesh" sympathies. Of the funeral ceremonies it is useless to speak. They were grand and appropriate. The procession was something to remember for a life time. Your humble servant formed a very humble part of it, and mourned really, as well as ostensibly. I will send you "Harpers Weekly" containing illustrations of the events of that and previous days which will give you accurate ideas, such as I could not convey in writing. The pictures are all correct—Especially that of President Lincoln at home, the boy of course being "Thad," and an exact counterfeit presentment of that enterprising youth. (By the way one of our clerks, Mr. Williamson, has been the tutor of the boy, up to the time of his father's death.)

Poor Mrs. Lincoln. How I pity her. She was proud of her husband, as well she might be, despite his plainness. And do you know that he was not half so plain as represented to be. His was a strong, rugged, honest face, beaming at the same time with gentleness and good nature. His smile was something to remember forever. It was positively beautiful. I never saw one like it on any other human face. It seemed to come from the heart and it certainly touched that of the beholder. Not withstanding his reputation as a "joker" his face was habitually a sad one. It almost always had a mournful, inexpressibly touching expression, so that you could not look upon it without pitying him. Could it be that it was prophetic of his sad end? I noticed this expression particularly on the evening of the assassination and saw him frequently cover his face with both hands as if busily engaged in thought. Of course this might not—have had any peculiar significance, yet when thinking of the later events of that horrid night. Such little acts appear magnified and imbued with a deeper meaning. He was a loving husband and father and one of the best men that ever lived, and when I think of his death there comes over me a feeling of personal loss. Of course, I could not be expected to be acquainted with him—I aspired to no such honor—but I had seen him often, and have taken him by the hand more than once. I heard him, too, deliver the inaugural address the fourth of March last, when he stood high on the East front of the Capitol and looked, with his fatherly smile and beaming spectacles like a real paterfamilias, and spoke words of gentleness and forbearance to "our misguided Southern brethren" such as they never deserved. I heard him too only a week before he died when he stood at an upper window in the "White House" and enunciated his views on the "Reconstruction" question.

He spoke too forgivingly, as I thought and that is what gives me resignation now. I think it "all for the best," and while I mourn the national loss as deeply as anyone, I yet think that we should rejoice that now the Rebel Chiefs will receive justice instead of mercy. The South will find to its cost that the wrong man has been killed, and will rue the day that Abraham Lincoln died and Andrew Johnson became president. To use an homely expression, the Southern people have "jumped out of the frying pan into the fire." I have seen and heard President Johnson and I am convinced he is the "right man in the right place" and when he said "the leaders (of the Rebellion) I would hang.", I knew that he meant it and will do it, if ever he catches them. . . .

Sincerely your friend,
John Downing, jr.

Clara Harris
Location: Presidential box
Letter reprinted in "Lincoln's Last Days," *New York Independent*,
Louis A. Warren Lincoln Library
April 29, 1865

Clara Harris was the daughter of Senator Ira Harris of New York. At the time of the assassination she was engaged to her stepbrother Major Henry R. Rathbone. Although Miss Harris failed to witness the shooting, she did observe the stabbing of her fiancée.

You may well say that we have been passing through scenes sad indeed. That terrible Friday night is to me yet almost like some dreadful vision. I have been very intimate with Mrs. Lincoln and the family ever since our mutual residence in Washington, which began at the same time, and we have been constantly in the habit of driving and going to the opera and theater together. It was the only amusement, with the exception of receiving at their own house, in which the President and Mrs. Lincoln were permitted, according to custom, to indulge, and to escape from the crowds who constantly thronged to see them, more than from any decided taste for such things. They were in the habit of going very often to hear Forest, Booth, Hackett, and such actors, when playing in Washington.

The night before the murder was that of the general illumination here, and they drove all through the streets to see it; a less calculating villain might have taken that opportunity for his crime, or the night before, when the White House alone was brilliantly illuminated, and the figure of the President stood out in full relief to the immense crowd below, who stood in the darkness to listen to his speech. He spoke from the center window of the Executive Mansion. I had been invited to pass the evening there, and stood at the window adjoining room with Mrs. Lincoln, watching the crowd below as they listened and cheered. Of course Booth was there, watching his chance. I wonder he did not choose that occasion but probably he knew a better opportunity would be offered. After the speech was over, we went into Mr. Lincoln's room; he was lying on the sofa, quite exhausted but he talked of the events of the past fortnight, of his visit to Richmond, of the enthusiasm everywhere felt through the country; and Mrs. Lincoln declared the last few days to have been the happiest of her life. Their prospects indeed seemed fair—peace dawning upon our land, and four years of a happy and honored rule before one of the gentlest, best, and loveliest men I ever knew. I never saw him out of temper—the kindest husband, the tenderest father, the truest friend, as well as the wisest statesman. "Our beloved President"—when I think that I shall never again stand in his genial presence, that I lost his friendship so tried and true, I feel like putting on the robe of mourning which the country wears. . . .

You were right in supposing the Major Rathbone who was with us to be the 'Henry' who you knew in Albany.

We four composed the party that evening. They drove to our door in the gayest spirits; chatting on our way—and the President was received with the greatest enthusiasm.

They say we were watched by the assassins; ay, as we alighted from the carriage. Oh, how could any one be so cruel as to strike that kind, dear, honest face! And when I think of that fiend barring himself in alone with us, my blood runs cold. My dress is saturated with blood; my hands and face were covered. You may imagine what a scene! And so, all through that dreadful night, when we stood by that dying bed. Poor Mrs. Lincoln was and is almost crazy.

Henry narrowly escaped with his life. The knife struck at his heart with all the force of a practiced and powerful arm; he fortunately parried the blow, and received a wound in his arm, extending along the bone, from the elbow nearly to the shoulder. He concealed it for some time, but was finally carried home in swoon; the loss of blood has been so great from an artery and veins severed. He is now getting quite well, but cannot as yet use his arm. . . .

Ever yours sincerely.
Clara H. Harris

Dr. G. B. Todd
Location: Dress circle
Letter to his brother, State Historical Society of Wisconsin
April 30, 1865

> *Dr. Todd, who served as the physician on the monitor USS* Montauk, *claims to have met Lincoln earlier that day when the president had toured Todd's ship at the Washington Navy Yard. His account provides a vivid description of the interaction between the "usher" and Booth outside the presidential box.*

Dear Bro. The few hours that have intervened since that most terrible tragedy of last night have served to give me a little clearer brain, and I believe I am now able to give you a clear account up to this hour. Yesterday about 3 P.M. the President and wife drove down to the navy yard and paid our ship a visit, going all over her, accompanied by us all. Both seemed very happy, and so expressed themselves,—glad that this war was over, or so near its end, and then drove back to the White House. In the evening nearly all of us went to the Ford's Theatre. I was very early and got a seat near the President's private box, as we heard he was to be there. About half past nine he came in with his wife, a Miss Harris and Major Rathburn and was cheered by every one. As soon as there was a silence the play went on, and I could see that the "pres." seemed to enjoy it very much. About 10:25 P.M. a man came in and walked slowly along the side on which the "pres." box was and I heard a man say "theres Booth" and I turned my head to look at him. He was still walking very slow, and was near the box door, when he stopped, took a card from his pocket, wrote something on it, and gave it to the usher, who took it to the box. In a minute the door was opened and he walked in. No sooner had the door closed, than I heard the report of a pistol and on the instant, Booth jumped out of the box onto the stage, holding in his hand a large knife, and shouted so as to be heard all over the house,—"Sic Semper Tyrannis" ("so always with tyrants") and fled behind the scenes—I attempted to get to the box but I could not and in an instant the cry was raised "The President is Assassinated."

Such a scene I never saw before. The cry spread to the street, only to be met by another, "So is Mr. Seward." Soldiers had gone. Some General handed me a note and bid me go to the nearest telegraph office and arouse the nation. I ran with all my speed and in ten minutes the sad news was all over the country. Today all the city is in mourning, nearly every house being in black and I have not seen a smile. No business and many a strong man I have seen in tears.

Some reports say Booth is a prisoner, others that he has made his escape, but from orders received here, I believe he is taken as a mob once raised now would know no end. I will not seal this until morning and I may have some more news.

April 24th.
I have had no time to write until now, as I have been a detective. We have now 7 that are implicated.

> Why don't you write?   Love to all,
> George.

Sheldon P. McIntyre
Location: Unknown
Wassau-Herald Record, Louis A. Warren Lincoln Library
Date unknown

> *McIntyre was a sixteen-year-old Union soldier stationed at Mount Pleasant Hospital in Washington, D.C., at the time of the assassination.*
> *McIntyre's description of Lincoln being denuded probably refers to the president's shirt having been removed by the doctors when they searched for a knife wound. Although the doctors had heard the gunshot, Rathbone's obvious knife wound led them to believe that Lincoln had been stabbed.*

I must tell you about Abraham Lincoln's death. I was at the theater when he was shot. I heard reports of the pistol when it went off and I spoke to the fellow that was sitting beside me and I told him that someone was shot and in a moment I saw a man jump from the box that the president was sitting in down onto the stage and he fell as he struck on the stage.

He sprang onto his feet. He held a pistol in one hand and a long dirk in the other hand and as he sprang to his feet said 'Revenge for the South' and he ran across the stage which is the distance of 39 feet. There was a man who attempted to stop him and he stabbed him in the clothes but did not hurt him.

Father, it was the greatest excitement that I ever heard. I never want to witness such a scene again. I was about three feet from the president when he was carried out of the theater. His clothes were all stripped off from him and he was as pale as death.

I was at the funeral. There was the greatest crowd of people that I ever saw. . . .

John H. Stevens
Location: Unknown
Letter, reprinted in auction pamphlet, Ford's Theatre National
Historic Site
Date unknown

> *Although it bears no date, this account was probably written within days of the assassination. The only inaccuracy was in placing Booth's words before the assassin's leap to the stage.*

At the theatre when Booth fired his shot and jumped from the box to the Stage everyone was wild with excitement. We were told to quietly leave the building. The President was carried to the house across the street where he lingered between life and death until morning . . . Booth took an opportune time to do his wicked work for just before he leaped from the box to the stage, with the words 'Sic Semper Tyrannis' all the actors had gone behind the scenes so there was no one to intercept his flight.

TWO

THE CONSPIRACY TRIAL
ACCOUNTS
MAY 1865

The conspiracy trial was held in a military court as the United States government attempted to prosecute those suspected of having assisted with Booth's plans. Numerous witnesses were questioned about the assassination, and several reliable accounts emerged.*

John Devenay
Location: Unknown
5/12/1865

Devenay was the first eyewitness to testify before the court concerning the events of the assassination.

The next time I saw of him was when he jumped out of the box of the theater, and fell on one hand, when I recognized him. He fell with his face toward the audience. I said, "He is John Wilkes Booth, and he has shot the President." I made that remark right there. That is the last I ever saw of him, when he was moving across the stage. I heard the words "Sic

*These accounts were also published in Benn Pitman, *The Assassination of President Lincoln and the Trial of the Conspirators* (New York: Funk and Wagnalls, 1954).

Semper Tyrannis" in the President's box before I saw the man. He had a knife in his hand as he went across the stage. If he made remarks as he went across the stage I didn't notice it. The excitement was great at the time.

John Buckingham
Location: Lobby
May 15, 1865

Buckingham was the doorkeeper who greeted Booth when he entered the Ford's Theatre lobby on his way to the presidential box. Buckingham's testimony indicates that Booth entered the theater the last time at 10:15 P.M.

I am night doorkeeper at Ford's Theater. In the daytime I am employed at the Washington Navy Yard. I know John Wilkes Booth by sight. About 10 o'clock on the evening of the 14th he came to the theater, walked in and out again, and returned in about two or three minutes. He came to me and asked what time it was. I told him to step into the lobby and he could see. He stepped out and walked in again, entering by the door that leads to the parquette and dress-circle; came out again and then went up the stairway to the dress-circle. The last I saw of him was when he alighted on the stage with a knife in his hand. He was uttering some sentence, but I could not understand it, being so far from him.

Major Henry R. Rathbone
Location: Presidential box
May 15, 1865

Because of his proximity to the president, Rathbone's description of the events in the box is probably the most reliable. His account before the court was almost identical with the one he provided on April 15.

On the evening of the 14th of April last, at about twenty minutes past 8 o'clock, I, in company with Miss Harris, left my residence at the corner of Fifteenth and H Streets, and joined the President and Mrs. Lincoln, and went with them, in their carriage, to Ford's Theater, on Tenth Street. On reaching the theater, when the presence of the President became known, the actors stopped playing, the band struck up "Hail to the Chief," and the audience rose and received him with vociferous cheering. The party proceeded along in the rear of the dress-circle and entered the box that had been set apart for their reception. On entering the box, there was a large arm-chair that was placed nearest the audience, farthest from the stage, which the President took and occupied during the whole of the evening, with one exception, when he sat down again. When the second scene of the third act was being performed, and while I was intently observing the proceedings upon the stage, with my back toward the door, I heard the discharge of a pistol behind me, and looking round, saw through the smoke a man between the door and the President. The distance from the door to where the President sat was about four feet. At the same time I heard the man shout some word, which I thought was "Freedom!" I instantly sprang toward him and seized him. He wrested himself from my grasp, and made a violent thrust at my breast with a large knife. I parried the blow by striking it up, and received a wound several inches deep in my left arm, between the elbow and the shoulder. The orifice of the wound was about an inch and a half in length, and extended upward toward the shoulder several inches. The man rushed to the front of the box and I endeavored to seize him again, but only caught his clothes as he was leaping over the railing of the box. The clothes, as I believe, were torn in the attempt to hold him. As he went over upon the stage, I cried out, "Stop that man." I then turned to the President, his position was not changed; his head was slightly bent forward, and his eyes were closed. I saw that he was unconscious, and, supposing him mortally wounded, rushed to the door for the purpose of calling medical aid.

On reaching the outer door of the passageway, I found it barred by a heavy piece of plank, one end of which was secured in the wall, and the other resting against the door. It had been so securely fastened that it required considerable force to remove it. This wedge or bar was about four feet from the floor. Persons upon the outside were beating against the door for the purpose of entering. I removed the bar, and the door was opened. Several persons, who represented themselves as surgeons, were allowed to enter. I saw there Colonel Crawford, and requested him to prevent other persons from entering the box.

I then returned to the box, and found the surgeons examining the President's person. They had not yet discovered the wound. As soon as it was discovered, it was determined to remove him from the theater. He was carried out, and I then proceeded to assist Mrs. Lincoln, who was intensely excited, to the stairs, I requested Major Potter to aid me in assisting Mrs. Lincoln across street to the house where the President was being conveying. The wound which I had received had been bleeding very profusely, and on reaching the house, feeling very faint from the loss of blood, I seated myself in the hall, and soon after fainted away, and was laid upon the floor. Upon the return of consciousness I was taken to my residence.

In review of the transactions, it is my confident belief that the time which elapsed between the discharge of the pistol and the time when the assassin leaped from the box did not exceed thirty seconds. Neither Mrs. Lincoln nor Miss Harris had left their seats.

This knife might have made a wound similar to the one I received. The assassin held the blade in a horizontal position, I think, and the nature of the wound would indicate it; it came down with a sweeping blow from above.

William Withers, Jr.
Location: Backstage
May 15, 1865

> *Withers, who was the orchestra director, had hoped to have "Honor to our Soldiers" — a piece that he had written — played at an early intermission. The intermission was delayed, and he went backstage to plead his case with the director. Although he was directly in Booth's escape path, Withers received only superficial wounds. "Honor to Our Soldiers" was not performed at Ford's Theatre until 125 years after the assassination.*

I am the leader of the orchestra at Ford's Theater. I had some business on the stage with our stage-manager on the night of the 14th, in regard to a national song that I had composed, and I went to see what costume they were going to sing it in. After talking with the manager, I was returning to the orchestra, when I heard the report of a pistol. I stood with the astonishment, thinking why they should fire off a pistol in "Our American Cousin." As I turned round I heard some confusion, and saw a man running toward me with his head down. I did not know what was the matter, and stood completely paralyzed. As he ran, I could not get out of his way, so he hit me on the leg, and turned me round, and made two cuts at me, one in the neck and one on the side, and knocked me from the third entrance down to the second. The scene saved me. As I turned, I got a side view of him, and I saw it was John Wilkes Booth. He then made a rush for the back door, and out he went. I returned to the stage and heard that the President was killed, and I saw him in the box apparently dead.

Where I stood on the stage was not more than a yard from the door. He made a plunge at the door, which I believe was shut, and instantly he was out. The door opens inward on the stage, but whether he opened it, or whether it was opened for him, I do not know. I noticed that there was nothing to obstruct his passage out, and this seemed strange to me, for it was unusual.

On that night the passage seemed to be clear of every thing. I do not think it was many minutes until the scene changed, and it was a time in the scene when the stage and passage way would have been somewhat obstructed by some of the sceneshifters, and the actors in waiting for the next scene, which requires their presence. I never remember seeing Spangler wear a moustache.

On May 31, Withers was recalled for further questioning. He informed the court:

The door leading into the alley from the passage was shut when Booth rushed out.

After he made the spring from the box, and ran across the stage, he made a cut at me, and knocked me down to the first entrance; then I got a side view of him. The door was shut, but it opened very easily; I saw that distinctly. He made a plunge right at the knob of the door, and out he went, and pulled the door after him. He swung it as he went out. I did not see Booth during the day.

James P. Ferguson
May 15, 1865
Location: Dress circle, north side

Ferguson's court testimony was similar to the testimony he gave Tanner. He was less sure of the statement "Revenge for the South" before the court and omitted the statement, "I have done it!" which he originally attributed to Booth.

Ferguson was correct in assuming that the hole in the door was bored, not the result of the pistol being fired through it. The .44 caliber derringer Booth used did not have the power to discharge a fatal bullet through the door. Either the Fords bored the hole to observe their patrons or Booth did it earlier in the day so that he could see Lincoln before entering the box.

I keep a restaurant adjoining Ford's Theater, on the upper side. I saw J. Wilkes Booth, on the afternoon of the 14th, between 2 and 4 o'clock, standing by the side of his horse—a small bay mare; Mr. Maddox was standing by him talking. Booth remarked, "See what a nice horse I have got; now watch, he can run just like a cat;" and, striking his spurs into his horse, he went off down the street.

About 1 o'clock Mr. Harry Ford came into my place and said, "Your favorite, General Grant, is to be at the theater to-night, and if you want to see him you had better go and get a seat." I went and secured a seat directly opposite the President's box, in the front dress-circle. I saw the President and his family when they came in, accompanied by Miss Harris and Major Rathbone.

Somewhere near 10 o'clock, during the second scene of the third act of "Our American Cousin," I saw Booth pass along near the President's box, and then stop and lean against the wall. After standing there a moment, I saw him step down one step, put his hands on the door and his knee against it, and push the door open—the first door that goes into the box. I saw no more of him until he made a rush for the front of the box and jumped over. He put his left hand on the railing, and with his right he seemed to strike back with a knife. I could see the knife gleam, and the next moment he was over the box. As he went over, his hand was raised, the handle of the knife up, the blade down. The President sat in the left-hand corner of the box, with Mrs. Lincoln at his right. Miss Harris was in the right-hand corner of the box, Major Rathbone sitting back at her left, almost in the corner of the box. At the moment the President was shot, he was leaning his hand on the railing, looking down at a person in the orchestra; holding the flag that decorated the box aside to look between it and the post, I saw a flash of the pistol right back in the box. As the person jumped over and lit on the stage, I saw that it was Booth. As he struck the stage, he rose and exclaimed, "Sic Semper Tyrannis!" and ran directly across the stage to the opposite door, where the actors come in.

I heard some one halloo out of the box, "Revenge for the South!" I do not know that it was Booth, though I suppose it must have been; it was just as he was jumping over the railing. His spur caught in the blue part of the flag that was stretched around the box, and, as he went over, it tore a piece of the flag, which was dragged half way across the stage on the spur of his right heel.

Just as Booth went over the box, I saw the President raise his head, and then it hung back. I saw Mrs. Lincoln catch his arm, and I was then satisfied that the President was hurt. By that time Booth was across the stage. A young man named Harry Hawk was the only actor on the stage at the time.

I left the theater as quickly as I could, and went to the police station on D Street, to give notice to the Superintendent of Police, Mr. Webb. I then ran up D Street to the house of Mr. Peterson [sic], where the President was taken. Colonel Wells was standing on the steps, and I told him that I had seen it all, and I knew the man who jumped out of the box.

Next morning I saw Mr. Gifford, who said, "You made a hell of a statement about what you saw last night; how could you see the flash of the pistol when the ball was shot through the door?" On Sunday morning Miss Harris, accompanied by her father, Judge Olin, and Judge Carter, came down to the theater, and I went in with them. We got a candle and examined the hole in the door of the box through which Mr. Gifford said the ball had been shot. It looked to me as if it had been bored by a gimlet, and then rimmed round the edge with a knife. In several places it was scratched down, as if the knife had slipped. After the examination, I was satisfied that the pistol had been fired in the box.

Captain Theodore McGowan
Location: Dress circle, right
May 15, 1865

> *Captain McGowan was seated next to Lieutenant Crawford, who also provided an eyewitness account and was also a member of the Veterans' Reserve. McGowan's account is one of only four that comment on the actions of the president's "messenger."*

I was present at Ford's Theater on the night of the assassination. I was sitting in the aisle leading by the wall toward the door of the President's box, when a man came and disturbed me in my seat, causing me to push my chair forward to permit him to pass; he stopped about three feet from where I was sitting, and leisurely took a survey of the house. I looked at him because he happened to be in my line of sight. He took a small pack of visiting-cards from his pocket, selecting one and replacing the others, stood a second, perhaps, with it in his hand, and then showed it to the President's messenger, who was sitting just below him. Whether the messenger took the card into the box, or, after looking at it, allowed him to go in, I do not know; but, in a moment or two more, I saw him go through the door of the lobby leading to the box, and close the door.

After I heard the pistol fired, I saw the body of a man descend from the front of the box toward the stage. He was hid from my sight for a moment by the heads of those who sat in the front row of the dress-circle, but in another moment he reappeared, strode across the stage, toward the entrance on the other side, and, as he passed, I saw the gleaming blade of a dagger in his right hand. He disappeared behind the scenes in a moment, and I saw him no more.

I know J. Wilkes Booth, but, not seeing the face of the assassin fully, I did not at the time recognize him as Booth.

John Miles
Location: Flies
May 15, 1865

Miles was working in the flies, which would have been twenty to thirty feet above the backstage. From the flies Miles would have assisted with the raising and lowering of the stage scenes.

Miles's testimony bolstered the prosecution's case against Edmund Spangler, who was accused of assisting Booth. The evidence was not overwhelming, but Spangler was sentenced to six months of hard labor.

Miles also refers to John Burroughs, also known as "Peanuts." He performed odd jobs around the theater and held Booth's horse after Spangler went backstage for a scene change. After exiting through a back door, Booth mounted his horse and gave Burroughs a sharp kick. Burroughs apparently did not know of Booth's plans, but he was suspected by some of having prior knowledge of Booth's intentions.

I work at Ford's Theater. I was there on the day of the assassination of the President. About 3 o'clock in the afternoon Booth put his horse in the stable, and Ned Spangler and Jim Maddox were with him. The stable is not more than five yards from the theater.

Between 9 and 10 o'clock that night, J. Wilkes Booth brought a horse from the stable, and, coming to the back door of the theater, called "Ned Spangler" three times. When Booth first called Spangler, some person told him that Booth called him, and he ran across the stage to him. I saw nothing more of Spangler or Booth until I heard the pistol go off. In a minute or two I heard the sound of a horse's feet going out of the alley. Before this I saw a boy holding the horse in the alley, perhaps for fifteen minutes. That was after Booth had called Spangler.

When Booth called Spangler I was up on the flies, about three and a half stories from the stage. It was, I think, in the third act; and from the time Booth brought his horse there until the President was shot was, I think, about three-quarters of an hour. I was at the window, John Peanuts was lying on the bench holding the horse; I did not see any one else holding it.

John Peanuts attended to Mr. Booth's horses. I have seen Spangler hold Booth's horses or hitch them up, but I never saw him put any gearing on them. Spangler's place on the stage was on the same side as the President's box, and he was there when Booth called him. There was another man working with Spangler to help him shove the scenes.

After the President was shot, I came down the stairs, and I saw Spangler out there at the door Booth went out of. There were, I think, two or three other or more men out there, some of whom were strangers. When I came down, I went toward the door, and Spangler came out, and I asked him who it was that held the horse, and he said, "Hush! don't say any thing about it;" and I didn't say any more, though I knew who it was, because I saw the boy holding the horse. Spangler, I suppose, when he said this, was about a yard and a half from the door, outside the door. Spangler appeared to be excited; every person appeared to be very much excited. By the time I got down stairs, the door through which Booth had passed was open. I never saw Spangler wear a moustache.

Joe Simms
Location: Flies
May 15, 1865

> *Like Miles, Joe Simms was in the flies, and thus he did not have the best vantage from which to view the events on stage, although he could see what happened backstage. Hence his testimony focuses more on Spangler than on Booth.*

I have worked at Ford's Theater for the past two years. On the day of the President's assassination, during the performance, while I was up on the flies to wind up the curtain, I heard the fire of a pistol, and looking down I saw Booth jump out of a private box down on to the stage. Between 5 and 6 o'clock that day, I was in front of the theater, when I saw Booth go into the restaurant by the side of the theater. Spangler was sitting out in front, and Booth invited him to take a drink. I did not hear a word spoken between them. Booth and Spangler were very intimate. I have often seen them together, and drinking together.

Spangler had charge of Booth's horses. There was a young man hired by Booth, but I suppose Mr. Booth thought he might not do right by his horses, so he got Spangler to see to their being fed and watered.

Spangler's place on the stage is at the back part of the stage, next to the back-door, leading out to the side alley. The President's box is on the left-hand side as you look toward the audience. My position is on the flies on the opposite side of the President's box, and Mr. Spangler's place was on the opposite side below, the side the President's box is on. I saw him in the first act. I do not remember seeing him in the second, but I was not looking for him. When I saw Mr. Spangler, he had his hat on. I never saw him wear a moustache. Mr. Spangler was on the stage attending to his business as usual that night. He was obliged to be there. From my position on the flies I could see him very well.

On May 18, Simms further testified:

On the afternoon of the day of the assassination, I saw Mr. Harry Ford and another gentleman fixing up the box. Mr. Ford told me to go to his bed-room and get a rocking chair, and bring it down and put it in the President's box. I did so. The chair had not been there before this season. It was a chair with a high back to it and cushioned. Mr. Spangler was at the theater during the afternoon. He worked there altogether, the same as I did.

I did not notice Mr. Spangler there in the afternoon, but his business was to be there. It was about 3 o'clock in the afternoon when Mr. Harry Ford and, I think, Mr. Buckingham were in the private box. I did not see Spangler in the President's box in the afternoon, nor did I see him when I came away from the private box.

John F. Sleichmann
Location: Backstage
May 15, 1865

As property manager, Sleichmann would have assisted in oversee-ing the physical property of Ford's Theatre. Like Simms's account,

Sleichmann's focuses more on Spangler's actions than Booth's. His comments concerning Booth clearly indicate that Booth had easy access to all parts of the theater.

I am assistant property man at Ford's Theater, and have to set the furniture, etc., on the stage. I was at the theater on the night of the assassination of the President. About 9 o'clock that night I saw John Wilkes Booth. He came up on a horse, and entered by the little back door to the theater. Ned Spangler was standing by one of the wings, and Booth said to him, "Ned, you'll help me all you can, won't you?" and Ned said, "O yes." Those were the first words that I heard.

I just got a glimpse of Booth after the President was shot, as I was going out at the first entrance on the right-hand side near the prompter's place. I saw Booth on the afternoon of the 14th, between 4 and 5 o'clock, in the restaurant next door. I went in to look for James Maddox, and I saw Booth, Ned Spangler, Jim Maddox, "Peanuts," and a young gentleman by the name of John Mouldey, I think, drinking there.

Booth spoke to Spangler right by the backdoor. I saw his horse through the open door, but as it was dark I could not see if any one was holding it.

I was on the stage that night, except when I had to go down to the apothecary's store to get a few articles to use in the piece, and when I went into the restaurant next door. Spangler's business on the stage is shoving scenes. I went to the front of the theater by the side entrance, on the left-hand side. When I was in front, I noticed the President's carriage there, but did not see Spangler; had he been there, I guess I should have seen him. I have never seen Spangler wear a moustache. I was in front of the theater two or three times, but was on the stage during the third act. I think it was ten or fifteen minutes before the close of the second act that I was in the restaurant next door.

After ten minutes, I suppose, after the assassination, Spangler was standing on the stage by one of the wings, with a white handkerchief in his hand. He was very pale, and was wiping his eyes. I do not know whether he was crying or not.

Booth was very familiar with the actors and employees of the theater, and was backward and forward in the theater frequently. He had access to the theater at all times, and came behind the scenes, and in the green-room, and anywhere about the theater, just as though he was in the employment of Mr. Ford.

When Booth spoke to Spangler, they were about eight feet from me, but Booth and Spangler were not more than two or three feet apart. After

Booth had spoken, he went behind the scenes. I do not know whether Booth saw me, but he could have seen me from where he was standing; no one else was by at the time that I noticed. Spangler is, I think, a drinking man; whether he was in liquor that night I do not know.

William T. Kent
Location: Unknown
May 16, 1865

> *One may well wonder why Kent gave the pistol to an Associated Press agent and did not deliver it to the proper authorities. Nevertheless, L. A. Gobright eventually gave the weapon to the metropolitan police.*

About three minutes after the President was shot, I went into his box; there were two other persons there and a surgeon, who asked me for knife to cut open the President's clothes. On leaving the theater I missed my night-key, and thinking I had dropped it in pulling out my knife, I hurried back, and on searching round the floor of the box, I knocked my foot against a pistol, which I picked up, and holding it up, I cried out, "I have found the pistol." I gave it up to Mr. Gobright, the agent of the Associated Press. The next morning I went round to the police station and identified it there. This is the pistol I picked up in the President's box on the night of the 14th of April.

Isaac Jacquette
Location: Unknown
May 18, 1865

> *Jacquette's testimony contains several points that need clarification. First, he probably did not enter the presidential box itself but rather entered the small lobby that led to the box. Second, the board to which he refers was used by Booth to brace the lobby door closed. It was removed by Rathbone after the assassination so that the doctors could attend to the president. Finally, the bloodstains on the board were most likely from Rathbone, not Lincoln, because Lincoln's wound clotted quickly while Rathbone's bled extensively.*

I was present at Ford's Theater on the night of the assassination. Soon after the President was carried out, I went to the box with several others.

The wooden bar was lying on the floor inside of the first door going into the box. I picked it up and took it home with me. There was an officer stopping at my boardinghouse, and he wanted a piece of it, which I sawed off for him, but he concluded afterward not to take it. It is nearly covered with spots of blood which were fresh at the time I found it.

Jacob Ritterspaugh
Location: Backstage
May 19, 1865

> *Jacob Ritterspaugh assisted with scene changes. The large man he mentions was probably Major Stewart, who had left his orchestra seat in an unsuccessful effort to capture Booth.*

I was a carpenter in Ford's Theater down to the 14th of April last, and was there on that night when the President was shot. He occupied the upper box on the left-hand side of the stage, the right as you come in from the front. My business was to shift wings on the stage and pull them off, and fetch things out of the cellar when needed.

I was standing on the stage behind scenes on the night of the 14th, when some one called out that the President was shot, and directly I saw a man that had no hat on running toward the back door.

He had a knife in his hand, and I ran to stop him, and ran through the last entrance, and as I came up to him he tore the door open. I made for him, and he struck at me with the knife, and I jumped back then. He then ran out and slammed the door shut. I then went to get it open. In a moment afterward I opened the door, and the man had just got on his horse and was running down the alley; and then I came in. I came back on the stage where I had left Edward Spangler, and he hit me on the face with the back of his hand, and he said, "Don't say which way he went." I asked him what he meant by slapping me in the mouth, and he said, "For God's sake, shut up;" and that was the last he said.

The man of whom I speak is Edward Spangler, the prisoner at the bar. I did not see any one else go out before the man with the knife. A tall, stout man went out after me.

When I heard the pistol fired I was standing in the corner of the stage, listening to the play, and Spangler was at the same place, just about ready to shove off scenes; I stood nearest the door. I am certain we both stood there when the pistol was fired. I did not at first know what had happened. Some one called out "Stop that man;" and then I heard some one say that the President was shot, and not till then did I know what had occurred. When I came back, Spangler slapped me there were some of the actors near who had taken part in the play; one they called Jenny—I do not know what part she took—was standing perhaps three or four feet from me; I do not know whether she heard what he said; he did not say it very loud. He spoke in his usual tone, but he looked as if he was scared, and a kind of crying. I heard the people halloo, "Burn the theater!" "Hang him and shoot him!" . . .

I saw Booth open the back door of the theater and shut it, but I did not know who he was then; I did not see his face right. I was the first person that got to the door after he left; I opened the door, but did not shut it. The big man that ran out after me might have been five or six yards from me when I heard him, or it might have been somebody else call out, "Which way?" I cried out, "This way," and then ran out, leaving the door open. By that time the man had got on his horse and gone off down the alley. I saw the big man outside, and have not seen him since. I did not take particular notice of him; but he was a tolerably tall man. It might have been two or three minutes after I went out till I came back to where Spangler was standing, and found him kind of scared, and as if he had been crying. I did not say any thing to him before he said that to me. It was Spangler's place, with another man, to shove the scenes on; he was where he ought to be to do the work he had to do. I did not hear any one call Booth's name. It was not till the people were all out, and I came outside, that I heard some say it was Booth, and some say it was not. Spangler and I boarded together; we went home to supper together, on the evening of the assassination, at 6 o'clock, and returned at 7.

Major Joseph B. Stewart
Location: Orchestra level, right
May 20, 1865

> Stewart's testimony indicates that Ritterspaugh probably directed the major. The small man Stewart encountered in the alley was probably John "Peanuts" Burroughs, the theater employee Spangler had asked to hold Booth's horse when he went to assist with a scene change. His testimony indicates that Stewart was probably the person who came closest to apprehending Booth.

I was at Ford's Theater on the night of the assassination of the President. I was sitting in the front seat of the orchestra, on the right-hand side. The

sharp report of a pistol at about half-past 10—evidently a charged pistol
—startled me. I heard an exclamation, and simultaneously a man leaped
from the President's box, lighting on the stage. He came down with his
back slightly toward the audience, but rising and fuming, his face came in
full view. At the same instant I jumped on the stage, and the man disappeared at the left-hand stage entrance. I ran across the stage as quickly
as possible, following the direction he took, calling out, "Stop that
man!" three times. When about twenty or twenty-five feet from the door
through which the man ran, the door slammed to and closed. Coming up
to the door, I touched it first on the side where it did not open; after
which I caught hold at the proper place, opened the door, and passed out.
The last time that I exclaimed "Stop that man," some one said, "He is
getting on a horse at the door;" and almost as soon as the words reached
my ears I heard the tramping of a horse. On opening the door, after the
temporary balk, I perceived a man mounting a horse. The moon was just
beginning to rise, and I could see any thing elevated better than near the
ground. The horse was moving with a quick, agitated motion—as a horse
will do when prematurely spurred in mounting with the reins drawn a
little to one side, and for a moment I noticed the horse describe a kind of
circle from the right to the left. I ran in the direction where the horse was
heading, and when within eight or ten feet from the head of the horse, and
almost up within reach of the left flank, the rider brought him round
somewhat in a circle from the left to the right, crossing over, the horse's
feet rattling violently on what seemed to be rocks. I crossed in the same
direction, aiming at the rein and was now on the right flank of the horse.
He was rather gaining on me, though not yet in a forward movement. I
could have reached his flank with my hand when, perhaps, two-thirds of
the way over the alley, brought the horse forward, down over the pummel
of the saddle. The horse then went forward, and soon swept rapidly to the
left, up toward F Street. I still ran after the horse some forty or fifty yards,
and commanded the person to stop. All this occupied only the space of a
few seconds.

After passing the stage, I saw several persons in the passage way, ladies
and gentlemen, one or two men, perhaps five persons.

Near the door on my right hand, I saw a person standing, who seemed
to be in the act of turning, and who did not seem to be moving about like
the others. Every one else that I saw but this person, seemed intensely
excited, literally bewildered; they were all in a terrible commotion and
moving about, except this man. As I approached the door, and only about

fifteen feet from it, this person was facing the door; but, as I got nearer, he partially turned round, moving to the left, so that I had a view of him as he was turning from the door and toward me.

The man [pointing to Edward Spangler] looks more like the person I saw near the door than anybody else I see here. He recalls the impression of the man's visage as I passed him. When the assassin alighted on the stage, I believed I knew who it was that had committed the deed; that it was J. Wilkes Booth, and so I informed Richards, Superintendent of the Police, that night. I knew Booth by sight very well, and when I was running after him, I had no doubt in my mind that it was Booth, and should have been surprised to find that it was anybody else. I felt a good deal vexed at his getting away, and had no doubt when I started across the stage that I could catch him. From the time I heard the door slam until I saw the man mounting his horse, was not over the time I could make two steps. I am satisfied that the person I saw inside the door was in a position and had an opportunity, if he had been disposed to do so, to have interrupted the exit of Booth, and from his manner, he, was cool enough to have done so. This man was nearest of all to the door, and could have opened and gone out before I did, as it would have been but a step to the right and a reach to open it.

The man I have spoken of stood about three feet from the door out of which Booth passed; I noticed him just after the door slammed. From the position in which he stood, he might have slammed it without my noticing it. The lock of the door, as I approached it, was on the right-hand side, the hinges to the left. If the door had been open and I had not been stopped, I could have had the range of the horse outside.

As I passed out of the door, a person, a small person, passed behind me, directly under my right elbow, [the witness was a tall man] and as I approached the horse at the nearest point, some one ran rapidly out of the alley. The one who passed me is not so tall as Spangler by, perhaps, four or five inches. . . .

I got to the door, Booth was just completing his balance in the saddle. I think from his position and the motion of the horse, that the moment he got one foot in the stirrup he spurred the horse, and, having the rein drawn more on one side than the other, lost control of him for the moment, so far as making more exertion than headway, but still going pretty fast.

Hearing the report of a loaded pistol, and seeing the man jump from the President's box with a dagger in his hand, my impression was that the person had assassinated or attempted to assassinate, the President, and every effort I made after I started to get upon the stage was under the conviction; so much so that I stated to the people in the tenement houses in the rear, before I returned to the theater, that the person who went off on that horse had shot the President.

James L. Maddox
Location: Backstage
May 22, 1865

Maddox offers little information about the events of the assassination. His testimony, like others, is focused more on Spangler's actions.

I was employed at Ford's Theater as property man. In December last, I rented from Mrs. Davis, for John Wilkes Booth, the stable where he kept his horse up to the time of the murder of President Lincoln. Mr. Booth gave me the rent money monthly, and I paid it to Mrs. Davis.

I saw Harry Ford decorating the President's box on the afternoon of the 14th of April, but do not remember seeing any one else in the box. I was in there but once.

I saw Joe Simms, the colored man coming from Mr. Ford's room, through the alley way, carrying on his head the rocking-chair that the President was to use in the evening. I had not seen that chair in the box this season; the last time I saw it before that afternoon was in the winter of 1863, when it was used by the President on his first visit to the theater.

My duties require me to be on the stage while the performance is going on, unless, as sometimes happened, there is nothing at all to do, when I go out. My business is to see that the furniture is put on the stage alright, and to get the actors any side properties that may be required for use in the play.

The passage way by which Booth escaped is usually clear. Only when we are playing a heavy piece, and when in a hurry, do we run things in there. The "American Cousin," which was performed on that night, is not a heavy piece, and the passage would therefore be clear of obstruction.

Spangler's position on the stage was on the left-hand side, facing the audience, and the same side that the President's box was on. I saw Spangler during nearly every scene. If he had not been at his place, I should certainly have missed him. If he had missed running off a single scene, I should have known it. Sometimes a scene lasts twenty minutes, but in the third act of the "American Cousin" there are seven scenes, the way Miss Keene plays it, and had Spangler been absent five minutes after the first scene of this act we should have noticed it. In the second act, I guess, he has a half hour, and in the first scene of the third act he has twenty-five minutes, and after this the scenes are pretty quick. I was at the front of the theater during the second act, but did not see Spangler there. I have never seen Spangler wear a moustache during the two years that I have known him.

I was in the first entrance to the stage, the side the President's box is on, at the moment of the assassination. Three or four minutes before that, while the second scene of the third act was on, I crossed the stage with the will, and saw Spangler in his place. After the pistol was fired, I caught a glimpse of Booth, when he was about two feet off the stage. I ran on the stage and heard a call for water; I ran and brought a pitcher full, and gave it to one of the officers. I did not see Spangler after that, that I remember, until the next morning. I may have seen him, but not to notice him.

I heard about 12 o'clock that the President was coming to the theater that night; I was told so by Mr. Harry Ford. I heard a young man, one of the officers connected with the President's house, say that night that he had come down that morning and engaged the box for the President.

James R. Ford
Location: Unknown
May 30, 1865

James R. Ford was one of the three Ford brothers who operated Ford's Theatre. His testimony supports the belief that the president was invited to the theater on April 14.

The Ford brothers did not continue the theater's operations after the assassination. The War Department closed down the theater and the Fords eventually sold it to the government and the interior was gutted.

In 1893, while the building was serving as a federal office building, the third floor collapsed. Twenty-two civil servants were killed and sixty-eight injured. In 1968, after a three-year renovation, the building reopened as Ford's Theatre, an active theater and a national historic site.

At the time of the assassination, I was business manager of Ford's Theater. I was first apprised of the President's intended visit to the theater on Friday morning, at half-past 10 o'clock. A young man, a messenger from the White House, came and engaged the box. The President had been previously invited to the theater that night, and I had no knowledge of his intention to visit the theater until the reception of that message. I saw John Wilkes Booth about half-past 12, two hours after I received this information. I saw him as I was coming from the Treasury Building, on the corner of Tenth and E Streets. I was going up E Street, toward Eleventh Street; he was coming from the direction of the theater.

The notice in the Evening Star that announced the President's intended visit to the theater, also said that General Grant would be there.

I wrote the notice for the Star in the ticket-office of the theater about half-past 11 or 12 o'clock, and sent it to the office immediately; I at the same time carried one myself to the National Republican. The notice appeared in the Star about 2 o'clock. Before sending the notice I asked Mr. Philips, an actor in our establishment, who was on the stage, to do it; he said he would after he had finished writing the regular advertisements. I also spoke to my younger brother about the propriety of writing it. I had not seen Booth previous to writing the notice, nor do I remember speaking to any one else about it.

I had sent the notice to the Star office before seeing Booth. . . .

Henry Clay Ford
Location: Unknown
May 31, 1865

> *If Ford was correct in asserting that it was not known until noon that the president was to attend the theater, then Booth and his conspirators had less than ten hours to prepare. According to H. C. Ford's testimony, the rocking chair was not placed in the box specifically for the president but only because it matched the other furniture. This statement clearly contradicts a commonly held belief that the rocking chair was placed in the box for Lincoln. It is also interesting that Ford had the box decorated not because Lincoln was to be in attendance but because Grant was expected to attend.*

On the 14th of April last I was treasurer of Ford's Theater. I returned to the theater from my breakfast about half-past 11 o'clock that day, when my brother, James R. Ford, told me that the President had engaged a box for that night. John Wilkes Booth was at the theater about half an hour afterward. I do not know that the fact of the President's going to the theater that night was communicated to Booth, but I think it is very likely he found it out while there. I saw him going down the street while I was standing in the door of the theater; as he came up he commenced talking to the parties standing around. Mr. Raybold then went into the theater and brought him out a letter that was there for him. He sat down on the steps and commenced reading it. This was about 12 o'clock. He staid there perhaps half an hour. I went into the office, and when I came out again he was gone.

I told Mr. Raybold about fixing up and decorating the box for the President that night, but he had the neuralgia in his face, and I fixed up the box in his place. I found two flags in the box already there, which I got Mr. Raybold to help me put up. Another flag I got from the Treasury Department. It was the Treasury regimental flag. I put this blue regimental flag in the center, and the two American flags above. There was nothing unusual in the decorations of the box, except the picture of Washington placed on the pillar in the middle of the box. This had never been used before. We usually used small flags to decorate the box; but as General Grant was expected to come with the President, we borrowed this flag from the Treasury regiment to decorate with.

The furniture placed in the box consisted of one chair brought from the stage and a sofa, a few chairs out of the reception-room, and a rocking-chair, which belonged to the same set, I had brought from my bed-room. This chair had been in the reception-room, but the ushers sitting in it had greased it with their hair, and I had it removed to my room, it being a very nice chair. The only reason for putting that chair in the box was that it belonged to the set, and I sent for it to make the box as neat as possible.

I received no suggestions from any one as to the decoration of the box, excepting from Mr. Raybold and the gentleman who brought the flag from the Treasury Department.

All that Spangler had to do with the box was to take a partition out. These are two boxes divided by a partition, which, when the President attended the theater, was always removed to make the box into one. Spangler and the other carpenter, Hake, removed it. The President had been to the theater, I suppose, about six times during the winter and spring; three or four times during Mr. Forrest's engagements, and twice during Mr. Clark's engagement. These are the only times I remember. I did not direct Spangler with respect to the removal of the partition; I believe Mr. Raybold sent for him. While we were in the box Spangler was working on the stage; I think he had a pair of flats down on the stage, fixing them in some way. I called for a hammer and nails; he threw up two or three nails, and handed me the hammer up from stage.

Spangler, of course, knew that the President was coming to the theater that evening, as he assisted in taking out the partition.

In decorating the box I used my penknife to cut the strings to tie up the flags, and left it there in the box.

Three or four times during the season Booth had engaged box No. 7, that is part of the President's box, being the one nearest the audience. He engaged no other box.

During the play that evening, the "American Cousin," I was in the ticket-office of the theater. I may have been out on the pavement in front two or three times, but I do not remember. I did not see Spangler there. I never saw Spangler wear a moustache.

None of the other boxes were occupied on the night of the President's assassination, and I do not remember any box being taken on that night. I certainly did not know that the boxes were applied for, for that evening, and that the applicants were refused and told that the boxes were already taken. The applicants did not apply to me. Booth did not apply to me, or to any one, for those boxes, to my knowledge, nor did any one else for him. There were four of us in the office who sold tickets. There were not, to my knowledge, any applications for any box except the President's. There may have been applications without my knowledge.

I knew nothing of the mortise in the wall behind the door of the President's box. I heard of it afterward, but have never seen it, nor did I see the hole to fasten the door, nor did I see the hole bored through the first door of the President's box, though I have since heard there was one. I have not been in the box since.

The screws of the keepers of the lock to the President's box, I understand, were burst some time ago. They were not, to my knowledge, drawn that day, and left so that the lock would not hold the door on it being slightly pressed. It was not done in my presence, and if it was done at all, it was without my knowledge.

I do not remember any conversation with Mr. Ferguson before the day of the assassination about decorating the theater in celebration of some victory.

The letter that Booth received on the day of the assassination, and read on the steps of the theater, was a long letter of either four or eight pages of letter-paper—whether one or two sheets I do not know, but it was all covered with writing. He sat on the steps while reading his letter, every now and then looking up and laughing. It was while Booth was there that I suppose he learned of the President's visit to the theater that evening.

There were several around Booth, talking to him. Mr. Gifford was there; Mr. Evans, an actor, and Mr. Gillet, I remember, were there at the time.

The President's visit to the theater that evening could not have been known until 12 o'clock, unless it was made known by some one from the Executive Mansion. It was published in the Evening Star, but not in the morning papers.

I am not acquainted with John H. Surratt.

I have never, to my knowledge, seen the prisoner, Herold.

The mortise in the passage-way was not noticed by me; the passage was dark, and when the door was thrown back against the wall, as it was that day, I should not be likely to notice it had it been there at that time. Had the small hole been bored in the door, or had the screws been loosened, it is not likely I should have noticed them.

I might have stated in the saloon on Tenth Street that the President was to be at the theater that evening, and also that General Grant was to be there.

Henry M. James
Location: Backstage
May 31, 1865

Henry James was employed as a backstage hand. His testimony was focused on Spangler's actions.

I was at Ford's Theater on the night of the assassination. When the shot was fired, I was standing ready to draw off the flat, and Mr. Spangler was standing right opposite to me on the stage, on the same side as the President's box, about ten feet from me. From his position he could not see the box, nor the side of the stage on which Booth jumped. I had frequently during the play seen Spangler at his post. I saw no one with him. The passageway was clear at the time; it was our business to keep it clear; it was more Spangler's business than mine.

I saw Spangler when the President entered the theater. When the people applauded he applauded with them, with both hands and feet. He clapped his hands and stamped his feet, and seemed as pleased as anybody to see the President come in.

I did not see Jacob Ritterspaugh near Spangler that evening. He might have been there behind the scenes, but did not see him. I can not say how long I staid in my position after the shot was fired; it might have been a minute. I did not see Spangler at all after that happened.

Jacob Ritterspaugh was employed there, and it was his business to be there behind the scenes, though I did not see him.

J. L. Debonay
Location: Backstage
May 31, 1865

> *According to Debonay, Booth went backstage before entering the theater lobby and meeting Buckingham. The passageway that Debonay refers to went under the stage to the alley. Booth used this passageway to reach the alley that led to Tenth Street. His description of Booth's exit does not mention a limp, and in fact, Debonay believed Booth moved faster than one of the pursuers.*

I was playing what is called "responsible utility" at Ford's Theater at the time of the assassination. On the evening of the assassination, Booth came up to the alley door and said to me, "Tell Spangler to come to the door and hold my horse." I did not see his horse. I went over to where Mr. Spangler was, on the left-hand side, at his post, and said, "Mr. Booth wants you to hold his horse." He then went to the door and went outside, and was there about a minute, when Mr. Booth came in. Booth asked me if he could get across the stage. I told him no, the dairy scene was on, and he would have to go under the stage and come up on the other side. About the time that he got upon the other side, Spangler called to me, "Tell Peanut John to come here and hold this horse; I have not time. Mr. Gifford is out in the front of the theater, and all the responsibility of the scene lies upon me." I went on the other side and called John, and John went there and held the horse, when Spangler came in and returned to his post.

I saw Spangler three or four times that evening on the stage in his proper position. I saw him about two minutes before the shot was fired. He was on the same side as the President's box. About five minutes after the shot was fired I again saw Spangler standing on the stage with a crowd of people who had collected there.

I saw Booth when he made his exit. I was standing in the first entrance on the lefthand side. When he came to the center of the stage, I saw that he had a long knife in his hand. It seemed to me to be a double-edged knife, and looked like a new one. He paused about a second, I should think, and then went off at the first entrance to the right-hand side. I think he had time to get out of the back door before any person was on the stage. It was, perhaps, two or three seconds after he made his exit before I saw any person on the stage in pursuit. The first person I noticed was a tall, stout gentleman, with gay clothes on, I think, and I believe a moustache. Booth did not seem to run very fast across the stage; he seemed to be stooping a little when he ran off. The distance he ran would be about thirty-five or forty feet; but he was off the stage two or three seconds before this gentleman was on, and of the two, I think Booth was running the fastest.

THREE

THE TRANSITION
1877–1908

The accounts written during this period are less reliable than the earlier ones. Booth's broken leg was first mentioned by eyewitnesses in these years. Mary Todd Lincoln's only written account of the assassination appeared in this period, as did two different accounts by John Buckingham that can be compared with his earlier one.

Mary Todd Lincoln
Location: Presidential box
Letter to Edward Lewis Baker, Jr., reprinted in Justin C. Turner and Linda Levitt, *Mary Todd Lincoln: Her Life and Letters* (New York: Knopf, 1972).
1877

> *In this letter Mary Lincoln made her only written reference to the assassination. She often wrote to Edward Lewis Baker, Jr., whom she considered a close friend, in the years after the death of her husband.*

My dear Lewis:

About ten days since, I received your very welcome letter and I am now sending you an immediate reply. Truly, the past winter, has brought much sorrow with it, and you can well understand how fully, I have sympathesized [sic] with you all, in your griefs, over the loss of those two sweet little girls. We are never prepared for these things & I sometimes wonder, if it is well, for us not to anticipate them, in a measure. God, gives us our beloved ones, we make them our idols, they are removed from us, & we have patiently to await the time, when, He, reunites us to them. And the waiting, is so long! My bereavements, have been so intense, the most loving and devoted of husbands, torn from my side, my hand within his own, at the time—and God has recalled from this earth, sons, the most idolising, the noblest, purest, most talented—that were ever given to parents—Their presence grand & beautiful—too good for this world, so full of sorrow—Yet the time will come, when the severance, will be over, together husband, wife and children—never more to be separated—I grieve for those who have been called upon to give up their precious ones, and until the sunlight of a happier clime dawns upon us, we will never know until then, why, we have been visited, by such sorrow. God wills it and we must bow to his irrevocable decrees. Prayers, tears, are unavailing, and we are left to our great desolation!! I am living through, a very sad time myself, this season of the year, with its reminiscences, renders me anything, but cheerful, I am leading a life of retirement and daily, send up my supplications to Him, the ruler over us all, to reconcile and soften the pathway, I have been called upon to tread within the last few years.

Colonel Pren Metham
Location: Orchestra level
Magazine article on unpublished biography of Pren Metham,
Coshocton County, Ohio, Historical Society
1881

> *As the article alleges, had Colonel Pren Metham opened the right door, he might be considered a hero today. Dr. Samuel Mudd remains a controversial figure to this day. Although some believe Mudd was only performing his duty as a physician by setting Booth's broken leg, others believe that Mudd knew Booth had assassinated the president. The phrase "your name is mud" was in use before 1865 and had nothing to do with the circumstances surrounding Dr. Mudd.*

Colonel Pren Metham, the man who missed being a hero by circumstances, was from a long line of military men, and the list of battles Colonel Metham participated in during the War of the Rebellion is long and impressive, ending with Sherman's march to the sea. He proved his bravery many times over and served his president and his country well.

In April of 1865, Colonel Metham was in Washington, D.C. In the course of his stay, he bought tickets for the play "Our American Cousin" and went the same night, April 14, that President and Mrs. Lincoln were in attendance.

Histories record the Lincolns were late, and the play was in progress when they arrived. A stir of commotion from the rear of the theater caused the actors to stop the performance, and the audience rose to greet the President and the First Lady. After they were seated, the play resumed, and Colonel Metham, as did everyone, turned his attention to the stage.

When the play was interrupted the second time by shots and a scream, "The President has been shot," Metham, the military man, acted. He elbowed his way to the aisle, hoping to stop the man stumbling across the stage. His way to the front of the theater was blocked with hysterical people, so the colonel whirled and raced toward the rear, planning to exit that way, circle the building and head off the gunmen.

Once he was free of the crowd, Metham spotted a side door that he assumed led into an alley near the rear of the building, and he charged through it only to find himself in the midst of the ladies' dressing room.

The fearless and brave colonel, from a long line of military men, was rendered helpless by the twist of the wrong doorknob.

One can only speculate how much history would have been changed if he had selected another door and succeeded in stopping John Wilkes Booth. He may have prevented a stigma from being attached to the name of Dr. Samuel Mudd, who innocently and compassionately treated Booth's broken leg, a stigma so great that even today when someone has done something less than honorable it is said, "His name is mud."

A. C. Richards
Location: Dress circle
Washington Critic, Louis A. Warren Lincoln Library
April 17, 1885

> *A. C. Richards's account is one of the very few that contends that Booth shouted "Sic Semper Tyrannis" twice. The young boy Richards questioned was probably John Burroughs, who had been holding Booth's horse. His account is especially interesting because he was the chief of police at the time of the assassination.*

"It was about 9 o'clock on the night of the assassination," said Major Richards, Captain M. Reed, now deceased, but then of the Metropolitan

Police force [was accompanied by Richards]. In making our usual rounds of the area we were in the vicinity of Ford's Theatre. Captain Reed suggested that as General Grant was supposed to be in the theatre to go in. We did so and took seats in the dress circle. We had been seated probably about 15 minutes, when at a time the stage in front of the scenery was nearly free of all persons, a shot was heard.

We could, at that instant, see no one nor any indications of any one who fired the shot. In a second or two a person was to scramble out of the front of the box in the second tier and let himself down by the aid of the flag staff to the center of the stage, dropping or leaping some four or five feet before reaching the floor. The next instant, Mrs. Lincoln appeared at the front of the box, and, with hands upward and downward in great excitement called out something which I did not fully understand; but I recognized the word, "Guerrillas." Of course I knew then that something serious had happened, but what, I did not know at that instant.

What was the first impression as to who has been shot?

In a few seconds word went round that General Grant had been shot. Then we [knew] it was President Lincoln was the one.

How did Booth act when he reached stage?

He seemed to drop upon one knee when he reached the floor. He then gathered himself up, faced the audience, drew his bowie knife, brandished it above his head, and with theatrical stride—his face all the time to the audience—cried out twice, I think, 'Sic semper tyrannis,' as he crossed the stage diagonally from the box to the rear and disappeared behind the scenery. He did not utter the words 'Sic semper tyrannis' while in the box, nor any words whatever. He did not crouch near the box with his knife in his hand and then run off the stage.

Did Booth seem to be excited?

No. He evidently intended that his performance should be a piece of tragic acting. He did his part coolly and deliberately, with no show of undramatic excitement or fear.

How long did all this take?

It all happened within a few seconds. As soon as Mrs. Lincoln appeared at the front of the box, and knowing that the person who sprang from the box had committed some serious act, I rushed from my seat to the stage.

I made my way through the now excited and tumultuous audience as quickly as possible. Upon reaching the stage I found J. B. Stewart, esq., formerly well-known in this city, but now deceased, already there. It is possible that one or two other persons were there then, but I think not.

Mr. Stewart and myself groped our way behind the scenery in search of the person who leaped from the box. We found an open doorway leading into the alley in the rear of the theatre. Stepping into the alley we came upon a colored boy who we questioned sharply. He disclosed the fact that the clatter of a horse's feet which we then heard some distance down the alley was that of a horse that a man had found some difficulty in mounting and which he (the boy) had been holding.

Was Spangler, the stage carpenter, there?

No, nor was he found for some time afterward. The boy did not complain of having been knocked down.

What was the first reliable information that you had as to the man who had fired the shot?

It was furnished by Miss Laura Keene herself. Spangler was not in haste at least to disclose anything.

They were exciting times, were they not?

They were. Of other wild, exciting and tumultuous scenes and incidents of that night I have not time now to talk. Of reports of the assassinations of Grant, Seward, Johnson, Stanton, Chase, and other public men there was no end that night. And it quite daylight before we knew really who had been assassinated and who were spared. Of the circumstances attending my visit to Mrs. Surratt's house that night with a squad of my men, at about 1 o'clock, of her manner of receiving from me the announcement of the assassination of President Lincoln, of her being in her usual dress, with no appearance of having retired that night of her cool and collected manner, and other incidents of that night and the few succeeding days I may talk hereafter.

Charles Forbes
Location: Dress circle
Affidavit, Chicago Historical Society
September 17, 1892

> *Charles Forbes was probably the president's messenger on the night of the assassination. It is impossible to determine his exact location at the time of the shot. In this account, Forbes claims to have been in the box when Lincoln was shot, but that statement and several others in this account disagree with numerous more reliable accounts. Either Forbes did not recall the events correctly or he was embellishing his acquaintance with Lincoln.*

I was the personal attendant of the late President Lincoln from shortly after his first inauguration up to the time when he fell by the assassin's bullet. . . . Tad had given me the picture in the afternoon [of April 14, 1865], and I still had it in my pocket when Mrs. Lincoln and her guests were ready to start for the theatre. The President was engaged, and told them to go ahead and send the carriage back for him. I accompanied them to the theatre and returned in the carriage for the President. When the last visitor had departed and I had helped him on with his great coat, I remembered the picture and said, "Mr. President, Tad gave me a photograph this afternoon, and I wish you would put your name at the bottom of it." "Certainly, Charley" replied the President, and picking up a pen he wrote his name on the photograph, and that is the last writing he ever did, for I accompanied him in the carriage, was with him from the carriage to the box in the theatre, and was in the box when the assassin fired his fatal shot.

J. E. Coyel
Location: Orchestra level, third row
Newspaper article, Louis A. Warren Lincoln Library
June 16, 1893

> *Coyel provides probably the best description of the actions of the main actress, Laura Keene. Other eyewitness accounts corroborate Coyel's statement that Keene attempted to calm the audience and then aided those caring for the president.*

Your interview with Captain R. S. Cullum, U.S.M.C., as to his experience as an eyewitness of the assassination of Abraham Lincoln, as published in a recent Sunday issue, I read with deep interest, but I fear that the captain has unintentionally been made to criticize most unjustly the conduct of Miss Laura Keene upon the memorable night. The honorable position which Captain Cullum holds warrants the belief that he would not intentionally do injustice to any one, but in view of the horrors of that night one might well be pardoned for any mistaken ideas one might have relative to the occurrence. With this explanation I ask permission to briefly comment on that part of the interview that relates to the conduct of Miss Keene.

Although more than twenty-eight years have elapsed since that dreadful tragedy was enacted every detail stands out in my mind with startling distinctness. I, too, was a witness.

With a friend I went to Ford's theater that April night, and we secured seats in the center of the house, in the third row in the orchestra, so were close to the stage and in good position to note what afterward occurred, and you will observe that, according to Captain Cullum's statement, I must have been some thirty or forty feet nearer the place where Miss Keene stood when she addressed the audience that he was. Her precise language as she strode to the front of the stage with outstretched hand and in a commanding voice, was, "Order Gentlemen: order gentlemen." She afterward obtained a glass of water from some source, and, as I was near at hand I helped her down from the stage, and she passed up to the box where the President was dying; the report at the time was that she took the dying President's head into her lap, the graphic description of which event will be remembered by all those who read the account at the time. The captain does not say that he saw her try to climb up in to the box from the stage, but head so [sic]; I am sure that such was not the case. I saw a gentleman standing on the front railing of the lower box trying to pass up a pitcher of water but with what success I do not know, as the flag used to drape the Presidential box was so disarranged but the passage of Booth that it hung so as to obstruct my view.

Harry Hawk
Location: Stage
Article in *Cincinnati Commercial Gazette*
1894

> *In this article, Hawk provided crucial evidence indicating the moment at which the assassination occurred. He did not provide a time, but he did recall the last lines spoken. Except for the expletive, the last line Hawk said on stage occurred in Act 3, scene 2.*

"We were giving good performance that night. Both the company and the audience seemed in the best of humor. President and Mrs. Lincoln and party came in during the first act. John Matthews, who was playing Lord Dundreary, had just asked one of his foolish conundrums, and then added in a listening way: 'They don't see it.' The people had turned and were rising in their seats to greet the president. I put in a 'gag' line and said, 'No, but they see him.' The house laughed and cheered, the orchestra played 'Hail to the Chief,' and there was great enthusiasm when the president and party came into the upper box at the right hand as you faced the stage. As I said before, the performance went very smoothly. In the second act it was a forest setting, with no furniture on stage. I was on the stage with Mrs. Muzzey, our 'old lady.' In the play it was supposed that I had lost my fortune, and so she refused to allow me, the American cousin, to marry her daughter. The dialogue was as follow, she speaking first:

'So it is plain to be seen you are not accustomed to the manners of good society."

"After speaking these lines she left the stage, and I said:

" 'Not accustomed to the manners of good society, eh? Well. I guess I know enough to turn you inside out, old woman; you damned old sockdologizing, man-trap.'

"Just as I had finished these lines and was standing toward the front of the stage opposite from the president's box, the shot was fired. The report startled me somewhat, but, as the report was muffled, I thought it came from the property-room of the theater. I did not recognize the sound as that of a pistol shot. Then I saw a man with a long dagger in the front of the president's box. He jumped to the stage, but before he jumped he shouted: 'Sic semper tyrannis,' although I did not understand the words at the time. The spur on his boot caught in the drapery of the box, and he fell to the stage. He dragged himself up on one knee and was slashing the long knife around him like one who was crazy and desperate. It was then, I am sure, I heard him say, 'The South shall be free.' I recognized Booth as he regained his rest and came towards me waving his knife. I did not know what he had done nor what his purpose might be. I did simply what any other man would have done—I ran. My dressing room was up a short flight of stairs, and I retreated to it. Booth followed me through the same and reached the back stage door, where his horse was in waiting.

"When I realized that Booth was not after me I ran back to the stage, and as I came on Colonel Steward, who had been seated opposite the president's party, jumped to the stage and grabbed me. 'Where is that man?' he asked. 'The man that shot the president.' Then I saw in the upper box the president leaning forward, unconscious, while Mrs. Lincoln supported his head. The members of the company surrounded me.

" 'An actor,' said I. 'What's his name?'

'I won't tell,' I replied. 'There'll be a terrific uproar, and I want to keep out of the trouble.'

"Phillips, our old man, turned to me and said: 'Don't be a fool; the man has shot the president, and you will be hanged if you don't give his name.'

'It was John Booth,' I said. They were amazed. It finally developed that only myself and a man named Ferguson positively identified Booth that night. Ferguson saw him go into the passageway behind the president's box. Booth barred the door behind him.

"Although the incidents connected with the tragedy followed one another with the greatest rapidity, every movement and the slightest action of those about me just before and after the shot, are stamped on my mind so that the picture stands before me to-day as vividly as though I had seen it just yesterday. I can see Lincoln unconscious in the box, the doctors being pushed up to him over the backs of two men who had made a sort of bridge of their bodies, as it was impossible to reach the president in the passageway. I can see the look of madness in Booth's face as he jumped to the stage, and that wild cry still rings in my ears. The excitement and uproar were followed by a sudden funeral hush, as the president was carried out of the theater to a house on the opposite side of the street. It was truly a night never to be forgotten.

James R. Morris
Location: Orchestra level
Letter reprinted in *Ohio Archaeological and Historical Publications*,
Louis A. Warren Lincoln Library
July 26, 1897

> *Morris was one of the few who alleged that Booth spoke the words "Sic Semper Tyrannis" from the box. Secretary of State Seward was attacked by Booth's accomplice Lewis Powell but survived. The doctor he referred to may have been Dr. Taft, who was also sitting in the orchestra level.*

I had gone to Washington with a friend, Captain W. M. Kerr, on some business of his connected with his service in the army. On Friday, April 14th, we had successfully concluded the business of our trip and decided to visit Ford's theater.

We were not aware that the President was to be present. As soon as I saw the President and Mrs. Lincoln enter the box in the balcony tier, I called Captain Kerr's attention to the fact. He had never seen the President before, and was, naturally, much gratified at this opportunity of seeing him. Another lady and gentleman accompanied the President, who I afterward learned were a daughter of Senator Harris, of New York, and a Major Rathbone.

Laura Keene and her company were playing "Our American Cousin," and the house was packed, as it was her benefit night. The play had progressed for some time, the curtain had just been rolled up for another act, and almost immediately thereafter the audience were startled by the report of a fire arm. I looked up to see if I could discover from whence the sound came.

I saw the assassin, as he proved to be, in the President's box making for the front. When he had reached it he placed his hand on the bannister and cried out: "Sic semper tyrannis," and, leaping over, alighted on the stage, bringing down with him some of the drapery surrounding the box. When he lit he sank nearly to his knees, as one naturally would in lighting on a solid floor from a height of eight or ten feet. He soon straightened up and ran diagonally across the stage and disappeared behind the wings or scenery and thus escaped.

Captain Kerr asked me: "Did you notice how deathly pale he looked?" and I answered affirmatively. When I first saw the assassin in the President's box after hearing the report of the pistol, I realized what he had done, especially so after hearing the words he uttered. I cannot describe the scene that followed. There was a dead silence for a few moments. The President fell or leaned forward, and I think his head rested on the bannister front. Mrs. Lincoln rose partly to her feet—extending her arms forward and upward, and uttering some mournful cries or words that I did not understand.

I jumped up on my chair and cried: "Hang the——— ———scoundrel!" (Using some expletives not very creditable to myself.) I did not then think he had had time to make his escape, but then think he would be arrested by some of the troup. As I saw no one on the stage when the assassin landed on it, it is not probable that any member of the company really knew what had happened until the assassin had left the theater; and this I have since seen stated in the public [indecipherable] is really the fact, although one or two of them saw him running across the stage and had heard the shot, but did not know until too late, that the President had been assassinated.

About this time Major Rathbone, (if I have the name accurately), rose in the President's box and called out: "Is there any surgeon in the house?" Then numbers were rushing for the stage—many getting upon it. Right before me was a gentleman, whom I took to be an army surgeon, and a lady. He started forward; the lady clung to his arm, exclaiming, "Oh, what will become of me!" I tried to pacify her, telling her to let the doctor go—that there was no danger now. Then the police came rushing in and commanded all to leave the theater. I called to one of them to take charge of the lady, which he did. Two persons were hoisted over the heads of those who were on the stage into the President's box whether the gentleman who had been seated in front of me was one of them I do not know.

The audience seemed to linger as if to learn if the President had been fatally wounded, but the police insisted on clearing the house. I went out with the crowd, but remained on the sidewalk until the President was carried down and across the street to the house where he died. I then made my way to the police office, and, being acquainted with the chief, I told him where I had been. He said: "Morris, it is reduced to a dot that the assassin is Wilkes Booth, but say nothing about it until you hear it from other sources." This was the first intimation I had who the assassin was. While in the chief's office other detectives came hurriedly in and told the chief that Secretary Seward had been assassinated. I left the chief and made my way back to the square where the tragedy occurred, but no one was permitted to pass the place. . . .

John Sears and John Busby
Location: Unknown
Newspaper article, Louis A. Warren Lincoln Library
March 14, 1900

> *This article identifies Captain John Sears and Captain John Busby*
> *as witnesses to the assassination. It is the first instance of two men*
> *who dubiously claimed, decades after the assassination, to have car-*
> *ried Lincoln from the theater.*

Editor Journal: On this anniversary of the assassination of Abraham Lincoln I took up Herndon's book and read the account of the great and distressing tragedy. Herndon closes by stating that but few people are to be found who were in Ford's theatre on that fearful night.

Capt. John Sears of this city and Capt. John Busby, now of Iowa, both still living, were in Ford's theatre on that night and carried Abraham Lincoln from the theatre to Peterson's [sic] home. Captain Sears preserves the blue coat he wore that night. It is still stained with a large spot, by the blood of the martyred president. This information may interest some of your readers who love the details of history. Your fellow citizen, Dr. George Kreider, is well acquainted with Captain Sears.

Roeliff Brinkerhoff
Location: Dress circle
Autobiography, pages 163–70, reprinted in article "Tragedy of an Age:
An Eyewitness Account of Lincoln's Assassination," *Lincolnian*, Ford's
Theatre National Historic Site
1900

> *It is unusual for an account such as Brinkerhoff's, which was re-*
> *corded decades after the assassination, to be so comprehensive. He*
> *readily admits that although some had speculated that Booth's leg was*
> *injured in the fall, he saw no indication of that. Major Potter assisted*
> *in escorting Mrs. Lincoln from the theater.*

I recall my own feelings by the closing paragraph of a letter written home
that morning, clearer medium than blinding tears:

It is with this letter as a verifier that I give my recollections of the
assassination. The morning papers, of April 14, had announced the arrival
of General Grant in the city, and the evening papers made the further
announcement that in company with the President he would be at Ford's
theater that night.

From want of inclination, or want of time, I have never been much of a
theater-goer myself, but I had a couple of friends who had never seen
General Grant. Therefore, for the first time, in Washington, I concluded
to go with them. We went early in order to select our position. The night
was dark, for there was no moon until after ten o'clock, and my recollection, also, is that it was cloudy, with a gloomy mist in the air. At any rate
as we came down the avenue from the war office and passed E street, we
noticed in front of Grover's theatre, which was a little distance to the left,
a large transparency, and as it was the only one visible, we gave it attention; but as the air was misty or smoky we could not make out the
inscription distinctly. At each end, however, there was a separate inscription: that on the left was "April, 1861, the cradle." That on the right was
"April, 1865, the grave."

"Rather ominous, that," said one of the party. "They must be rebels,"
said another. Of course it meant the cradle and grave of the rebellion, but
its indistinctiveness confirms my recollection of the mistiness of the night.
We remembered it afterwards as an omen of evil.

We passed on to Tenth street, and having entered the theater, we took
seats diagonally opposite the President's box, and upon the same floor.
The President's box was upon the second floor, which was twelve feet

eight inches above the stage. The two boxes upon that floor had been thrown into one by removing the partition between them. The box was festooned with flags, so that we knew it was the President's.

The play commenced and had been in progress quite a while, perhaps half an hour when the President came in. He was greeted with a storm of applause as he passed on to his box. He was accompanied by Mrs. Lincoln, Miss Harris, and Major Rathbun (sic). General Grant had concluded not to come and was then on his way to Philadelphia.

Mr. Lincoln took a seat in an armchair (a rocking chair) at the side next to the audience, Mrs. Lincoln was at his right, near the center of the box, and Miss Harris at the further side. Major Rathbun was seated on a sofa near Miss Harris, a little back from the front. Mr. Lincoln, for the first time during my knowledge of him, seemed cheerful and happy. I had seen him often during his presidential term, commencing with his inauguration in 1861, and a sadder face I never saw. But now the load seemed lifted and every vestige of care and anxiety had passed away. He seemed to enjoy the play very much. The play was the American Cousin, and Laura Keene was the star of the evening.

Everything passed on very pleasantly until about ten o'clock or a little later. It was in the third act, in the milkmaid scene, when one of my friends called my attention to the President's box, with the remark, "there's a reporter going to see Father Abraham." I looked and saw a man standing at the door of the President's box, with his hat on, and looking down upon the stage. Presently he took out a card case, or something of that kind, from his side pocket and took out a card. It is said he showed it to the President's messenger outside, but I saw nothing of that kind, in fact I saw no other man there aside from those seated in the audience. He took off his hat, and put his hand upon the door knob, and went into the little hall or corridor, back of the box. I then turned to the play. Presently, I cannot say how soon, it may have been two, three or five minutes, I heard a pistol shot. I turned to the President's box and saw a man flash to the front, with face as white as snow, and hair as black as a raven.

My first impression was that it was a part of the play. The man put his left hand upon the front railing and went over, not with a clean sweep, but with a kind of a scramble, first one leg and then the other. It evidently was his intention to swing over a fence, but his spur, as appeared afterwards, caught in the flag, and hence the scramble.

As he went over, or possibly after reaching the stage, he shouted very clearly and distinctly, "sic semper tyrannis," and then for the first time it flashed upon me that the whole thing meant assassination. The Virginia coat of arms, with its device, had been familiar to me from childhood, and of course with "sic semper tyrannis" ringing clearly through the hall, I understood it at once. The man struck the floor, and sunk down partially, but immediately rose up and brandishing a double-edged dagger, which glittered in the gas light, he passed diagonally across the stage, with his face to the audience, and went out. He did not run, it was a swift stage-walk, and was evidently studied beforehand, like everything else he did, for effect. It is said his leg was broken by the fall, but I saw no evidence of it in his gait.

For a moment there was a stillness of death. The audience seemed paralyzed. No sound whatever came from the box that I heard. It is said in the various accounts the Mrs. Lincoln shrieked. I heard no shriek. Major Rathbun testified that he shouted "stop that man." I heard nothing of that kind, and I believe I could have heard a whisper. I saw Mr. Lincoln sitting in his chair with his head drooped upon his breast, but in all other respects he retained the position he had before he was shot.

Quite a little interval passed before anything was said or done. By interval I mean twenty, thirty or forty seconds, which under such circumstances seem a long time. Then some of the audience rose up, others sat still. Here and there inquiries came as to whether the President was hurt.

In company with Major Potter (a paymaster in the army) I started for the box, but before we got there others had found that it was barred inside. In the meantime Miss Keene had gone into the box from the stage entrance, and perhaps one or two others; at any rate an inquiry was made for a surgeon, and a crowd gathered around the box. There was no uproar or confusion at any time. After a few moments the door was opened and Mr. Lincoln was carried out along the back side of the dress-circle and out at the front. I was close behind, and as we went down stairs I noticed a plash [sic] of blood on every step. His face was very pale, and the stamp of death upon it, which once seen rarely deceives us.

As we reached the street the news began to come of other assassinations. The vice president had been killed; Mr. Seward had been murdered, also Mr. Stanton. In fact the air was full of rumors of blood, and for a short time it looked as if there might be a second Saint Bartholomew in progress. I immediately passed down Tenth street for a sight of the signal station upon the Winder building, and soon saw signals to the army and answers from the fortifications, and knew that any uprising would be quickly suppressed. Mr. Lincoln was taken into a dwelling house across the street from the theater, where he lingered until morning of April 15, and then died. . . .

As to the impelling causes of a deed so desperate, yet so useless, as the assassination of Mr. Lincoln, it is difficult to answer. Booth, himself, doubtless, was actuated by various motives. He was steeped to the lips in the spirit of the rebellion, but I am inclined to think that ambition was the strongest influence. . . .

It may be that Booth had worked himself into the idea that Mr. Lincoln was a kind of representative tyrant, and that in killing him he was playing the role of Brutus, but I think not, for the entire affair was entirely too stagey, at least for the spirit of Brutus. He was acting a premeditated part from the beginning to end, it is true, but it was entirely for stage effect, and for the glorification of the actor. His "sic semper tyrannis" was stagey. His whole attitude and walk before the audience at the theater were stagey. His double-edged gladiatorial dagger had been prepared purposely for stage effect. In fact, it was all a part of a play which was to make John Wilkes Booth immortal in history.

Henry Williams
Location: Unknown
Newspaper article, Ford's Theatre National Historic Site
1900

*Henry Williams describes Booth as "limping" across the stage, infer-
ring that Booth broke his leg in jumping from the president's box.
This speculation became fact in some twentieth-century accounts that
were recorded a few years after Williams's account.*

Henry Williams, great uncle of Howard Arnold, Sr. of North Scituate, Rhode Island, was standing in that long line as the sun was setting at 7 P.M. There was reason to celebrate. This day, Good Friday, was the first time the Civil War would be referred to in the past tense. Henry was alive, whereas over 600,000 Americans, from both North and South, had given their lives. He was AWOL from I Company, U.S. Artillery, to see this great man who spoke of "malice toward none, with charity for all." Williams paid for his ticket and received his change—a 50-cent piece, dated 1831. He was one of 1700 persons who strolled into Ford's theatre and saw the President enter his special box. The audience rose and applauded, and Mr. Lincoln bowed in acknowledgement.

As the play proceeded, Henry Williams often glanced at the Lincolns' lavishly decorated box. The last act was almost over when he heard a dull report. The President's head sagged forward and Williams was halfway out of his chair when the assassin, Booth, scrambled down from the balcony, caught his spur in the treasury flag, and fell to the stage.

While the audience sat, dumbfounded for the moment, Booth was limping toward the back door. He made it to his saddled mare and spurred his animal through Ninth Street to Pennsylvania Avenue. Williams was one of the first to get back to his company fast. Racing his mount down Louisiana Avenue, he passed a scant few feet from Booth, riding in the opposite direction. (Williams did not recognize the assassin, but knew it to be Booth upon hearing a detailed description later that evening.) He returned to his quarters, still stupefied with the horror of the witnessed act. Then Williams remembered the 50 cent piece. He took it out of his pocket, looked at it, turning it over and over, put it back, took it out and looked it over once more.

For the next 40 years the coin remained on his person, a treasured symbol of a tragic event—a small monument to a President to be revered. Henry Williams would remember, and the haunting words of his beloved President would come back: "To do all which we may achieve and cherish a just and a lasting peace among ourselves, and with all nations."

John Buckingham
Location: Lobby
"Today's Anniversary," *Washington Evening Star*, Library of Congress
April 14, 1903

> *John Buckingham's earlier account claimed that Booth entered the lobby twice. Because the previous one has greater credibility, it is more likely that the assassin entered the lobby twice, not five times. Buckingham also admits to being a personal friend of the Booth family. Buckingham was seventy-seven years old in 1903.*

"It was in the latter part of 1862 that I became doortender at Ford's. I came to Washington from Baltimore at the request of John T. Ford. I was on the main door of the theater at nights and days I worked at the navy yard.

"The night of the assassination I remember with distinctness. The President and Mrs. Lincoln and Maj. Rathbone and Miss Mary [sic] Harris, the daughter of Senator Harris of New York, came to the theater together.

I passed them within and saw them disappear in to the box where Mr. Lincoln received the fatal shot. Miss Harris was on the arm of the President, and Mrs. Lincoln was escorted by Maj. Rathbone. The President seemed to be unusually bright in appearance.

"I should say it was about 20 minutes after 10 o'clock, and I was putting away my checks and tickets and getting ready to close up when the show was over, when I heard the noise of a pistol shot. I should think it was about a hundred feet from the stage to my door. I stepped back to the door leading to the parquet and there saw John Wilkes Booth in a stooping position.

"I did not see him jump, but I saw him when he was going across the stage. The slouch hat he had been wearing he dropped on the stage. He had a large knife in one of his hands. As he ran across the footlights he shouted 'Sic semper tyrannis.' Booth rushed through the flats and made his exit through the back door. I was confused utterly in the excitement that followed the shooting of the President. I was trying to let the people out of the house and at once began to unfasten the doors leading to the street. I remember that some one called to me and asked who it was that had done the shooting and I replied it was John Wilkes Booth. As I walked back to the main door Harry Ford, the brother of John Ford, the manager, came up to me and said, calling me by a nickname:

" 'Buck, step out to the curb and get Mayor Wallach. You will find him there. Ask him to come in and request the people to leave the theatre.'

"I found Wallach and he came in. He wedged his way around through the crowd to the stage from which he addressed the audience. He told them that the President had been shot and asked them to leave the theater as quietly as possible. In a short time the house was empty.

"President Lincoln was carried out of the theater and across the street to the Peterson [sic] House, where he died the following morning. I recall how the President looked as he was being taken from the theater. Several persons carried him. I opened the door leading to the pavement and through which the President and his bearers passed.

"I recall particularly the presence of Laura Keene, the actress, in the lobby. She stood there, back toward the ticket office window, and, raising her hand, exclaimed:

" 'For God's sake try and capture the murderer.'

"In closing the door after President Lincoln had been taken out I was stooping down to press the bolt when an army officer rushed past me with a big pistol in his hand. As I turned to look up the pistol struck me on the back of the ear. I called to him, but got no response. I don't know to this day who it was. In those days there were always a number of army officers at the performances. I managed to close the door, in fact, all the front doors. In a little while a provost guard took possession of the theater."

Mr. Buckingham said today, as he was telling his story of the tragedy, that Wilkes Booth entered Ford's Theater that night five different times.

"Booth had the entree to the theater. He came in and went away when he pleased. Sometimes he would stand at the door a minute and chat. The last time he came into the theater that night, only a minute or so before he shot the President, he shook two fingers of my hand. I had placed my hand out for a ticket, not noticing who it was. He pressed my fingers and said:

" 'Buck, you don't want a ticket.'

"Booth was thinking that evening. He had vacillated between the theater and the saloon a few doors away. I did not notice that he was particularly under the influence of drink, but knew he had been drinking."

Captain Isaac Hull
Location: Orchestra level
Newspaper article, "Recalls Tragedy of Event," Louis A. Warren
Lincoln Library
1906

> *Captain Isaac Hull claimed to have met personally with Lincoln at the White House on April 14, 1865. His account is one of the few that place the shot at ten o'clock, and it is one of the first to state that Lincoln had been seated in a rocking chair.*

"I had arranged to leave Washington for Baltimore that night, and had all my luggage ready to take a late train. After settling with the clerk, I walked down Pennsylvania avenue, and as I came to Ford's Theater, I suddenly determined to go in and witness the performance until it was time for me to go to the railroad station. I had heard much of Booth and the play, 'Our American Cousin,' and felt that it was an opportunity not to be missed. The seat I purchased was unsatisfactory, and so I went to the box office and had it changed to one within two or three rows of the stage.

"While I was getting my ticket changed I hear somebody said 'There's Booth,' and for the first time I saw the noted actor. I took a good look at him, and then went into the theater and occupied my seat in what was known as the orchestra row. I could not have been more than fifteen or twenty feet from the box in which President Lincoln and his party were sitting. From where I sat I could see the President moving to and fro in a rocking chair which had been placed in the box especially for his comfort.

"It was about 10 o'clock when I heard a shot fired, and strange to say, I thought on the instant that it had been fired from the gallery. It seemed to me that nobody paid much attention to the report for a few moments. Then I heard a woman scream, and the next instant almost I saw Booth appear in the front of the box, place his hands on the railing and vault over to the stage with a knife in his hand. He went down on one knee as he alighted, and then arose waving the knife. I heard him say something but I could not understand him because of the confusion that had arisen. Others claim to have heard him say 'Sic Semper Tyrannis' but his words failed to reach my ears. Then he dashed behind the scenery and disappeared.

"Four or five men, with myself leaped out of our seats and made our way to the stage over the footlights, all animated by the same desire to capture Booth, but he had escaped. I recall encountering Miss Laura Keene, the leading lady, as I ran across the stage and hearing her say, 'My God, it's Wilkes!' and of hearing other exclamations from members of the company who were huddled behind the scenes. I had left my hat in my seat, and it suddenly struck me that I ought to get it before the theater lights were extinguished, so I ran for my seat by the way I left it. By the time I secured my hat nearly everyone had left the theater.

"A strange scene was presented when I emerged on the street. The lights in many dwellings had been extinguished. People were standing in little groups on the sidewalks talking about the great plot to kill the executive officers of the government. I heard the news of the murderous attack on Secretary Seward. I heard the stories that there was a conspiracy to kill every Union soldier in Washington. Squads of calvary were galloping up and down the avenue, and small bodies of infantry were tramping up and down Pennsylvania avenue. The hunt for Booth already had started.

"I was unable to get a train out of Washington that night for all of them were suspended until the next morning. There was an atmosphere of uncertainty in Washington that I cannot describe. As long as I live I shall not forget that night."

John Buckingham
Location: Lobby
Newspaper article, Ford's Theatre National Historic Site
1907

*As Buckingham recollects, the Fords were unsuccessful in attempting
to reopen the theater. Sixty-one years after this article, Ford's Theatre
would reopen as an active theater.*

I was tending the door at Ford's Theater the night that Lincoln was shot.
The impression it made upon my mind is still so vivid that I don't like to
talk about it, but for all that there was nothing of the horrible scene often
described. The soldiers, who were almost immediately upon the spot, did
not charge upon the crowd with fixed bayonets, as is sometimes erro-
neously stated. There was very great difficulty in making the people leave
the house. Hardly two minutes after the shot was fired the audience
seemed to flow over into the orchestra and upon the stage. This state of
things lasted for some time until, at the request of Mr. Harry Ford, I went
out to the sidewalk and spoke to Mayor Wallach, for many years the
Mayor of this city. He came in, and going as far as he could down one of
the aisles, addressed the crowd and asked them to leave. He was well
known and the people obeyed with tolerable promptness, and that is the
way the throng was really dispersed. When they were finally gone, I
locked the doors and quitted the building.

All this, of course, is more or less widely known to the public. What is
less familiar is the subsequent history of the old house. A provost guard
was put in charge, and the soldiers made sad havoc with the appearance of
the theater. We had, for instance, a pretty little waiting parlor for ladies;
here the guard cooked and ate their rations, until floor and furniture were
covered with grease. They damaged the boxes, too, a great deal, and
altogether left the place in a sorry condition. Mr. Ford obtained permission to open again on the fourth of July. The play was the Octoroon, and
was billed all over the city. The provost guard was not ordered out until
the last moment, and after that we attempted to put things in order as best
we could. The theater was cleaned, and I brought out a roll of crape and
draped the box which President Lincoln had occupied. We were busy all
day on the 10th, and I hurried home late to dress for the evening's business. A little before time for the performance I came back and found a
row of soldiers on the steps. Mr. Ford came up and told me that he had
been summoned to appear at the War Department, and that there could be

no performance that evening. He went to see Secretary Stanton. The building was bought by the Government for $100,000 and has not been used for theatrical purposes since.

Laura H. Freudenthal
Location: Dress circle, front row
Washington Star, Louis A. Warren Lincoln Library
February 13, 1908

> *Laura Freudenthal was unusual in claiming that the shot occurred during intermission. Also, Mrs. Lincoln was sitting directly to the president's right so it is unlikely that she would have had to clamber over the chairs. Freudenthal was eighty-seven years old when she recalled the event.*

"You know my sister was visiting us from New York," Mrs. Freudenthal will begin. She wanted to see the President and the papers said he'd be at that show —it was 'Our American Cousins,' you know—so we thought that would be a good time to see him well, and thats how we came to be there that night."

"There was my husband and my sister and I and we were in the first row of the first balcony where we were right across from the President's box and we could see him perfectly."

"They had turned down the gas—you know they used that for illumination then—and everybody was waiting for the second act to begin," she recalls. "Suddenly we heard a pistol shot but everybody thought at first it was part of the play. Then I saw Booth jump out of the President's box. There was a big flag draped about the box, though, and Booth's foot caught in it and he fell down to the stage. He recovered himself quickly there, and before a soul could move he stood down there in the dim light—he was really handsome, I thought then—and he cried 'Sic semper tyrannis.'

"You know he had a great big knife in his hand and after he shouted from the stage he turned to run off and he swirled that knife around in front of him and if anybody had gotten in his way they'd have gotten it. Then somebody cried out 'the President is shot!' and oh it seemed awful. Everybody was frightened and surprised and for a minute they didn't move. Then I saw Mrs. Lincoln clambering over chairs to reach Mr. Lincoln and by that time the people in the audience were milling about excitedly. And then—they took him out of the theater."

"We all felt we needed something to quiet our nerves; we just couldn't go home like that for we were nearly frantic, so we walked down to Harvey's— you know that place was famed for its steamed oysters and a glass of wine.

When we had quieted down a bit, we went outdoors again to go home and I never saw such a sight as long as I've lived.

Everybody seemed to be out; soldiers were milling about and the excitement was something terrible to behold! But we went right home to our house over on Capitol Hill."

W. H. Taylor
Location: Dress circle
"A New Story of the Assassination of Lincoln," *Leslie's Weekly*,
Library of Congress
March 3, 1920

> *W. H. Taylor's is one of the few twentieth-century accounts that contains more nonfictional information than fictional information. It is truly remarkable that his voluminous account reads with the accuracy of an 1865 one.*

The programme shown here of a performance at Ford's Fifth Street Theatre in Washington, D.C., was obtained by me under peculiar circumstances. I was a young man, about twenty years of age, and living in Washington at that time. Having been away on a trip to Chicago and points in the West, I was returning home on the forenoon of April 14th, 1865, when, on reaching the Relay House, nine miles from Baltimore, I noticed in the morning paper an announcement that President Lincoln, General Grant, and other notables were to attend Ford's Theatre that night. This caused me to resolve upon going to the theatre, as I had never seen General Grant, whose fame had for some time been so well established. Quite early in the evening I started out at the solicitation of a young friend of mine, John Danser of Trenton, N.J., to witness a street parade in honor of recent passage of eight-hour law, etc. We could hear the bands playing, and directly came to a point where we could discern floats, torchlights, etc. coming down Louisiana Avenue. After watching the procession we proceeded to the theatre. We selected seats in the dress circle, which was as yet almost vacant, and secured places where no more than two or three dozen others were able to see as well as ourselves the arrangements of the President's box, which was situated immediately across from our position and on the same level.

About the middle of the first act the President and party arrived and were received with loud and hearty applause. The band played "Hail to the Chief!" which stopped the performance for a few minutes while they were proceeding to their seats. On reaching the box the President took a large arm-chair in front and to the left as they entered, Mrs. Lincoln took a chair in front and to the right, and Miss Harris one near Mrs. Lincoln, but not quite as far forward. Major Rathbone was seated further back than the ladies on an old-fashioned sofa that ran along the wall on the extreme right.

About the middle of the third act a shot was heard and immediately thereupon rang out John Wilkes Booth's cry, "Sic semper tyrannis"; not after he reached the stage, as has been stated in some accounts; neither did he jump from the box full height with arms outspread and upstretched, as we often see him in illustrations. On the contrary, he placed both hands upon the rail of the box and swung himself over in that manner, thereby lessening the fall by the distance of his own height. One of his spurs caught in the American colors with which the box was draped, and he probably landed his whole weight on one foot. On striking the stage he pitched forward on all fours, and I then saw the blade of a long stiletto or dagger glisten in the footlights, as his hand lay on the floor. He quickly rose to his feet and took one or two uncertain steps, then, turning to face the audience, drew himself up in theatrical attitude, and, swinging his arm in a half circle made a grand flourish with the dagger, and was off stage in a flash. Next came the piercing and horrifying shrieks of Mrs. Lincoln, and then arose a fearful commotion. Directly efforts were made by some parties to get into the box from the outside, but the door was barred from the inside. I next noticed a military officer standing on the shoulders of another man and endeavoring to climb up to the box from the stage. Meantime, the President had remained sitting in his chair with his head bent forward, but I distinctly saw him rise once to his feet and in a dazed sort of way attempt to take a step or two. He was not upright but half erect. Just then Major Rathbone came to his assistance, and supported by the latter, he sank back into the chair. About this time I noticed Miss Laura Keene who had reached the box from the private way back of the stage, and who was said to have brought a glass of water which might refresh the President. The bar against the door having been removed from the inside, several people went into the box from the dress circle, and little more could be distinguished thereafter.

Strangely enough, an assassination plot seemed to have been under-stood at once, for word was passed around that the place would be blown up. There was a general rush to vacate the theatre, and from our position we were necessarily about the last ones that could possibly leave the place. On nearing the doorway we saw men approaching from the passage-way back of the box with the form of the President, carried on an improvised stretcher—as it now seems to me a window shutter or something of that nature—and we stopped to let them pass. They were hastening from the building as well as they could, and the President's head was thrown back and hanging somewhat down. He was quite unconscious, seemed perfectly limp, and was bleeding slightly from the wound in his head. Just as they passed by I glanced on the floor, and seeing a crimson blotch on the piece of paper herewith illustrated, I picked it up. That the marks thereon are the life-blood of Abraham Lincoln is as certain as that he was shot on the date and in the place mentioned.

As the place remained brilliantly lighted and there seemed to be no immediate danger, we went back to the President's box, where almost the first thing that attracted the notice of my companion and myself was the pistol which Booth had used, lying on the floor only about three or four feet back of the chair in which Mr. Lincoln sat. I recall the weapon as a single-barreled percussion-cap affair of the Deringer type, shorter and more compact than the dueling pistols so much in favor among gentlemen of the old school in those days. As we started to leave the theatre we met, at the head of the stairway, a policeman, who inquired if we were present at the time of the shooting, etc., and said we had better give our names and addresses as it might be necessary to call us as witnesses. I drew the pistol out of my pocket and gave it to the policeman to take charge of against the chance of its being called for as evidence.

The blood-stained programme has never been out of the hands of my immediate family. . . . It always seemed to me extremely doubtful that Wilkes Booth could have been the accredited representative of the governing body of the Southern Confederacy, notwithstanding that Jefferson Davis in a speech at Charleston, S.C., when he received a dispatch from John C. Breckinridge announcing Lincoln's murder remarked to the audience, "If it were to be done, it were better that it were done well." The brutal frankness of such a statement made in public was almost sufficient evidence that he was not directly knowing to the infamous plot. . . . At the time of Booth's capture he was found to have kept, in his flight, a diary, in which his egotism was seatly in evidence. It was rather a disjointed affair, full of wild and ardent expressions. He had seen newspaper comments and was surprised and deeply grieved at not finding himself glorified in the affair.

Isaac Walker Maclay
Location: Unknown
New York newspaper, Louis A. Warren Lincoln Library
December 31, 1908

> *Isaac Maclay is another eyewitness who claimed to have carried*
> *Lincoln from the theater. His claim is not supported by any other eye-*
> *witness accounts.*

On the night of the assassination of President Lincoln at Ford's Theatre in
Washington by J. Wilkes Booth, Major Maclay with two other officers of
the Washington Arsenal attended the theatre, and after the shooting he
and his fellow officers carried the President to the Peterson [sic] house
and placed him on a bed in a rear room. This house is now known as the
Lincoln Museum. Then Major Maclay went for Dr. Todd, the President's
family physician, after which he was detailed to guard the residence of the
Secretary of War.

Captain Edwin Bedee
Location: Orchestra level, second row
Source unknown, Louis A. Warren Lincoln Library
1908

> *The physician Edwin Bedee assisted into the box was probably Dr.*
> *Charles Sabin Taft. He is one of the few eyewitnesses to claim that*
> *Booth said, "Revenge for the South," as he crossed the stage.*

He was seated in the second row on the left side of the theatre in back of
the orchestra. A command view could be had of President Abraham
Lincoln watching the play. The sound of a shot rang out above the actor's
voice on stage. Captain Edwin Bedee stared as a man vaulted from the
President's box to the stage. . . .

When Captain Bedee saw the man drop onto the stage from the Presi-
dent's box, his first reaction was to pursue the fleeing murderer. Instead,
Bedee, like the rest, listened as Booth boldly uttered the incredible words,
"Revenge for the South!"

Sensing a catastrophe, Captain Bedee sprang from his chair, climbed
over some rows, bolted past the orchestra and footlights and across the
stage in the direction Booth had disappeared.

A scream shattered the mounting house. "They've got him!" Bedee
presumed the assassin was caught. Another scream. It was Mrs. Lincoln

"My husband is shot!" A doctor was called for. Captain Bedee reeled around and bounded across the stage toward the box, a man appeared and stated he was a physician. Captain Bedee stepped aside, pushed the doctor up to the railing and followed directly behind. Had the captain not given assistance to the surgeon, he would have been the first to reach Lincoln. The only entrance to the box was believed locked by Booth when he slipped in to do his foul act, which apparently kept anyone from hastily entering from the outside passageway. . . .

The play was "Our American Cousin." It was being performed for the last time. Captain Bedee was fortunate to obtain a seat, for the house was sold out. In fact, his seat gave him full view of the President's box and its occupants. Because the audience was laughing at the antics on stage at the time few heard the shot that felled the President.

FOUR

THE LAST ACCOUNTS
1909–1954

The plethora of accounts stand as testament to Lincoln's popularity and the public's interest in the assassination. These accounts contain numerous discrepancies. In almost all cases, the eyewitness was the focus of the account. Although the eyewitnesses were probably in the theater on the night of the assassination, their recollections were based on an event witnessed decades before and thus are highly suspect. Nelson Todd's account is probably the best example of one that lacks credibility.

I have not reproduced several accounts because they provide scant information on the assassination. Those accounts are those of Herman Newgarten (*Harrisburg Telegraph*, November 26, 1910), Myron L. Story (*Washington Post*, Febuary 15, 1915), Benjamin F. Judd (newspaper article, 1940s), Sarah N. Eastman (newspaper article, date unknown), Henry Edward Riley (*Washington Times-Herald*, August 2, 1942), William E. Widrick (newspaper article, 1934), Levene C. B. Stewart (newspaper article, 1932), Charles H. Quimby (newspaper article, September 9, 1930s), Emmanuel Obendorfer (newspaper article, 1930s), John Revord (newspaper obituary, 1930s), Samuel Kirby Gleason (*New York Times*, August 5, 1930), Albert W. Boggs (newspaper obituary, 1930), Mary E. Smith (newspaper article, April 14, unknown year), and Henry C. Harris (*Madison County Record*, Huntsville, Arkansas, June 24, 1920).

Some of these accounts, however, contain interesting information. Riley claimed to have been arrested by police after he left Ford's Theatre because he had a sprained ankle. Widrick and Newgarten both maintained that they witnessed the assassination and assisted with Booth's capture. Gleason claimed to have pursued Booth in the theater. Although Major Stewart never mentioned her, his wife was also in Ford's Theatre. Boggs, formerly a Union army sergeant, attended the theater with Major General Thomas M. Vincent and also witnessed the conspiracy trial, the execution, and Lincoln's funeral. Mary Smith, who worked as a nurse during the Civil War, visited Ford's after meeting Lincoln during one of the president's hospital visits.

Captain Oliver C. Gatch
Location: Dress circle, right
Newspaper article, Louis A. Warren Lincoln Library
February 5, 1909

This is one of the more inaccurate eyewitness accounts. Neither Taft nor Leale mentioned another doctor besides Dr. King. Gatch's account is in clear contradiction with the reliable ones of Taft and Leale and thus must be considered erroneous.

He is Captain Oliver C. Gatch, now in his 74th year, a retired farmer, whose home is near the city. He was the first man to enter Lincoln's box in Ford's Theatre after John Wilkes Booth had fired the bullet that stilled the heart of the great emancipator.

Until recently Captain Gatch has been reticent upon the subject. With even his closest friends he refused to discuss the great tragedy. Recently, however, he was prevailed upon to give an account of the shooting, and the history making incident he witnessed on the fatal night.

Captain Gatch and his brother, Dr. Charles Gatch, now dead, left Washington during the excitement following the assassination of Lincoln without giving their names to the authorities, and it never occurred to them that their testimony was wanted. "It wasn't necessary," says Captain Gatch.

Captain Gatch, while hardly more than a boy, enlisted by the Confederate troops and imprisoned until March, 1864, when he escaped from his captors and returned to his home, which was then at Milford near here. There he met his brother, Dr. Gatch. Together they went to Washington on official business. On Friday night, April 14, 1865 Good Friday—they went to Ford's Theatre, attracted thither by the announcement that President Lincoln was to be a guest.

"Our seats were in the balcony, and, had we desired, we could have touched the sentry stationed at the entry of the box to be occupied by the President," Gatch declares. "In fact, we were so close to the President's box that we could hear his chuckle at the jokes of the play, but we couldn't see him."

During an intermission in the play, which was the elder Southern's great success, "The American Cousin," Captain Gatch and his brother, cramped from sitting in one posture, stretched themselves. As they did so they noticed a handsome young man watching the show from a position against the wall near Lincoln's box. It was John Wilkes Booth, who murdered Lincoln.

"I saw him edge toward the box," Gatch says. "Suddenly he entered the passageway. A few seconds later we heard a shot. Bedlam reigned in the audience.

"A man—Major Rathbone, Lincoln's guest, it was—rushed from the President's box and shouted: 'Get a doctor.' My brother said he was a physician, and he and I were dragged into the President's box. My brother raised Lincoln's head to probe for the bullet, and the index finger of his left hand came in contact with a jagged hole in the back of Mr. Lincoln's head. When he withdrew his hand it was filled with the President's brain, which was oozing out at the ghastly hole."

Captain Gatch's brother told those in the box that the wound was fatal, and advised that the President be taken to a private residence near the theatre, and not to the White House, as was suggested.

A shutter was hastily secured as a stretcher and Captain Gatch and his brother, with others, raised the President from the floor of the box and carried him down the stairs and out of the theatre.

The sobbing of the people and the hoofbeats of the approaching cavalry regiment, which was hastily summoned, was the only sound on the street. Lincoln was tenderly carried to a little house across the street from the theatre, and the great men of the nation called to look at him before death came. His wife, too, was at his bedside.

Gatch and his brother then returned to the theatre and measured the distance Booth had leaped from the President's box to the stage. It was 144 inches.

"We saw Booth fall on the stage, the spurs on his boots having caught in the folds of a flag which was draped about the President's box.

"He brandished a dagger, shouting: 'The South is avenged.'

Captain Gatch and his brother obtained the cuffs worn by Lincoln on the night he was shot, but they were stolen 15 years ago. Gatch works on his farm every day and lives alone with his wife.

"The events of the night are burned into my mind," he said.

Earl Stirling
Location: Backstage
"Tell Original Lincoln Tales," *Chicago Daily Journal*, Library of Congress
February 13, 1909

> *Earl Stirling was an actor who told his story of the assassination to the media long after the event.*

In connection with the anniversary of the birth of America's greatest statesman, Abraham Lincoln, it is interesting to note that there is playing in Chicago at this time an actor who was a member of the staff at Ford's Theatre at the time that the emancipator was felled by an assassin's hand, and who was a close associate of Edwin Booth.

This actor is Earl Stirling, character man at the College theatre, on the north side. On the night of April 14, 1865, Mr. Stirling was standing in the wings when Booth fired the fatal shot.

The next instant he was hurled to the floor. Booth had jumped to the stage, and in an effort to reach an exit had knocked him over. Mr. Stirling says that for fully fifteen minutes he was not aware of what had happened "out front." He was among those arrested the following day, but because of his age, he being only 20 years old, he was discharged. Mr. Stirling is now wrinkled and bent from the weight of sixty-four years, forty of which have seen service on the stage.

Lieutenant William Ennis
Location: Orchestra level
Newspaper article, Louis A. Warren Lincoln Library
Date unknown

> *Ennis was one of the few who attended Ford's Theatre who did not know until after the assassination that the president was in attendance. He evidently arrived after the Lincolns did.*

General William Ennis, U.S.A. (retired), now residing in this city, was one of the few, if indeed he is not the only one living in this vicinity who was present in Ford's Theatre, Washington, April 14, 1865, when President Lincoln was shot by John Wilkes Booth. General Ennis was then a lieutenant in the United States artillery and was on duty with his battery a short distance from Washington. He attended the theatre with an old classmate at West Point, Lieutenant Maclay of the ordinance corps, who was then on duty in or near Washington. Lieutenant Maclay, who was retired from the army several years ago and was engaged in business in New York, died in that city quite recently and was then spoken of as the last survivor in that city who was at Ford's Theatre on that fateful night.

Lieutenant Ennis and Lieutenant Maclay occupied seats about six or seven rows from the stage. The play was "Our American Cousin," which was being presented by the Laura Keene Company, in which the elder Southern played the part of Lord Dundreary. It had advanced to the point where the American cousin, Asa Trenchard, appears on the stage alone and soliloquizes whether he shall destroy the will which would make the English cousin heir to the property which would otherwise fall to him. General Ennis does not recall the name of the actor, but he is spoken of in other accounts as a player named Watts.

While the soliloquy was in progress and the audience engrossed in listening to the actor's words, a pistol shot rang out in the theatre, causing a slight disturbance. Immediately another person was seen on the stage, as a tall man came from the direction of the boxes and with a theatrical stride walked rapidly towards the opposite wings. So intent had been the audience on the actor on the stage that the appearance of a new actor was scarcely realized, and none knew what it meant. General Ennis says he recalls having seen the glint of a knife which the man carried in his hand, though he did not thoroughly appreciate what it was, as he supposed the man was a part of the play. In an instant both the actor and the assassin had disappeared, and it was learned the actor, seeing the strange man on the stage, carrying a knife in a threatening sort of a way, made good his escape.

General Ennis says that up to the time the man appeared on the stage he did not know President Lincoln was in a box, but that soon after Booth's appearance and disappearance the news rapidly spread through the theatre and the audience dismissed itself in great excitement. He went at once to a hotel, where all sorts of rumors were current, that not only had

President Lincoln been assassinated but also the Vice President, Secretary Stanton, Secretary Seward and other members of the cabinet had been killed. Everybody was naturally much excited and it was impossible to learn the exact truth that night, and it was not until the next day at camp that he learned that President Lincoln had died and that the other reports were unfounded.

William H. Flood
Location: Orchestra Level
"First to Aid Lincoln," *Washington Post*, Library of Congress
February 15, 1911

This account contains numerous discrepancies. It is highly unlikely that Flood could have been the first to enter the presidential box because his seat was on the orchestra level. Furthermore, like Gatch's account, Flood's is in clear contradiction with Dr. Leale's and Dr. Taft's concerning who was in the president's box after the assassination and who found the President's wound. The article also claimed that Flood was a personal friend of Abraham Lincoln's.

Flood refers to the Petersen house as the Oldroyd house. Years after the assassination, Osborn Oldroyd, a Lincoln collector, purchased the house and used it as his residence. After it was purchased by the federal government, Oldroyd departed and the house was again known by the Petersen name.

I was an ensign in the navy at the time and was attached to the U.S.S. Primrose, stationed in the Potomac. On the evening of April 14, I was invited to Ford's Theater by my captain, Silas Owen. He had heard that President Lincoln would attend the performance, Our American Cousin —and, of course, I accepted the invitation.

We went in uniform, but I did not carry arms. We sat in the third row from the stage and could see the President's box. Immediately after a man jumped to the stage, shouting 'Sic semper tyrannis,' I recognized him at once as John Wilkes Booth.

In getting to the stage he nipped over some bunting and fell, but immediately picked himself up and rushed across the stage, waving a long knife. No one moved until he was out of sight. I jumped from my seat and, brushing past the people in the aisle, ran to the President's box, where the women were screaming.

I grabbed the side of the proscenium arch and 'shinned' up to the President's box, where Miss Harris, who was in the presidential party, assisted me over the railing. Mrs. Lincoln threw her arms around me as I got in and cried:

They've murdered papa! They've murdered papa! See if you can't do something.

I looked into the back of the box and there—there sat the President in a big chair. His hands rested on his lap and his head was bent forward. One woman in the box was hysterical. I opened Mr. Lincoln's vest and felt for some signs of a wound, but could find none.

Then I discovered he had been shot in the head. My hands were covered with blood. Below there was a panic, with women screaming and fainting and the men shouting. Then a surgeon came with some soldiers and placed the President on a stretcher. As they did this, I stepped on the edge of the box and called to the audience:

"The President is not dead, but is mortally wounded." I took my place at the head of the stretcher, and with Capt. Owen, walked to the Oldroyd house, where the President breathed his last. A little later we started to the ship, and as we reached the street saw a crowd of wildly excited people gathered on the sidewalk. My uniform was covered with blood, and a report started that I had been connected with the assassination.

I left Washington the next day under orders. Later I returned to identify the body of Booth, and this talk that it was not Booth's body is foolish. I knew him, and am willing to swear that it was his dead body that I saw at the inquiry.

E. A. Emerson
Location: Backstage
Theatre Magazine, Library of Congress
June 1913

> *Emerson provides more information concerning Booth's polite nature. The bloodstains on the program were probably from Rathbone's wound because Lincoln bled little in the box.*

"It was near the beginning of the third act. I was standing in the wings, just behind a piece of scenery, waiting for my cue to go on, when I heard a shot. I was not surprised, nor was anyone else behind the scenes. Such sounds are too common during the shifting of the various sets to surprise an actor. For a good many seconds after that sound nothing happened behind the footlights. Then, as I stood there in the dimness, a man rushed by me, making for the stage door. I did not recognize Booth at the time, nor did anyone else, I think, unless perhaps someone out on the stage, when he stood a moment and shouted with theatrical gesture, 'Sic Semper Tyrannis!' (So perish all tyrants!). Even after he flashed by, there was quiet for a few moments among the actors and the stage hands. No one knew what had happened.

"Then the fearful cry, springing from nowhere it seemed, ran like wildfire behind the scenes:

" 'The President's shot!' "

"Everyone began to swirl hither and thither in hysterical aimlessness. Still the curtain had not been rung down—for no one seemed to have retained a scintilla of self-possession—and the actors on the stage were left standing there as though paralyzed.

Then someone dropped the curtain and pandemonium commenced. The police came rushing in to add to the chaos, and for what seemed an hour, the confusion was indescribable. One incident stands out plainly in my memory from the confusion of men and sound that turned the stage into chaos. As I was running aimlessly to and fro behind the scenes—as everyone else was—a young lady, coming out from a dressing room, asked the cause of all the uproar.

"President Lincoln has just been shot!" I replied.

"Oh!" she exclaimed and, closing her eyes, was sinking limp to the floor in a faint when I caught her and carried her into her dressing room. She was Miss Jennie Gourlay, one of the then well-known family of actors, and that night playing the part of Mary Trenchard. This little episode exhausts my recollection of anything coherent during the time immediately after the shooting.

"Those who first attempted to aid Mr. Lincoln tore his clothes from him in the most frantic manner in their efforts to locate the wound. I was told by several of the men connected with the theatre, among them young Mr. Ford, who had charge of the ticket office, that, when he was brought out, he had been practically denuded of all his outer garments. Later on, when the place was cleared, I went into the box where the assassination had occurred. Just by the side of Lincoln's chair was a program half crumpled. On it was a dark wet spot, which I do not say positively was the life-blood of the President, but in my own mind I am convinced it was."

This program, which no doubt was that held in the hand of Mr. Lincoln at the time the fatal shot was fired, is carefully preserved by Mr. Emerson. The spot referred to, though faded to a dim brown, is still plainly visible. "I knew Wilkes Booth very intimately," continued Mr. Emerson, "and acted with him a great many times. We were much the same size, dressed alike, and were of the same general physical characteristics—whereby hangs a tale as I'll tell you later. I first played with him some time before the outbreak of the war, at the Sycamore Street Theatre, in Cincinnati. He played the part of Evelyn, in Bolwer's comedy, 'Money.' In the fourth and fifth acts he was the best Richard III that I ever saw. In the earlier acts, he was not sufficiently self-contained. He was also the gentlest man I ever knew. He was not feminine, yet gentle as a woman. In rehearsal he was always considerate of the other actors, and if he had a suggestion to make, made it with the utmost courtesy, prefacing it with; 'Now, Mr——don't you think that perhaps this might be a better way to interpret that?' In this he differed from his older brother, Edwin, who was always harsh and commanding, showing little feeling for the young actor.

"Wilkes Booth's first appearance on the stage was at the old Richmond Theatre in that city. He played under the name of 'John Wilkes,' because, he told me, his father had told him that he would never make an actor and, if he turned out a failure, he did not want the family name to be entangled in it. Only after he made a success did he use his own name. The last time I played with him in Nashville in 1864, after the fall of Nashville. I was with a dramatic company, playing there, and Wilkes Booth, who was not engaged with any troupe at the time, was there. I next saw him in Washington the following April, after Lee's surrender—the week of the tragedy. He made his headquarters in a way about Ford's Theatre. I do not think that, even at that time, he had made any plans of assassination in his mind. Indeed, all his friends wondered, after the act, that one of his gentle nature could conceive such a bloody deed. Yet an incident I myself witnessed may possibly have first excited his disordered brain to committing the dreadful crime. At the time I thought nothing of this occurrence. It was only in after years that the full significance of it dawned upon me.

"About eleven o'clock on Friday morning—the fatal day—I was standing with Booth in the lobby of the ticket office as we then called it. A courier from the White House came in and stated to Mr. Ford, who happened to be in the box office, that the President desired to know if he and a party could get seats for that night's performance. This was the first intimation anyone had that he could attend that night.

" 'Certainly,' replied Mr. Ford; 'The President and anyone he cares to bring are always welcome at my house at any time, and, taking out some box seats he gave them to the courier, at the same time crossing them off the cardboard plan of the house that lay before him. That was before the days of coupon tickets, you know, and the seller crossed off the seats as they were sold. At the same time, he wrote across the margins of the plan in large letters, for the benefit of the public, the following: 'The President and party will attend tonight's performance.'

"Wilkes Booth, seeing him write, took the plan, swung it around and read the notice. Then, without another word, he walked out of the theatre. I have since become convinced that then, for the first time, the idea of assassinating the President occurred to him. An abduction would have been useless, since there was no longer any question of an exchange of prisoners. But his thoughts evidently had been so long directed against Lincoln that it had become a morbid obsession in his mind and, with his romantic temperament, he did not stop to think of the heinousness of this deed he contemplated. I do not stop to think of the heinousness of the deed he contemplated. I do not say this in palliation of the crime, but merely in explanation. No doubt it occurred to him that, from his position as an actor, he could have the run of the theatre, both before and behind the curtain, without exciting comment, and thus his way to the shooting was rendered easy.

"I was not directly entangled in the subsequent proceedings, but I came very near being. There were some negroes living in the alley just back of the theatre next to the stable where Booth kept his horse. On the morning after the assassination they reported to Chief Baker of the Secret Service that, about ten o'clock on Friday morning, just preceding the fatal night, they had seen Booth talking to a lady in the alley near the rear door of the theatre, explaining his plans to her and pointing up to various places in the building. They described her as dressed in a blue silk skirt, with a dark-gray jacket and wearing a hat with a white plume in it. On inquiry at the theatre, Chief Baker found that this description fitted the street dress of Miss May Hart, who had, on the night of the assassination, played the role of Georgina. She had left for Baltimore just after the tragedy, he learned, and was staying at Barnum's hotel there. That evening he went over to Baltimore with a force of his officers and, going to Miss Hart's room in the hotel, knocked loudly. The young lady had retired and called to them to wait until she had put on a wrapper before opening the door. So intense was the feeling at that time, however, that they burst open the door and compelled her to dress before their eyes, not trusting her to a moment's privacy. Nor did they tell her why they had thus summarily arrested her until she was safely lodged in the Old Capitol prison in Washington.

"The following morning a strange man came to see me. Roughly, he demanded:

"'Are you Edwin A. Emerson?,'

"'I am,' I replied.

"'Where were you,' was the curt query, 'at ten o'clock last Friday morning?'

"'None of your business,' I replied with equal curtness. In those parlous times men were not answering a stranger's impertinent question offhand. "'It is some of my business,' exclaimed the stranger, and throwing back his lapel, disclosed his badge of office. 'And a human life may depend upon your answer.'

"'Why, certainly I will tell you,' I replied. 'At that time I was standing in the alley near the rear door of the theatre with Miss May Hart, who was to play the part of Georgina that night. I was to play Dundreary, and as we had never played together, we wished to rehearse some of the dialogue between us. The stage was cold and black that morning, so we came out into the warm sunshine of the alley and went over our lines together there. Now why?'

"'Oh, that explains things!' he ejaculated with a smile, and then told me of Miss Hart's misadventure, adding that he had kept her under strict watch since her arrest so that she could not communicate with anyone, and hence my story must be correct, as she had given the same account. He went immediately to the prison and released the young woman.

"The mistake of the negroes—who had added the part about the conspiracy talk from their imaginations, as negroes will—was not without reason. Booth and I, as I've said, were much alike. That morning, I wore a hat identical in appearance with the one Booth was wearing, and also the same sort of cape cloak he wore; what was known in those days as a Talma. Hence the negroes, who had seen Booth oftentimes at the stables, mistook me for him."

Mr. Emerson was born in Alexandria, Virginia, on December 27, 1837. His first appearance on stage was with a dramatic club of that city in Otway's "Venice Preserved."

"I remember telling our negro orchestra of two fiddles and a clarinet to play some appropriate music when the curtain fell on the awful tragedy," said Mr. Emerson with a smile.

" 'All right boss,' said the leader, 'We knows.' And when the curtain fell on that awful tragedy they merrily struck up, 'Hail Columbia!' He evidently thought I meant patriotic music."

John L. Bolton
Location: Orchestra level
Norfolk Virginia Ledger/Letter, Louis A. Warren Lincoln Library
1914

> *Bolton's actions in the presidential box cannot be confirmed, but his account provides a fascinating view of the assassination from the perspective of a provost guard.*

In 1864, I was stationed in Washington, commissioned as Lieutenant in the 7th Regiment, U.S. Veteran Reserve Corps, and detailed as Lieutenant of the Provost Guard for the city. In this service there were three Lieutenants, who among other duties had to visit the different theatres and examine the passes of all officers and soldiers attending. From the fact that a large part of the audiences of the theatres was composed of army men and Washington was under military law, the Provost Guard was kept in charge of the law and order, the police having no authority to arrest soldiers. On the night that a lieutenant was on duty at Grover's theatre he had to leave there about half past eight; after most all the audience had come in, put a sergeant in charge with a detail of guards and meet a reinforcement of his patrol at 7th street and Pennsylvania Avenue. From there he went to a place of amusement called the "Canterbury," then to 9th street, to the "Varieties," and to other resorts, examining passes. It took him until two or three o'clock in the morning to complete the route. But on the next night when he went on duty at Ford's Theatre, after examining the passes, by placing a sergeant in charge of the guard he could consider himself off duty, if he so desired.

It happened that on the night of April 14th, 1865, I was on duty at Ford's Theatre and remained to see the performance, taking a seat in the orchestra about thirty-five feet from the stage. The play "Our American Cousin" was being presented by Laura Keene. It had been announced in a newspaper that President Lincoln, Mrs. Lincoln, General and Mrs. Grant would attend the performance there that evening. General Grant left

Washington that afternoon, it was reported among the officers that a dispatch had called him to Baltimore. The President and his wife arrived accompanied by a major and a young lady, I have since been told that they were Major Rathbone and Miss Harris, a daughter of Senator Harris. They occupied an upper box on the left-hand side of the stage, and as they entered the orchestra struck up "Hail to the Chief," the audience all rose to their feet and applauded the President.

I was well acquainted with John Wilkes Booth, as I was with many other actors, my duties frequently throwing me in their company. While I was standing at the door that night examining passes, he passed in and out several times. I noticed nothing peculiar about his countenance or actions. As he was a very familiar figure there and had access to the theatre at all times, his being there was taken as a matter of course.

A few minutes after ten o'clock, during the third act of the play, the report of a pistol shot rang out through the building; immediately a man emerged from the President's box, lowered himself by his left hand from the plush cushion on the railing in front of the box and dropped to the stage, coming down on one knee and hand. He sprang to his feet at once and limped across the stage shouting "Sic Semper Tyrannis." I thought that all of this was a surprise in the play, and so did everyone there that I conversed with about it afterward. Not another sound was heard nor any outcry made,—. . . . The first intimation we had was after Booth had crossed the stage, when "Bill" Ferguson, who kept a saloon next door to the theatre, rose from his seat in the orchestra near the stage and pointing to the President's box, cried out: "My God—The President's shot." The whole audience was on their feet in an instant and the aisles were immediately filled with a bewildered and excited throng. I rushed over the empty orchestra seats, got on the stage and made for the entrance. I was told there that the assassin had escaped on horseback.

My duty was then with the President. There was no way of reaching the box by the entrance, on account of the crowd that blocked the way, and running across the stage just under the box a number of citizens lifted me until I could reach the railing of the box, which was nine feet above the stage. I climbed in and found the President lying at full length on his back—his right eye was black and swollen and he was breathing heavily. Three or four persons had already come into the box from the dress circle entrance, and we immediately stripped his clothing to find where he was wounded. Mrs. Lincoln was not in the box when I entered it; she came back while we were searching for the wound, and grasping my elbow, exclaimed, "My husband, my husband." I led her to the adjoining box and returned to the President. In turning him over on his side, we located the wound. He was shot in the back of his head, a little to the left and about two and one half inches from his ear, the bullet—as was found later— lodging just behind his right eye.

At this point I went to the front of the box and ordered the house cleared. This was practically a waste of breath. The women as well as the men made no attempt to leave, but held their ground in their anxiety to learn where it were a reality that such foul murder had been done. A few of my guard had reached the box by this time, and calling upon a few citizens to help them, I ordered the President carried out of the theatre so that he could be taken to some place where he could receive medical attention. This was accomplished with great difficulty; those in front of us were willing to give way, but those in the rear under the terrible excite- ment were pressing forward, and I had to threaten them and actually use the flat of my sword before a passage way was opened. We finally suc- ceeded in getting him out of the building, and as we reached the sidewalk a young man coming from across the street called out; "Bring him over here." There was no other place that we knew of to take him, so we accepted the invitation and carried him across the street into this young man's room, which was on the floor above the basement and at the end of the hall. The bed was pulled out from the corner and placed near the center of the room, and we laid the President upon it. Some surgeons had come in with us, and leaving him in their charge I returned to the street and made an effort to clear the block. While I was so engaged, a vidette approached on horseback, exclaiming; "A plot, a plot! Secretary Seward's throat is cut from ear to ear; Secretary Stanton is killed at his residence; General Grant is shot at Baltimore and Vice-President Johnson is killed at the Kirkwood House." The excitement then was intense; words fail to de- scribe it. I have in mind now an army captain in the street who lost his rea- son, becoming raving mad, and I was compelled to place him in charge of two of my guards and send him to the central guard house. Finding it under my command, I asked the vidette just referred to, to ride with all speed to the "Circle" and tell them there to send a squadron of cavalry. These soon arrived and the block was cleared and guards stationed across the street above and below Mr. Peterson's [sic], house, where the President lay.

Soon after the guards were established with orders to let no one pass, Secretary Stanton made his appearance and I escorted him to the bedside of the President. I afterward took orders from and reported to him at intervals during the night. His orders were "Admit only general surgeons." No one knew how far the plot extended or who was involved in it, and as an extra precaution I placed a guard at the rear of the house, not knowing but that an attempt might be made on the lives of some of those present. From time to time I was called by the guard, to find different people who wanted admittance, claiming to be Senators, Congressman, friends of Mr. and Mrs. Lincoln &c. I told them of my orders from Secretary Stanton, and some of them asked to have their names mentioned to him. In some instances he would say "Admit him quietly." In others he would make no reply. A few minutes after seven o'clock on the morning of April 15th, Mr. Lincoln breathed his last. Mrs. Lincoln was summoned from the front parlor, where she had been waiting all night, to the death chamber. At this time I was in the hall and I recall very vividly the words she said as she passed me;—they were "Oh, why didn't you have me to him." After he died, Colonel Vincent—since promoted to General—asked me if I could get him a silver half-dollar; one of the officers had one and he wanted another to place over the President's eyes, to keep them closed after death. I obtained one from the landlady of the Falstaff House next door, giving her a dollar greenback for it, which was then the value of silver as compared with paper currency. This coin is still in my possession.

Forming my guard in line, we presented arms to the body of the President as it was carried past us to the hearse, after which I was relieved from duty.

James N. Mills
Location: Dress circle, second row, left
Boston Sunday Globe, Louis A. Warren Lincoln Library
April 12, 1914

> *Both Mills and Major Rathbone claim to have escorted Mrs. Lincoln across Tenth Street to the Petersen house. Rathbone's account is given greater validity because it was recorded earlier than Mills's.*

The great Civil War ended.

Gen. Lee had surrendered only a few days preceding on April 9, and the great general officers had left the field and were in Washington. The soldiers were pouring in and the capital was thronged with them.

The country was wild with joy over the ending of the long struggle. It was given over to rejoicing. Bonfires were blazing from every hilltop, but in no place was the rejoicing greater than in the capital city of the Nation whose foes had submitted.

"A performance of the play of "Our American Cousin" was given on that night at Ford Theatre by Laura Keene's company. It was to be a gala night. Gen. Grant, whose face was not then so familiar in Washington as it subsequently became was to attend in the company of President Lincoln.

The announcement was published in the local newspapers that the "President and lady" and the "Hero of Appomattox" would be present. The theatre therefore was packed.

But Gen Grant suddenly changed his plans and with his wife went to Philadelphia. To the day of his death Gen. Grant regretted that change of plan. Years after he said to John Russell Young that he believed that had he been present he would have noted the approach of the assassin and prevented the deed.

The theatre was full of soldiers. Among them was James N. Mills, a Brooklyn boy, who had served as drummer boy in Co 1, 67th New York Infantry, and who had only less than two months previously been mustered out of the service with the Army of the Potomac, and a month later had enlisted in the United States General Service and was at that time serving as clerk in the office of the Adjutant General of the Army, with headquarters in the War Department.

The regiment in which young Mills served was known as the 1st Long Island Regiment, and also as the Brooklyn Phalanx and known throughout Brooklyn as "Beecher's Regiment" because under the auspices of Plymouth Church its enlisting force was greatly augmented during the early years of the Rebellion.

Henry Ward Beecher's son was adjutant of the regiment during the first year of its service in camp at Washington. Young Mills, not then 17 years old was fired with the ambition to go with it.

His enlistment had been refused because of his youth, but he followed it to Washington and supported himself by selling papers to the soldiers encamped in the immediate surroundings of Washington. Young Mills was a daily visitor to the 1st Long Island Regiment selling his newspapers to the boys at Camp Proctor, and his final appeal for permission to enroll as a drummer boy was accepted by Lieut. Thomas M. K. Mills (no relation, however) of Co I 67th New York Infantry, and on Feb. 6, 1862 young Mills became a full-fledged member of Uncle Sam's Army.

Having enlisted at Washington, D.C. he was returned there at the expiration of his term of service Feb. 6, 1863, and a month later he had again enrolled as a private in the United States general service and served as a clerk under Samuel S. Breck, Assistant Adjutant General, for a period of three years.

It just happened that on the night of April 14, 1865, young Mills attended the performance of the play, "Our American Cousin," and it fell to his part to perform an important service in guarding Mrs. Lincoln, who was distracted and overwhelmed by the awful tragedy of the night.

"I was in the dress circle of Ford's Theatre that night, drawn thither more by a desire to see the two great men of the Nation than to see the play. The theatre was packed, standing room only, and the immense audience anxious to see the President and Gen. Grant, who were expected to be present.

"After the President and his wife accompanied by Col. Rathbone had taken their seats the cheering was long continued. The party occupied the right hand box off the dress circle and I sat in the second row of the dress circle on the left side and my view of the immediate surroundings was unobscured.

"The third act of the play had just opened, and Harry Hawk, an actor in the East, had just appeared entering on the stage from the left when there was a report of a pistol shot, and on looking over at the Presidential box I saw a man gesticulating at the occupants. Suddenly he faced the stage and jumped through the window to the stage floor, and limping slightly, disappeared through the back entrance of the theatre leading into an alley which led through to F st.

"Instantly the audience arose, the whisperings of the moment became a roar as it dawned on it that the President had been assassinated. The confusion was indescribable.

"I quickly made my way to the head of the dress circle stairs and shouted that the President had been shot and passing out onto 10th st gave the alarm to the provost guards at the door.

"The provost guards at that time were stationed at all places of amusement in Washington to examine the passes of uniformed soldiers who were in the city after nightfall. Gen. James R. O'Beirne of New York city was in command of the guards on that occasion.

"I returned to the theatre a few moments later and made my way to the dress circle, and to the box of the Presidential party.

"As I reached the box President Lincoln was being carried out on the shoulders of two men, one of whom I recognized as the proprietor of a saloon adjoining the theatre. He was in his shin sleeves and the head of

Mr. Lincoln was resting on his shoulder and the blood trickling down the sleeves and back of his shirt.

"The President was carried across the street and up the front stoop of the house of Mrs. Peterson [sic] and into a room adjoining the parlor. This room was sparsely furnished and rarely used for permanent roomers.

"Mrs. Lincoln, distracted beside herself with grief, was apparently overlooked by everybody. She was nearly unconscious, hysterical and crying and sobbing. There was no one to care for her.

"I took her by the hand and we followed the men carrying Mr. Lincoln across the street to the Peterson house, and there in that extension room on a bed our martyred President died the following morning."

Mr. Mills, with the exception of Gen. James R. O'Beirne, provost marshal of the District of Columbia at that time, is now thought to be the only man alive who was in close touch with the tragic event of over 48 years ago. All others have followed the man whose untimely death plunged a rejoicing Nation into mourning.

George C. Read
Location: Unknown
"George C. Read's Story," *New York Sun*, Library of Congress
September 1, 1914

> *George C. Read provided some unique information concerning Booth's activities in the hours before the assassination. His account again shows the personal popularity of Booth; he was not disliked by his contemporaries, as some writers have contended.*

Sir: I recently picked up a clipping from your valuable paper containing a statement of James N. Mills, who claims to have been present at the time the lamented Abraham Lincoln was shot.

I, too, have a story that has never been related in the public prints. It also has to do with little things that I witnessed at the time the President was assassinated, and also something that occurred the afternoon prior to it.

I was only a boy at the time, scarcely 10 years of age. I had been in the army since August, 1862. Was enlisted in Company H, One Hundred and Fortieth New York Volunteers, as a drummer. I was detached from my company nearly all the time from the spring of 1863 to the time I was discharged from the service as a foot orderly at brigade headquarters. I served in that capacity under the Colonel of my regiment, who for a time commanded the Third Brigade, Second Division, Fifth Corps, Colonel P. H. O'Rourke, who, by the way, was killed at Gettysburg; also under Colonel Girard of the One Hundred and Forty-sixth New York Volunteers, commanding the brigade. In 1863 and up to the close of the war I was with General Griffin and General Ayres. As I said, I was only a foot orderly, consequently did not have the confidence of the officers attached to head-quarters, still was among them, ready to obey any orders given me day or night. I was in the front most of the time, but did not have the honor of capturing a whole brigade of the enemy, or performing any heroic acts others tell about.

Some time in the latter part of March, 1865, I was sent to Washington on account of the loss of my voice. I remained there most of the time in barracks on east Capitol Hill. On the afternoon of the fated April 14, 1865, I happened in the saloon next door to Ford's Theater to see the barkeeper, one Jim Peck. While standing near a stove about the center of the room three men came into the place laughing and talking loudly. They all went to the end of the bar nearest the door and ordered a drink. One was a tall, handsome fellow, dressed in the latest fashionable clothes. I remember rightly, and the others appeared like workmen of some kind. Both were carelessly dressed, and I think one was in his shirt sleeves. They had their drink, and then the fine-looking man turned toward where I was standing and said, "Come up, soldier, and have a drink." I declined, for the reason that I had not at that time become addicted to the habit of social drinking. He then approached me and took me by the arm and said, "Have something; take a cigar." This I did not refuse, and he put his hand in his vest pocket and, pulling out a cigar, handed it to me without any further remarks. He then returned to his companions at the bar. They remained, if I remember correctly, about five minutes after, and then, all laughing at something that Peck said, left the place. As soon as they were gone I asked Peck who the big man was, and he said that he was an actor—one of the Booth family—John Wilkes Booth. I had heard of him before, but paid no further attention to it except to remark that he seemed to be in a happy frame or mind, when Peck stated that he was on a "drunk," and associated with the stage mechanics in the theater all the time.

As I was about to depart, little thinking what history would develop in a few short hours, Peck asked me to accept a couple of tickets to the theater for that night. I was glad to get them, having no money to purchase the same, and knowing that the President would be at the play. Later I found a young man, like myself, broke, and invited him to accompany me to the play. We were on hand early, and having good reserved seats about the center of the house, were elated over our good luck.

Suffice it to say that the curtain went up and "Our American Cousin" was introduced. I was intently interested and cannot remember positively what act it was that was on, except what is told in history, when I heard a shot, and immediately a man appeared at the front of the President's box and, without waiting, jumped to the stage beneath. I, as well as all others in the theater, was astonished. He ran to about the center of the stage and raised his left hand and said something I did not catch and then disappeared behind the wings. As soon as I saw him I recognized the handsome man I had seen in the saloon that afternoon and turned to my comrade and said: "That's Wilkes Booth, the actor, and I think he is on a drunk." Before I had finished even this a cry went up that President had been shot. "Stop that man!" and many other exclamations I have forgotten. It was all done so quickly that he had hardly time to think. Immediately, the audience rose as one person and cries were heard all over the house, "Stop that man." "The President has been assassinated." and many others. The people began to crush each other and try to get out of the theater, but they were quieted to a certain extent and the provost guard on duty there fought to make them keep their places. Soon there was a movement on the side aisle running from the President's box, and from where I was standing on my seat I could see what appeared to be a party of men carrying some one. Later the rest of the party were conducted out of the theater, and when I managed to head outside I saw a crowd looking up at a house opposite. On asking what it meant, I was told that the President had been carried there and was dying. I lost my comrade in the crowd and I have never met him since.

Captain William Greer
Location: Unknown
Newspaper account, Louis A. Warren Lincoln Library
December 1, 1914

Some of the information Greer provided shows the effect of time on the human memory. He claimed that Booth shot Lincoln during the final act of the play, rather than in Act 3, and he contended that Booth "walked" across the stage.

Captain Wm. Greer, who died here Monday morning, was a witness of the assassination of President Lincoln at Ford's theatre, Washington, in April, 1865. The Captain was just recovering from the amputation of his arm, an operation made necessary by Confederate balls while he was a member of the 100th Pennsylvania was charging Longstreet's legions. Captain Greer was with several convalescing army comrades, who went to the theatre more for the purpose of seeing the President than to witness the play.

Within recent years some parties have put in claims for injuries said to have been received while trying to stop the assassin. One man filed a claim stating he had clutched Booth by the throat, and tried to hold him until aid came, but that the assassin wild with excitement had thrown the claimant fiercely from him and made his escape through a rear door.

"Nothing of the sort occurred in view of the audience," declared Captain Greer. "Not a hand was laid on Booth while he was on the stage. He disappeared at the side of a curtain, leaped to his waiting horse and was away like the wind.

"The shooting of President Lincoln by Booth occurred towards the close of the play. The President occupied a box on the west. Some army comrades and myself were to the east. The soldier boys all sought places where they could get a good look at Mr. Lincoln. A great many of them were in the audience. Never in all his life was President Lincoln more beloved by the army than he was then.

"The curtain had just risen for the final act. I have forgotten many things that happened since that night, but what occurred then has always remained in my memory.

"The first thing that beckoned something unusual was the sinister crack of a pistol. There was no shooting in the play, and there was an oppressive silence for a moment or two while the people looked about to see what it meant.

"Suddenly a man leaped from the President's box to the stage walked to the center of it, flourished something over his head that glittered in the light. It is said Booth carried a revolver and a knife when he attacked the President. He cried to the audience: 'Sic semper tyrannis!' ('So may it be with all tyrant!'—the motto on the seal of Virginia.)

"It was all so sudden that the human mind was incapable of keeping up with events. There were many active resolute men in the audience, but the first impulse was to run to the President. Before they took in the situation and knew that Booth was a murderer he was gone. Then there was a tumult! Women fainted and men screamed. Somebody from the balcony on the north side first made the public announcement: 'The President is shot' 'Where is the murderer?' I doubt if the National Guard could have saved him had the people got hands on Booth.

"Instead of retreating that way some fool hardy notion made him seek to made his deed as public as possible, and he escaped by way of the stage.

"The crowd, wild with grief and rage, made its way to the street, then waited to see them bring the President out. At last they came along with the stretcher. A gentleman and myself followed closely across the street. A hat and shawl dropped from the litter and we picked them up. The sufferer was taken to a three-story house, and carried to one of the rooms on the second floor. The crowd attempted to force its way in, but was thrust back. My companion and I, as the bearers of something belonging to the President, were permitted to enter the room. I had a yearning desire to see his face, as something told me it would be the last time, although at that time no one knew whether the wound was fatal or not. Had you been in the Army of the Potomac you could appreciate the depth of feeling we all had for 'Father Abe.' He was unconscious. We looked at the well known features, muttered a prayer and left. Down stairs we were besieged by a crowd of fully 3,000 people, all asking the same eager questions: 'Is he dead?' 'Will he get well?'

"And how they did grit their teeth and wish that Booth was in reach! It was a time when people's passions were easily aroused, and they were inclined to do almost anything that promised a reckoning for the cowardly act."

Captain Greer's family have a historic war record. The Captain's father, James W. Greer, was killed while the Pennsylvania "Round-head" regiment was trying to break through Stonewall Jackson's battle line.

Henri Oliver, Captain Greer's son, enlisted when he was 17, in Company G, 18th U.S.A., and was killed in the Philippines the 4th of March, 1900. The boy died working his gun and facing the enemies of his country. Captain Greer's uncle and grandfather were soldiers in the Mexican war. The ancestry all the way back to the American Revolution has been loyal to the government and characterized by promptly shouldering a musket on the first call to arms.

Daniel Dean Beekman
Location: Orchestra level
Magazine article, Louis A. Warren Lincoln Library
February 11, 1915

> *The surgeon Beekman mentioned was Dr. Charles Sabin Taft, who entered the box after being lifted from the stage. His description of the medical attention given to the president appears to be accurate.*

Dr. Taft did not throw the president's head back for fear that Lincoln was choking.

Tomorrow will be Lincoln's Birthday, and I wish to give you an account of what I saw and heard on the night of April 14, 1865, in Ford's Theatre, In Washington, fifty years ago, this coming April, when I was in my thirtieth year. I was in Washington that week on business with a friend of mine, and hearing that Lincoln and Grant were to be at Ford's Theatre the night of the 14th, I decided to stay over another day, so I could see them. We secured tickets in the Second Row Orchestra, left-hand side, of the house, the stub of which ticket, I have here between these two pieces of glass, fastened together.

The play, was "Our American Cousin" which I had seen before, here in the city, where I had often see Edwin Booth, brother of John Wilkes Booth, play and who resembled each other so much, that I mistook him for the great actor as he leapt out of the President's box that fatal night. I have never been inside a theatre since; [I] said that night I would never go again.

I was in my seat at 7:30 facing the President's box when he came at 8:30 with his wife, Miss Harris (Senator Harris' daughter), and Major Henry R. Rathbone—Grant and his wife leaving the city at six o'clock that night. As the President walked along the gallery to his box, the orchestra played "Hail to the Chief" and the audience arose and cheered him. I remarked to my friend, "He is the homeliest man I have ever seen," but when he acknowledged the applause by bowing and smiling, it so changed his countenance, that I said, it was the most heavenly smile I ever saw on a man's face. He sat in the right-hand corner of the box, in a rocking chair, his head resting on his hand, elbow leaning on the arm of his chair, looking utterly worn out and apparently in deep thought.

Upon the closing of the second scene in the third act of the play, about twenty minutes past ten, I heard the report of a pistol, and I said to my friend, "that is strange, there is no shooting in this play," and just as I said that, Wilkes Booth, whom I took to be Edwin Booth, (the actor), threw one leg over the President's box, brandishing his dagger, crying out in a loud voice, "Sic Semper Tyrannis," Virginia's motto, which means, "Thus always with Tyrants." Booth's spur caught in the flag which decorated the President's box, and he fell on his knee, a distance of nine feet, causing him to limp as he ran across the stage, still theatrically brandishing his dagger, then disappeared behind the curtain before anyone in the audience realized what had happened.

Then I heard a woman scream, and some one called out, "The President is shot"—and then, there was an uproar. The man sitting ahead of me was on the stage second, and I was the third one. I noticed a surgeon of the army, standing beside me, whom I knew by his straps, (having two brothers in the war, both Lieutenants, serving under Sherman, in the 135th N.J. Regiment) looking anxiously up to the President's box, and I said to him, "Do you want to get up there?" and he said, "Yes." I told him to put his foot on my hand, the other foot on my shoulder, and I boosted him up into the President's box, which was about nine feet from the stage. No one could get in the box from the back, as Booth had barricaded the door after he got in by putting a piece of plank across, one end of which was secured in the wall, the other against the door.

The President was shot in the head, back of the left ear, so the surgeon told me after.

Everyone rushed out of the theatre as the report was circulated around that there were conspirators in Washington, and that all the Cabinet were killed. I told my friend, I was going to stay to see the President carried out which I did, taking hold of his elbow, lifting up his arm and putting my other hand on his wrist. I knew by his pulse, which was very irregular and weak, that he was fatally shot, which remark I made to my friend. They carried him across the street, where he died twenty minutes past seven the next morning just nine hours after he was shot, and where Mr. Oldroyd, has the Lincoln Memorial Collections.

As my friend and I went out of the Theatre, we saw it was surrounded by the Invalid Corps, soldiers who had been wounded and were convalescent enough to do Guard duty in Washington. They mistook us for a couple of conspirators, as I heard the Captain of the guard say, and my friend, exclaimed, "Let us run" but I replied, "No, your life wouldn't be worth a cent if you did that" and turning, faced the Captain and his guard, of about twenty-five men. He looked at us sharply and said, "These are no conspirators, rightabout-face," and we walked down leisurely to the Metropolitan Hotel, where we were stopping. As we entered, I saw the surgeon whom I helped in the President's box, in the parlor of the Hotel, with a crowd of men around him. Looking up he saw me and said, "Come here, you are the man who helped me up in the box, see what I have here." It was a small piece of bone, about the length of my forefinger, and on the end of it, were two small eggs, resembling Shad Eggs. He said, "This is part of the President's brain, and I am going to preserve it in alcohol." He then went on to say, "When I got in the President's box, I saw blood on the back of his collar, and thinking he was choking, I threw back his head in my hand, to undo his collar, and this dropped in my hand, then I knew he was mortally wounded. . . .

I have related to you the most tragic event of our country's history, of which I was a witness. I thank you for your close attention. Follow Abraham Lincoln's example of truthfulness, honesty and justice, have malice toward none and charity to all, and you will be useful citizens.

Katherine M. Evans
Location: Green Room
"Recalls Vividly Details of Lincoln's Death," *New York Tribune*, Louis A. Warren Lincoln Library
April 1915

> *Katherine M. Evans's is the second eyewitness account, with the no-table exception of Booth's diary, that asserts that Booth broke his leg in the jump from the presidential box. She is also one of the first to assert that Lincoln was sitting in a rocking chair.*

"I was in the green room . . . chatting with 'Maggie' Gourlay, the Skillet of the play, and waiting for my cue, when I heard a shot ring out. I was dressed in my stage gown—the crinoline of the period. Miss Gourlay was making a tidy. I had just said, using a stage expression, 'Wake me up when Kirby dies.' Hawk had the scene to himself, and the other players were grouped at the entrances ready for their turns. I knew when I heard the shot that it couldn't be a part of the play. We dropped our work and ran to the first entrance, where there was a good deal of excitement.

"A moment before young Booth had leaped to the stage and had caught his spur, as you remember, on one of the flags that draped the presidential box. In falling he had broken a small bone in his leg, a wound that during his flight must have given him excruciating torture. I heard somebody shout, 'Stop that man!' I learned later that it was Major Lovejoy.

"Booth, being an actor, was familiar with the stage. He ran between Hawk and Billy Ferguson, struck at Withers, our orchestra leader, with his knife, and made his way out through the stage door into the alley when 'Peanut Johnnie' the boy who sold peanuts in the gallery was holding his horse.

"I looked and saw President Lincoln unconscious, his head dropping on his breast, his eyes closed, but with a smile still on his face. Mrs. Lincoln had risen from her seat beside him and was stroking his cheeks.

"She wore an old fashioned black coal scuttle bonnet, the chin bow of which had become untied. She did not wear a wreath of red flowers and a low-necked gown, as many people believe.

"Miss Clara Harris, Senator Harris' daughter, and her fiancee, the young Major Rathbone, who had accompanied President and Mrs. Lincoln, stood beside them. Miss Harris was as pale as a sheet. The major, breathing heavily from his struggle with the assassin, was trying frantically to open the door which Booth, as you remember, had closed with a block of wood.

"In an instant the theater was in an uproar. It was crowded to the topmost gallery, and every one had risen in his seat. Men were shouting and climbing out into the aisles. Miss Keene was making her way up to where the president lay wounded, and several doctors from the audience were trying to force a passage through the crowd. Dr. Charles Taft was lifted up into the box from the stage, while many persons, some of the physicians, were crowding into the narrow aisle which led into the box and were pounding on the door, demanding admission.

"Lincoln lay back in rocking chair. Dr. Taft had to open his shirt and was looking for the wound. He found it finally behind the left ear. Then they laid the president on a shutter and carried him out of the theater to the house across the street where he died at 7:30 o'clock the next morning.

"After the tragedy I ran upstairs into the dressing room. The stage was filled with secret service men, who seemed to have gone crazy. They had arrested 'Peanut Johnnie' as an accomplice. 'Poor Peanut!' He did nothing more than hold Booth's horse. They were looking for Ned Spangler, our stage carpenter, who had innocently held the door open for the assassin. My husband was also under suspicion.

"I rubbed my makeup off and thought that every moment a detective would rap at the door and place me under arrest. Finally 'Jimmie' Mattox, our property man, called me.

" 'What are you doing up there?' he asked.

" 'I'm waiting.'

" 'Waiting for what?'

" 'To be arrested.'

"He assured me that everything was all right, and I ventured down. The theater was empty by that time. The last audience it was ever to see had departed after witnessing a scene more tragic than ever was played behind the footlights."

Charles H. Johnson
Location: Unknown
Boston Post, Ford's Theatre National Historic Site
April 11, 1915

> *Lincoln was seated in the far left corner of the box, not the center as Johnson recalls. Johnson was one of the few eyewitnesses to claim that the assassination occurred during the second act, and he was the second eyewitness to claim that Booth crossed the stage with a "noticeable limp."*

"The audience was slow to grasp the significance of the pistol shot," Mr. Johnson says, and he as well as others, thought it, for a few seconds, perhaps, a part of the play.

Seated in about the center of Ford's Theatre, Mr. Johnson had an excellent chance to see nearly all that happened. He was, at that time, regimental quartermaster sergeant of the 3d Massachusetts Heavy Artillery. He had ridden into Washington from Ft. Bunker, about five miles northwest of the city, to witness the torchlight parade in celebration of the surrender of Gen. Lee's army.

In company with a sutler's clerk named Webster, from Rockland, Mass., the young soldier, now a white haired veteran of 72, viewed the parade and was about to get his horse and return to the fort, when, by the merest chance, he decided to visit Ford's Theatre.

The two young men learned that Gen. Grant was expected to be in the Presidential party, and they decided they wanted a look at the famous leader, who had not, up to that time, been seen much in Washington. Grant, however, did not attend the performance.

"Lincoln occupied a seat in about the center of a box," said Mr. Johnson, "and was not visible to people in the body of the theatre. We could only see Maj. Rathburn [sic] and two ladies who occupied seats in the front of the box.

"As the curtain went down on the second act, we heard a pistol shot from the President's box and then saw a dark, striking-appearing man who was the center of a commotion in the box. We later learned this was John Wilkes Booth.

"Maj Rathburn grappled with the assassin, but dropped him when Booth nearly cut his arm off with a dagger. We saw Booth leap from the box to the stage, and sprawl on all fours, having caught one of his spurs in the flag which draped the front of the box. He was up in an instant, and stalked with a noticeable limp off the stage. Booth looked every inch the actor and never more so than in his intensely theatrical exit after fatally wounding President Lincoln.

"For an instant after the assassin disappeared there was silence. Then a woman uttered a shriek: 'The President is shot!' The audience went crazy. We surged toward the stage, but the assassin had fled. There were cries of 'Lynch him! 'Shoot him!' and the like. Doubtless he would have been torn to pieces had the frenzied audience laid hands on him.

"Laura Keene, the leading lady, came before the curtain and finally was able to make herself heard above the shouts of the maddened audience.

"The President is hurt. Please clear the theatre as quickly and quietly as possible,' she said.

"Among the last to leave the theatre was Mr. Johnson, and this resulted in his being able to see the dying President as he was borne from one of the basement exits in the arms of several men. The young soldier stood in a porch over the exit from which the party emerged.

"The form of the President had been divested of clothing to the waist," said Mr. Johnson, "in an effort to find a supposed stab wound. As Mr. Lincoln was brought out, I gazed straight down into his unconscious but still placid face, not six feet away."

J. F. Troutner
Location: Family circle
Iowa Journal, Louis A. Warren Lincoln Library
June 10, 1915

> *J. F. Troutner's account perpetuates the theory that Booth broke his leg jumping from the box. He is incorrect in stating that George Atzerodt was supposed to assassinate Grant. Atzerodt was assigned to assassinate Vice-President Andrew Johnson. Troutner is the only eye-witness who claims to have been seated in the family circle, which contained the least expensive seats at Ford's Theatre.*

On the night of April 14, 1865, I went to the Ford theater, where the president was to be. The title of the play presented that night was "Our American Cousins," and many soldiers were present. I was seated in the family circle about five or six rows from the stage.

Lincoln and a party of his friends were seated in a box not far from me. Everyone seemed to be interested in the play. After the conclusion of the first act—it was customary for us to do so—we left our seats to take some refreshments. Shortly after I returned to my seat I saw Booth edging near the president's box. He paused there for a moment and then leaned toward his victim. The second act had not yet started and Booth's presence caused no interest, as he was often seen at the theater. Having seen him in plays a number of times I recognized him.

While waiting for the second act to start, the report of a pistol was heard, but this was nothing unusual. It was shortly after the close of the war and shooting in the city still was common. It appeared as though someone in the rear of the theater might have fired, but the audience exhibited no interest.

No one knew that Lincoln had been shot until Maj. R. Rathbone, who had accompanied the president, arose and requested that some soldiers come to the box. He then announced that Lincoln had been shot. We rushed to the front, but Maj. Rathbone advised us that only six soldiers were wanted.

Booth was observed climbing over the railing of the box near Lincoln. In an effort to hurry away and make his escape he caught his left foot on a flag below the railing. Losing his balance, he fell to the stage eight or ten feet below, suffering a broken leg. In a desperate attempt to flee, he brushed the stage curtain aside and struggled out, running over the stage and escaping through the rear entrance.

Having the murder well planned he mounted a horse in the rear of the theater and rode away. Edward Spangler, a supenumery for the ford theater, who later was sentenced to prison as an accomplice, was given $10 for watching the animal during the absence of Booth, I am told.

In the meantime, Lincoln, mortally wounded, was laid upon a window shutter and carried to a little lodging house across Tenth street from the theater. The soldiers were ordered to form a guard so that the president might be carried away quickly to a place where medical aid could be administered.

Citizens were excited. Pandemonium had broken loose. Hardly had we crossed the street when a throng of excited people came rushing down the street toward us, crying the news that an attempt to assassinate Secretary of State, William H. Seward and his son, Frederick, had been made by Lewis Powell. All was not yet ended, for terror was added when another mob of persons came rushing from the Baltimore and Ohio station with information that Grant had been shot. Grant was to have been included in the president's theater party, and had he arrived as he had planned, George A. Atzerodt probably would have killed him, for he was waiting at the station. Missing his connections at the Relay house probably saved Grant his life.

Atzerodt had been stationed at the railway terminal to await the arrival

of Grant and to assassinate him. With all this news coming simultaneously, the inhabitants were wild with fear that the entire cabinet of
the president was to be killed. Terror, sorrow, and anger prevailed for
many days and the city was placed under guard, while the search for
Booth and his accomplices went on. I was one of the guards who watched
the city until July 15.

Fred W. Schwarz
Location: Orchestra level
Knickerboker, Louis A. Warren Lincoln Library
February 20, 1916

> *By the early twentieth century, the belief that Lincoln had been oc-
> cupying a rocking chair was accepted.*
> *The motion picture to which Schwarz referred was probably* The
> Birth of a Nation. *This highly controversial film promoted the erro-
> neous belief that Lincoln's guard had left his position outside the pres-
> idential box.*

I could scarcely see President Lincoln from my chair, which was on the
first floor of the theatre and not far from the orchestra. . . . We could all
see Mrs. Lincoln and also Miss Harris, who was in the upper right hand
box with the presidential party; but the President's rocking chair was so
far back in the box that many in the audience could not get a glimpse
of him.

The moving pictures now displayed the lulling of Lincoln distort facts
in making him appear conspicuously before the audience.

I talked with Harry Hawk, leading man in the company. . . . He confirmed my own recollection that it was in scene two, third act, of "Our
American Cousin," which was the name of Laura Keene's play.

Hawk himself was speaking when Booth's pistol shot put a permanent
period to the play. As Asa Trenchard, Hawk was delivering the words of
his dialogue with Mrs. Montchessington as follows:

Well, I guess I know enough to turn you inside out, old gal, you
sockdologizing old mantrap—

He [Booth] didn't leap, but he fell. There was confusion in the President's box. I saw Booth there with his dagger after he had shot Lincoln. I
saw him fall upon the stage, not afraid to do something because it. He
dramatically waved his hand and exclaimed, 'Sic Semper Tyrannis!' and
hurriedly limped to the back of the stage.

Hawk told me that he had talked that very afternoon with John Booth—

he always called him John—but that the assassin had not intimated what his dark intentions were.

John Reagan
Location: Unknown
Omaha World-Herald, Ford's Theatre National Historic Site
1916

The most tragic thing in connection with the long army life of this old soldier was when he witnessed the escape of Booth after he had shot President Lincoln at Ford theater. As often related to his family and friends, Sergeant Reagan ran the lines the night of the tragedy and took a seat near the center of the theater to see "Our American Cousin" played. During the performance when all eyes were on the stage, he heard a sharp report and a moment later there was great commotion, for it was immediately known that President Lincoln had been shot. He saw the president sink back in his seat and a man jump down from the president's box and over onto stage, dashing aside those who tried to stop him. A moment later Booth, the assassin, had disappeared. The people began a mad fight for the exits and soon the street in front of the theater was a surging mass of humanity.

Leaving the theater, Mr. Reagan ran all the way to where his quarters were and got through the line in the excitement, without being seen. Immediately he had reached his quarters the bugle sounded and a general alarm was given. Soldiers were tolled off rapidly in squads to search for the murderer, Reagan being one of them. All that night he was on his feet, here, there and everywhere, but Booth had escaped. Speaking of the event, Mr. Reagan once said: "It was truly a night of horrors. Had Booth been captured that night I am sure he would have been literally torn limb from limb. But we could not find him and it was great news when the word came that Booth had been captured. It relieved a tension that existed among all the men in the ranks and officers' quarters that seemed at times too great to bear. The nation at large loved Lincoln, but no more than the boys in blue, who adored him."

Discussing the night hunt for Booth, Mr. Reagan told his family not long ago: "I have served twenty-eight years in the army and never fell asleep but once on picket duty. That was the night following the assassination of Mr. Lincoln. I hadn't had any sleep for so long that I just wilted and was asleep before I knew it. Hardly had my head, however, dropped over my breast when the guard mount came by and I heard his step and was on the job when he arrived, so I was not reprimanded."

W. H. Roberts
Location: Unknown
Newspaper article, Louis A. Warren Lincoln Library
February 12, 1917

> *W. H. Roberts mistakenly recalls that members of the audience ascended the stage before John Wilkes Booth had made his escape.*

Roberts, then a cavalryman, declared he was seated about thirty or forty feet from the President's box. Lincoln took his place in the flag-draped box and bowed as he received the ovation of the packed theatre, he said, and a moment later the curtain was rung up for the presentation of "Our American Cousin."

"The shot came in the midst of the play without warning," Roberts said. "Nearly every one feared, I believe, that the President had been the target of the gun.

"All appeared dazed for a moment, and then the confusion prevailed as enraged spectators dashed toward the stage, to the street or toward the spot where Lincoln had fallen."

It was then, Roberts declared, that Wilkes Booth, the assassin, leaped on the stage and disappeared.

"A man leaped from the President's box to the stage and a spur becoming entangled in the flags threw him heavily to the floor. Flourishing a dagger, Booth sprang to his feet and made his escape through the wings and a rear entrance."

Roberts said his unit was assigned to search for Booth, and was on duty when he was found and shot. He is commander of the Findlay G.A.R. Post.

Henry W. Mason
Location: Unknown
Newspaper article, Louis A. Warren Lincoln Library
1919

> *Mason's account contains several interesting points. First, although the orchestra seats were more expensive than those in the dress circle, Mason indicates that the dress circle was more fashionable.*

Second, the anti-Lincoln English newspaper to which he refers was probably the London Punch. *Yet after Lincoln was assassinated, the paper performed an about-face not only by publishing a moving tribute to Lincoln, written by Tom Taylor, the author of* Our American Cousin, *but also a moving caricature on Lincoln.*

Captain Henry W. Mason of the Union Army was looking forward with extra-special interest to seeing Laura Keene in "Our American Cousin" at Ford's Theater, Washington, that night of April 14, 1865. President Lincoln was scheduled to attend, adding an extra thrill to the ones expectable on stage. That pleasant evening turned into a nightmare and Captain Mason found himself an eyewitness, instead, to the assassination of President Lincoln.

A native of New York, the captain later came to live in New Bedford, served as chief of police here from 1896 to 1914 save for one year, 1906. After he retired from the force, he was named a Deputy sheriff, died in 1928. In 1919, he told the story of that tragic night in 1865 to an Evening Standard reporter. His account appeared in The Sunday Standard April 13, 1919 and is reprinted here today.

The irony that turned a pleasant evening into one of horror touched others in the theater beside the young Union Army officer. Laura Keene held the dying President's head in her lap, tried vainly to staunch the flow of blood, kept her head while many others present panicked. But the shock brought her to the edge of a complete breakdown.

She bought a farm in Acushnet and lived a life of semi-seclusion, enjoying what some said were the happiest years of her life there. The home burned down years ago and only a little street, Laura Keene Road, remains to tell the curious that one of America's greatest 19th-Century actresses once lived there.

"Our American Cousin" was written by Tom Taylor and there is irony here, too, for Taylor, as editor of the famed British upper class had savagely attacked Lincoln in a magazine. But after the President was assassinated, Taylor belatedly realized the greatness of the man whom he had slandered and wrote a moving and repentant poem which still stands as one of the finest poetic tributes paid the martyred President.

Here is Mr. Mason's story:

I had been sent from the Shenandoah Valley, where I was on duty with my regiment, to Washington on business for the quartermaster's department. I calculated the work would take about two days. I arrived in

Washington April 13th and finished my work in the forenoon of the 14th. I did not want to return to my regiment at once, so I looked up a close friend, a Captain Sweet of an Ohio regiment, who was in Washington at the time.

We were both well-acquainted with two young ladies by the name of Carpenter, whose father was dead, and we asked them to go with us to the show that evening. As they accepted the invitation, we went to Ford's Theater where the play, "Our American Cousin" was showing. We bought seats in the very front of what was known as the dress circle. In those days, that was the most fashionable part of a theater and we had to be in style.

Some time after the play had started, the President's party entered the box by way of a door leading from a corridor. Every eye was instantly turned to the President. His box was on our right and we watched the party as interestedly as any of the civilians. There were four people in the party, a major of the regular army whose name I cannot just now recall, and a Miss Harris, daughter of Senator Harris, a close friend of the President. Following this couple came President and Mrs. Lincoln.

We were able to see all that went on as the box was in the second tier and on a level with the dress circle. The President seated himself near the door through which he had entered the box and proceeded to watch the play. Interest in the presidential party waned after this and all eyes returned to the stage. The play went on till the end of the act; the curtain dropped and the audience started to discuss the play or to indulge in the usual between-the-act chatter. Suddenly a shot was heard and a man appeared in the door of the President's box. He stepped to the front of the box, threw his leg over the edge, and jumped to the stage.

Daniel H. Veader
Location: Orchestra, third row
Source unknown, Louis A. Warren Lincoln Library
1920

> *Daniel H. Veader states that there was no guard and infers that there was no one stationed outside the presidential box, which is contrary to the reliable eyewitness accounts.*

Luckily I had been able to procure seats in the third row of the orchestra and so found myself in an excellent position to view whatever happened in the president's box, which was located on the right side of the house and in the second tier. Just as the play commenced Lincoln arrived, accompanied by three other persons whom I afterward deamed to be Mrs. Lincoln, Major Rathbone, USA, and his fiancée, a Miss Harris. There was no guard at the door of the President's box or even in the vicinity, or the tragedy that was soon to occur might never have taken place.

Well, the play started on time and everything proceeded without a hitch into about 10:30 as near as I recall it. The scene had just been shifted and the curtain was up, when, without warning a pistol shot rang out. Naturally, the audience . . . looked toward the stage. But oddly, I had been gazing directly at Lincoln as he leaned on his elbow over the rail of his box had seen a man, or a shadow, rush into the box, and then the president fell backward. Here was the tragedy which but a handful in the whole assembly had witnessed.

But now the assassin called the attention of everyone to himself by jumping out of the box, scrambling somewhat as he did so, and brandishing a small dirk. There was but a second in which to notice an extraordinarily handsome young man who faced the audience and uttered these famous words: "Sic semper trannte." [sic] Then, before even the actors realized what had happened, he crossed the deserted stage and was gone.

Everything had been so sudden that hardly anyone had more than a lethargic understanding of what had transpired. At someone's shouting, "The president's shot," the theater was instantly in a state of commotion and I was forced to seek safety on the stage itself. Many women fainted and above all there was a veritable babel of shouts and screams of excitement and fear.

To add to the scene of confusion the theater exits were ordered closed until the removal of the president. This suggested the possibilities of fire or hostile troops, or the theater, a rumor ran about that General Mosby and his Confederate troops had taken possession of the city.

After leaving the theater, I learned that an attempt had been made on the lives of Seward, the secretary of state, and Andrew Johnson, vice president. And a hundred and one other exciting tales, both true and false, were started and died out. It was several days before order was again restored in Washington.

Dr. George C. Maynard
Location: Unknown
Source unknown, Louis A. Warren Lincoln Library
1920s

> *The song to which George C. Maynard refers, "Honor to Our Soldiers," was supposed to debut that night at Ford's Theatre. It was not played at Ford's until 125 years later.*

"That evening (April 14, 1865) I went to Ford's. As everybody knows, the play was "Our American Cousin." My seat was in the first gallery, on a level with and in full view of the upper right-hand box, which was reserved for President Lincoln and his party.

"The occasion was an unusual one. The war had come to be regarded as an interminable conflict, something which would always engulf this country. Those in the theater that night were giving vent to perhaps their first real enthusiasm that the war had actually ended. It was to be a gala night. An atmosphere of festivity pervaded the place. Also, it was Laura Keene's benefit.

"Naturally, it was a patriotic performance. I still have a small scrap of paper on which I wrote the musical program. 'The Star-Spangled Banner,' 'Red, White, and Blue,' and 'Marching Along' were played, while the entire company was to have sung 'Honor to Our Soldiers,' a patriotic song of the times.

"The President and his party did not arrive before the curtain rose. It was during the dairy scene when they came in. Miss Hart, playing Goergiana, was telling an American joke to Mr. Emerson, taking the part of Dundreary drawled: 'They ought to see it, you know.'

"It was about 10:30 when the pistol shot which sent the bullet at Lincoln was fired. Booth suddenly slid down the from the front of the box onto the stage and rushed diagonally across, disappearing. He caught his foot in the flag decorations and made some exclamation which I did not understand, but no such dramatic speech as has popularly been accredited to him. Had he done anything of that kind I believe he would have been mobbed before he could have escaped. As it was, J. B. Stewart a man of athletic build, sprang onto the stage and was after Booth immediately.

"There was no panic, such as a fire would have caused. The entire audience was stunned, the real significance of the tragedy coming only after several minutes. The theater people swarmed upon the stage. An officer in military uniform managed to get to the President by climbing up from the stage into the box, the door having been barred. Laura Keene came quickly through the gallery with a pitcher of water, lending an odd note to the scene with her costume and make-up. The door of the box by this time was opened and she entered.

"Intense excitement reigned, yet no lack of self-control. There seemed to be a desire to lend whatever assistance was possible, while the air was electrical with a spirit of vengeance against Booth for the crime just committed. Several people climbed over seats, I myself helping one lady thus making her exit. Some seats were broken. Yet, withal, the people left the theater slowly and quietly. It was about ten minutes before the President was removed, followed by Mrs. Lincoln supported by two gentlemen. A crowd of people filled Tenth Street.

"At that time I was a member of the military telegraph corps of the War department, being a cipher operator. I rushed to the office. Persons I met on the way were ignorant of the tragedy. At the office the news had been learned, but no details, and D. H. Bates, manager of the office, asked for particulars.

"A full force of telegraphers spent the night in the office, sending out reports of the President's condition. It was eight o'clock on the following morning before I left for my lodgings. I walked along G street. The morning was rainy, raw and cheerless. Between Thirteenth and Fourteenth streets, almost in front of Epiphany church, I met a small squad of cavalry, accompanied by a few military officers and civilians on foot. The band was proceeding quietly and with an evident desire to avoid public notice. They were escorting the President's body to the White House.

Andrew Jackson Huntoon
Location: Unknown
Reprinted in *Surratt Courier,* Ford's Theatre National Historic Site
January 1, 1923

> *Andrew Jackson Huntoon provides strong support for the story that Booth said, "Sic Semper Tyrannis." He was contradicting eyewitness W. J. Ferguson, who later wrote the book* I Saw Booth Shoot Lincoln, *in which he contended that Booth said nothing as he crossed the stage.*

"I turned to my wife . . . and told her that Lincoln was shot. When Booth reached the stage, I distinctly heard him say: 'Sic Semper Tyrannus.' [sic] I know, of course, that this has been denied, particularly by W. J. Ferguson, who was a member of the theatrical company playing at Ford's that night, but they don't know what they are talking about. Booth positively did make that remark. I'll swear to it.

When Booth leaped to the stage, he fell, but quickly recovered himself, and before the audience fully realized what had happened he had disappeared back of the stage, and escaped through the alley. I never witnessed such an exciting and distressing scene in all my life. All was in an uproar. Many men and women were crying like broken-hearted children. Several women fainted, and determined men hurled strong words at the brute who had shot our beloved President. I observed several agile men climbing up over the stage lights in an effort to find the assassin.

I was nearby when the men carried Lincoln down. At first, they were carrying him headfirst, and then turned him the other way, and thus carried him across the street to the house where he passed to his reward the following morning. I stood close enough to the stricken leader, when they reversed the position of his body, to have laid my hand upon his head.

Never has there been such a wildly exciting night in Washington. Soon all sorts of terrible rumors were in circulation on the streets and homes. It was claimed, by some, that Secretary of State Seward and General Grant had both been murdered. It was a sleepless night for the people of Washington. I can never forget the awfulness of it.

Helen Truman
Location: Unknown
Source unknown, Louis A. Warren Lincoln Library
February 17, 1924

> *Many of the later eyewitnesses claim to be the last surviving one.*
> *As Helen Truman correctly stated, several were still living at the time*
> *of her article. The last eyewitness would live until 1956.*

In your paper of today there is an article from your New York correspondent about Mrs. Struthers—"Jennie Gourlay"—which claims that she is the only surviving woman member of the company that played at Ford's Theater on the night that Abraham Lincoln was assassinated.

Permit me to state that the writer is still alive and was a regular member of the company at Ford's Theater, and played that night the part of Georgina. I had just left the stage to go to my dressing-room to change my dress for my next scene when I heard a shot, and knowing there was no shooting in the play, I hastened back to the first entrance and heard the screaming and other sounds of voices, and saw President Lincoln fall over from his chair. I had noticed Booth previously as he had bowed to me as I went on from my scene, from where he was standing back of the President's box and wondered what he was doing there but dismissed the thought, as Booth had run of the theater, front and back, and was acquainted with all the company.

Miss Laura Keene, the star that week, was the first one to reach the box from the back of the stage, and knelt down and raised up the President's head.

Harry Hawk, one of the company, claimed for a few years before he died to be the only surviving one, and then W. H. Ferguson (Billy) who was the prompter that night was "the only one," and now Mrs. Struthers is "the only one."

I don't want to be killed off so young as I am still able to come up smiling, and don't want to be "the only one," although there are not many left either. But I have not cared for the notoriety of it, as I had always wished it had never occurred as it was a terrible tragedy to go through.

I have lived in Los Angeles for the past fourteen years, and wrote to Jennie Gourlay a year ago, when I read the article you had in The Times magazine about her being alive and residing in Milford, Pa. but have had no reply. Jennie Gourlay left the company at that time to be married to Mr. William Withers the leader of the orchestra. The remainder of the company played at the National Theater as we were not allowed to leave Washington, being subject to the supervision of the War Department, under Gen. Burnett, until after the trial of the assassin.

Yours respectfully,
HELEN TRUMAN
(at that time)
No. 1 182 West Thirty-first street

Annie P. Wright
Location: Unknown
New York Times, Library of Congress
April 9, 1924

As this article states, Dr. Taft, who was one of the doctors who attended Lincoln, was accompanied to the theater that evening by Annie P. Wright and was lifted to the presidential box.

Annie P. Wright, who was a member of the audience at Ford's Theatre, Washington, D.C., when Abraham Lincoln was shot, died here last night. She was 86 years old. Her husband, the late John B. Wright, was stage manager of Ford's Theatre at the time of the tragedy. Mrs. Wright was accompanied by Dr. J. S. Taft on the night the President was shot. When a call for a doctor was sent out, Dr. Taft was lifted from the orchestra into Lincoln's box and attended the dying President. She was on the stage for many years under the name of Annie Cushing.

John Davenport
Location: Dress circle
National Republican, Ford's Theatre National Historic Site
April 22, 1922

> *John Davenport incorrectly calls Major Rathbone a doctor and places the pistol shot at a moment when the stage was empty. Furthermore, he erroneously contends that the orchestra level was cleared by soldiers, whereas, according to most accounts, the patrons departed in an orderly manner.*

That eventful Friday evening, April 14th, after the General [Grant] had left on the afternoon New York train, and having nothing particularly to do, I remembered that the newspapers of that day had stated that the President and General Grant with their wives, were to attend Ford's theater, so I drove directly there from the depot. But starring on the same train with General Butler was General Grant, he being destined to Burlington, N.J., to visit his family. Therefore, I knew he would not be present at the theater. Arriving at the theater, I found the outside of the building hung with bunting in honor of the guests, and I succeeded in obtaining a seat in the first balcony, to the right of the center, about eight rows back from the front.

The box of the President's party was on the same floor, about thirty feet at my right. It was hung overhead and at its sides with draperies and lace curtains, while beneath the railing several American flags had been festooned. When I reached my seat, there was no one in this box, but the audience were constantly craning their necks in expectation, and several false alarms of "here they come" were given until after the curtain was rung up and the play of "Our American Cousin" had begun. Miss Laura Keene, the star, was then at the height of her fame and popularity. I had never seen the play—and I have never seen it finished.

The first act was nearly over, when behind me and either side the people for the minute lost their interest in the play. The President's party had arrived and all eyes had been turned toward them as they passed to their box, the President's face beaming with smiles in response to the ovation. The commotion spread to the first floor, and when those of the audience there caught sight of the party as they were about to enter the box, their enthusiasm knew no bounds and the play was stopped until the party was lost to view. Within the box the President sat in the first chair, but the farthest one from the stage, so that no view except to the few who sat well up toward the front on the opposite side of the theater.

The party consisted of President and Mrs. Lincoln, Dr. Rathbone [sic] and his fiancee, Miss Harris, the daughter of Senator Harris.

Although it was Good Friday the presence of the illustrious guests had crowded the house to the doors. The war was over, and our beloved ruler who for four years had borne his great burdens with such meekness and resignation, was to unbend for the moment to laugh and enjoy himself in common with us all.

The third act of the play closes when the hero has been rejected by his lady-love because of the disparity between them in their social position; she is poor, but by the will of his grandfather he has inherited a large fortune. The girl has refused his proposal of marriage, and passed off the stage, leaving her lover alone. As he soliloquizes over the blighting of his future, there comes to him a happy thought; he will gain her for his wife at the sacrifice of his own fortune, and suiting the action to the thought he takes from his pocket his grandfather's will and burns it in the lighted grate before him. Happy in the belief that the last barrier to their union is thus removed, he continues the soliloquy as he saunters off the stage to the left. For four or five seconds not a soul is on the stage.

The sharp crack of a pistol—Is it part of the play? Where did the report come from? Look at that curly-haired young man within the President's box! He is vaulting over the rail to the stage below, a distance of about ten feet. The spur on his foot catches in the festooned flag below; he falls heavily one-fourth of the distance across the stage, but in a second he is up and swinging a dagger over his head exclaiming "sic semper tyrannis," follows the last actor behind the scenes out of sight. The audience sits spellbound—they can neither move or speak. Only one man has his full presence of mind, he sat in the front row on the right side beneath the President's box and close to the orchestra. He climbs quickly to the stage and follows but a few steps behind the assassin, only to see him in the alley in the rear of the theater, and the horse and rider vanish. Had the pursuer been armed, he could have shot him in his tracks as he mounted.

Within the theater the screams of Mrs. Lincoln caught the attention of the audience, and in an instant pandemonium reigned. Everybody arose to their feet, the cry "The President is murdered" rang throughout the theater. Women screamed, fainted and went into hysterics. Men cursed the assassin, gesticulated as though they would tear him to pieces, and not a few shed tears as only excited men can do. Laura Keene came from her dressing room, and thinking it an alarm of fire tried to quiet the audience.

The next moment soldiers rushed in from the rear over the stage and with their bayonets for clubs cleared the first floor. While those about me were frantically leaving the theater, I, scarcely knowing what I was about, made my way to the front part of the balcony in an effort to get close to the box. As I neared it I saw two or three men in citizen's dress pounding upon the outside of the door of the box for admission, at the same time stating that they were army or navy surgeons. About the time I reached the box (at the end of the row of seats) some one from within removed the heavy bar of wood which held the door fast. This stout brace the assassin had secreted in the box during the day, to prevent any one from following him should he be detected when entering the box from the gallery; at the same time he bored a small peephole in the door through which he could see how each occupant within was seated.

In a few minutes after gaining admission the surgeons came out carrying Mr. Lincoln between them as best they could; the remainder of the President's party following behind. They made their way down stairs and out of doors across the street into a private house. My first collected thoughts were to send a dispatch to General Butler, intercepting him on the train. Having done this I went into the street again in a dazed condition. The long roll was being beaten, the clatter of cavalry, the clanking of sabres, the rumble of artillery and the hoarse shouts of common men were heard in various directions.

I wandered back to Willard's then to learn of the attempt made upon the life of Secretary Seward. Rumors of the assassination of Secretary Stanton and Vice President Johnson were on every hand.

The next morning af half past seven, the tolling of the bells told us that our Commander-in-Chief had joined the hosts of his boys in blue who had crossed the dark river before him. Meanwhile, alarms had been sent out by telegraph, through the signal corps of the army and by the police of the city. With the tolling of the bells, flags were at once set half staff and the whole city went into mourning, which was heartfelt and universal everywhere.

All government departments, stores and shops were closed, and on every hand—from the humblest negro quarters to the finest residences—were to be seen the emblems of grief; and, as if to add to the solemnity of the scene, nature shed tears of rain also.

W. H. Roberts
Location: Unknown
Washington Evening Star, Ford's Theatre National Historic Site
February 12, 1927

> *Roberts correctly places Booth's escape before the audience ascended the stage. Roberts was a sixteen-year-old Union soldier at the time of the assassination.*

I was with a group of comrades in a restaurant in Washington early that evening.

Someone suggested we go to Ford's theater. I hesitated at first, for I was not in the habit of going to theaters, but decided to go.

We were admitted free. I guess it was because we were soldiers. The president and his company came in a few minutes after we were seated. He bowed to the audience from his box and received quite an ovation. His box was some ten feet above the stage at one side. . . .

The shot came in the midst of the play without warning, startling the audience as anything like that would. Nearly every one feared, I believe, that the president had been the target of the gun. All appeared dazed for a moment. Then great confusion began to prevail, of course. Cries of "get him" went up on all sides. Some rushed to the stage, from which Booth, the assassin, had fled. Others went into the street, while others rushed toward the box.

Just after the crack of the gun we saw a man leap from the president's box. A spur attached to his boot became entangled in the flags around the railing and he fell heavily to the stage. As he leaped, he flourished a dagger. He muttered something in a strange language, which I afterward learned was the famous "Sic Semper Tyrannis." The assassin quickly recovered himself and disappeared through a stage door, despite a bad ankle.

As cavalrymen we joined the hunt for Booth and were on the scene when he was finally captured and shot several weeks later. . . .

Anyone who said a word that might be regarded as condoning the act was dealt with harshly. I recall a soldier shooting to death one man who said he was glad Booth had shot Lincoln.

Edward Holy
Location: Unknown
Chicago Daily News, Ford's Theatre National Historic Site
April 14, 1927

> *Edward Holy, who was seventeen years old in 1865, had the unique claim of witnessing both the assassination of Lincoln and the Chicago fire.*

But, of course, that event [Laura Keene's thousandth performance] was greatly overshadowed by the announcement that Lincoln was to be present. He was my ideal and I could hardly help talking about it in advance. I had a kind of "flunky" job helping my uncle since I had come to this country from what is now Czechoslovakia and the possibility of sitting in the same theater with President Lincoln overawed me.

I paid little attention when I saw a man entering the box . . . but it seemed that in a moment the whole theater was in uproar. I realized what had happened and wanted to do something. Some men who were able to get away gave chase, but the whole crowd was taken by surprise.

I didn't know how to feel . . . I know I felt a deep void and I guess I cried, too, when I went to look at the body lying in state at the white house, but it was too big a thing for me to understand fully.

Caleb Milligan
Location: Unknown
Cleveland Plain Dealer, Ford's Theatre National Historic Site
April 15, 1928

> *Milligan was another eyewitness who claims that Booth broke his leg in the jump from the box to the stage. She was a second cousin of Jefferson Davis. She was seventeen at the time of the assassination.*

It was in my mind as though it were yesterday . . . though I did not realize what had happened until several minutes after it was over.

When we heard a shot fired in one of the boxes we thought it was a part of the play. Then John Wilkes Booth jumped from President Lincoln's box to the stage, but his spur caught in some bunting and he fell, injuring his leg. . . .

It seemed to me that minutes passed while all we heard was the commotion attending Booth's escape . . . before some man appeared on the stage and announced that Lincoln had been shot.

There was a deathly silence, finally broken by a gasp which seemed to come simultaneously from every throat. Then the name of every member of the audience was taken and they all filed out. There was no panic, contrary to the popular supposition.

Mrs. Milligan was personally acquainted with John Wilkes Booth, for her parents' home was but a short distance from the Ford Theater, and she also knew Mrs. Mary E. Surratt, at whose home the assassination plot was formed and who was hanged for her part in the crime.

Charles Francis Byrne
Location: Unknown
Evening Bulletin, Louis A. Warren Lincoln Library
February 12, 1929

> *This account states that Booth broke his leg in the fall, which indicates that by the 1920s that had become part of the accepted story.*

A twenty-year-old youth stood in the wing of Ford's theatre, Washington, D.C., on the night of April 14, 1865, nervously awaiting his entrance as "Captain De Boots," a minor character in the play, "Our American Cousin."

As he strode out before the footlights, hoping to do his best on this particular night, a shot rang out from the President's box, and he, with the rest of the cast, and the entire audience remained transfixed with horror as they saw the beloved President Lincoln crumple forward in his chair, and the assassin, John Wilkes Booth, leap to the stage and disappear. . . .

And for that ambitious Charles Byrne, that tragic curtain was the last. So distressing were the thoughts which forever were associated in his mind with the theatre that he has never uttered an actor's line or set upon a stage since that night.

"Booth, whom we all knew well, shot President Lincoln from behind . . . and then jumped to the stage, catching his foot in some bunting and breaking his leg as he fell. A guard tried to hold him just before he jumped from the President's box but Booth wrenched himself loose. He picked himself up and was crying with pain as he ran past me."

After the first shock, Mr. Byrne ran to the box, climbed up the side, saw the blood flowing from the President's wound. Laura Keene, the leading lady of the cast, had also rushed to the box and had Lincoln's head in her lap, Mr. Byrne relates:

"I took one look and then fled," he continued, "all of us did. We didn't want to be implicated in the terrible affair."

Mr. Byrne had seen Lincoln frequently. He was a friend of the president's son, Tad, and the two young men frequently went to dances together.

W. J. Ferguson
Location: Backstage
I Saw Booth Shoot Lincoln (Boston: Houghton Mifflin, 1930)

> *William J. Ferguson was assigned backstage on the night of the assassination. Ferguson hoped that his book would be the final word on the Lincoln assassination. Yet some of his conclusions, such as his claim that Booth said nothing from the stage, were contradicted by the reliable eyewitness accounts of 1865.*
>
> *He wrote numerous accounts of the assassination. This one was selected because it provides the most comprehensive detail.*

To reach his box, Mr. Lincoln, first entering the theater by its main doorway from Tenth Street, passed through the lobby to the right stairs, which he climbed to the level of the balcony floor; thence down the slope of the aisle next to the right-hand brick side, or south wall, of the building to a door giving into the narrow private hallway, three feet wide, which was a sort of antechamber to the box. On entering this hallway, the solid back wall of the theater was on the right hand, while on the left a permanent wooden partition there were two small doors which gave admittance.

The party with the President followed the same path, and any visitor or intruder, because of structural conditions, had to do the same. There was no other way to reach the box, except by the obviously improbable course of climbing from the apron of the stage to the railing at the auditorium side. (Pp. 23–24.)

It is repeatedly stated in published accounts of the evening that when Mr. Lincoln appeared at the box front he was greeted with salvos of applause and prolonged cheers, and that the orchestra, according to different testimonies, played "Hail to the Chief" and "See, the Conquering Hero Comes." Though at this time I was on the stage, along with other characters, I heard neither great expressions of enthusiasm nor martial music. (P. 27.)

Mrs. Lincoln accompanied the President to the theater. On the night of the assassination, he was also accompanied by Major H. R. Rathbone and his fiancee, the daughter of Senator Harris.

I have no recollection of ever seeing a bodyguard with President Lincoln at the time of his visits to Ford's, even though I often saw the presidential party enter the box from the hall at the back. (P. 30.)

Mr. Lincoln did not struggle or move, save in the slight backward sway. I saw no blood flowing from the President's body then, or afterward when I was close beside him. This again is a point to be understood, when I come to the discussion of certain assertions.

The President stayed perfectly still.

The stage was set with a front scene, in which was a center door with curtains. Mrs. Muzzy "old woman" of the company, had just made an exit through the curtains. Harry Hawk, playing the part of Asa Trenchard, was left alone on the stage and about to leave it, following Mrs. Muzzy. With Miss Keene, I would have made an entrance after the slight pause Miss Keene would have held to give time for the laugh which was expected after the comedian's exit. Booth, I am confident, knew the stage would be untenanted for a moment, and chose it to carry through his intention.

Booth fired the shot with not more than five feet separating him from Mr. Lincoln. An instant afterward he was at the box railing, mounting it in preparation for jumping to the stage. Major Rathbone seized him by the coat from behind. The assassin wore a sack suit of dark-colored material. Feeling himself held back, he slashed behind him with his knife. Major Rathbone's wrist was cut, as I learned within a few minutes.

Booth leaped. One of his spurs caught in the folds of the draped American flag on the front of the box, throwing him out of control of his movements. He fell to the stage, landing on his left knee. The next day I saw the semicircular indentation made by one of his spurs in the floor of the apron where he struck. Already I have noted the coincidence of his having been wounded previously at this very spot.

Almost without pause, he recovered himself and arose, in spite of the fracture of his ankle that it was later known he had suffered. Apparently unhurt, three feet to a stride, he rushed across the stage toward the point in the first entrance where Miss Keene and I were standing. Less than half a minute, I judge, had passed since the pistol shot. He came on when once he started, without the least pause or hesitation, and, reaching the prompt entrance, ran between Miss Keene and myself, so close that I felt his breath on my face.

I stepped back into the prompter's space, a mere foot or so. Immediately after he passed me, I followed a few feet to the offstage end of the tormentor and watched him till he disappeared. He was not out of my sight three seconds. Without pausing, he ran through the first entrance to the angle of the north wall, ten feet on, and followed it back thirty feet to the little door in the back wall communicating with the alley, and opened it.

Outside was revealed the yellow mare I had often seen him ride. Peanut John, the basket boy, mounted, and I heard the beat of his horse's hoofs on the cobble-stones of the alley. In all, possibly a minute had passed between the time of the pistol report and the moment when he rode out of sight.

I think I have made it clear that there was no time for the slightest delay in Booth's progress from the time of his fall to his disappearance in the alley, the distance on the stage level, about seventy-five feet, having been covered, at a running pace, in not more than half a minute. Yet set down in history as facts are testimonies that, in those thirty seconds, two sensational incidents, requiring much time for accomplishment, occurred, in addition to what I have told. First, there is the story that Booth stopped at the center of the stage, raised a hand aloft holding a dagger, and shouted, "Sic semper tyrannis!" Major Rathbone testified afterward in the course of the official investigation that Booth hissed the words in his ear while still in the box. He probably did so, either in passing Major Rathbone or when he was on his way to jump over the box rail. It is the only fact on which to base the fable and pictures which have been printed in so many schoolbooks. I have seen the copy of the "New York Herald" of the day after the assassination, which says there are rumors to the effect that Booth shouted the words while crossing the stage. In the same column it is twice said that the assassin was thought to be Booth, but that no one had identified him positively. The doubt shows how unreliable were early reports of the catastrophe. (Pp. 36–39.)

Rejoining Miss Keene, and my eyes turning again to Mr. Lincoln's box, I know now that I took note of Miss Keene standing as one in a trance. My thoughts at the time naturally were not so ordered as they appear now in words, after long reflection on what I witnessed.

Mrs. Lincoln was advancing to the front of the box, in great excitement and evident anguish. This fact confirms my statements regarding the extremely short time between the pistol shot and Booth's disappearance.

Mrs. Lincoln was calling to the audience. I did not know what she was trying to say, nor did the audience. She exclaimed incoherently rather than spoke in words. Her efforts at appeal or explanation made no immediate impression on her hearers. So completely hidden had been the tragedy that the hundreds in the house had not the least idea of the profound seriousness of the happening.

A man had been seen to leap from the box, fall, and rush away.

Booth was well on his way before those who crowded the stage fell to asking each other, "Who was it?" Some thought they recognized the man as John Wilkes Booth, others did not identify him.

It seems to me now, as then, that Mrs. Lincoln continued to call for a long time before the audience as a body was roused. I have distinct recollection of absolute quiet, except for the voice of the President's wife. My own comprehension was just becoming clear as to the awful realization of the commission of a crime of crimes.

Major Rathbone joined Mrs. Lincoln at the front of the box. It was testified that he called out, "Stop that man! Stop him!"

Suddenly there was realization. It came to the audience and all with inflaming demand for retribution. In an instant there was great confusion. Practically as one, the audience stood up. A few persons rushed to the lobby to ascend to the box. Scores climbed over the footlights and poured onto the stage. Pistols were drawn. Search for Booth then commenced.

Miss Keene and I stood where we could see everything, and for some short moments she held her place by my side. I saw her start toward the footlights. Following, I assisted her over them to the floor of the orchestra pit. We went rapidly to the lobby stairs, and thence up to the box, arriving as Major Rathbone was opening the hall door, after pulling away the obstructing bar placed by Booth.

We pushed our way to the front of the small group gathered before the door, and on into the hall and into the box. Some one called for a doctor. Soon several medical men were around Mr. Lincoln, who remained seated, as when I saw him from the stage, his head leaning forward on his chest. I stood close to the doctors and saw the wounded President plainly.

Noises from the main auditorium and stage broke in on the profound gravity of the group about Mr. Lincoln. I well remember the almost silent solemnity with which the medical men noted the dangerous location of the wound. Mrs. Lincoln, I recall, sat on a sofa with her arms outstretched in an attitude of astounded despair. Miss Harris sat beside her, speechless.

Miss Keene stood near by, silently watching, as I was. Mr. Lincoln remained in the rocking-chair, and was lifted in it and carried past me by the doctors. I saw what they had been examining so gravely—a little dark spot no larger than the head of a lead pistol, just under the left ear. I saw no blood issuing from the wound.

Through the theater, out onto the street, and across to a house with which I was very familiar, which was occupied by Mr. William Petersen, I followed the doctors carrying Mr. Lincoln. They entered the front door and went up the front stairs. (Pp. 50–53.)

John Lindsey
Location: Unknown
Newspaper article, Louis A. Warren Lincoln Library
1930s

The first, last and only time John Lindsey, 90-year-old retired farmer of Bridgeton, N.J., ever attended a theatre was the night of April 10, 1865, he disclosed here today.

It was that evening Abraham Lincoln was shot by John Wilkes Booth, and Lindsey was among those who saw the tragedy in Ford's Theatre, Washington.

Since then, the aged farmer said, any thought of a theatre visit has been repugnant.

"I can still see Booth, as he jumped from the President's box to the stage," he said. "His face had a hideous and fiendish expression as he brandished the dagger with which he stabbed Major Rathbone. And I can still hear Booth's shout as he fled behind the scenes."

Mrs. Nelson Todd
Location: Unknown
Monthly Agency Review, Library of Congress
May 1935

> *Mrs. Todd's account is one of the most unusual. Many of her statements are not supported by any other eyewitness accounts. For example, there is no evidence that Booth was whisked from the theater by a rope after bleeding on the stage. Todd's account is the best example of an inaccurate twentieth-century recollection.*

From time to time we have published letters of appreciation from Sun Life annuitants who, on account of their advanced age, have generally had a background of interesting reminiscence. When Mrs. Todd recently visited our Newark branch and expressed the pleasure it would lead to us having the opportunity of publishing an item of such historical interest as subsequently transpired. It appears that on Lincoln's birthday commemoration of 1934, she broadcasted from New York over a national hook-up the story of her experience on that memorable night at the theatre. Mrs. Todd is, despite her age, very healthy and active, and insisted upon calling at our Newark office rather than have them wait upon her at her home for these details. As to the story itself, we think we had better let her tell it in her own words as recounted in the American press of February 1932, when she faced the microphone for the first time at the news reel studio. She was then ninety-two years of age.

In Newark today there is a woman who is believed to be one of the few persons now alive who saw Abraham Lincoln assassinated.

Mrs. Nelson Todd of 39 Lincoln Park, oldest living member of one of the oldest families in Newark, yesterday recalled the circumstances of the tragedy which shocked the nation on the night of April 14, 1865.

Despite the fact that she is in her ninety-third year Mrs. Todd does everything but sit at home peacefully. She is in the habit of walking from her modern apartment to the vicinity of the Four Corners at least once or twice a day, dining out, and going out for an automobile ride when the spirit moves.

Motion picture theatre patrons throughout the country will have an opportunity to see and hear Mrs. Todd in a "talkie" within the next few days, telling her story of how Lincoln was shot. A leading news reel concern requested her to describe the tragedy before its camera and microphone.

The picture was taken at the concern's New York studio one day last week. Her first experience before a movie camera evidently turned out well, because on the following day Mrs. Todd again went to New York for the purpose of lengthening the film.

Not only has Mrs. Todd shaken hands with Abraham Lincoln, but she was personally acquainted with John Wilkes Booth, the actor who fired the shot which ended the career of the Great Emancipator.

"I have shaken hands with every President since William Henry Harrison, who died in 1841, also with Henry Clay, Daniel Webster and Kossuth," said Mrs. Todd. "I have known many splendid and distinguished people, and of all I have known there was not a finer man than John Wilkes Booth, a fine looking, mannerly chap about my own age.

"I have heard that he had fallen into bad company. We all knew his sympathies were with the Southern States, and we learned later that he was a member of a set of fellow radicals we would call them today—who drew lots to see which one should kill Lincoln. It just happened that the lot fell to Booth.

"I shall never forget the first time I saw Lincoln—nor the last. The first time was just a little before his second inauguration, when he passed through Newark by train. I was horse-back riding and rode through side streets so that I saw Lincoln not once but several times on the rear platform. My persistence must have attracted President Lincoln's attention. William Coulter, a friend of my father's, the conductor of the train, told me later that the President pointed me out and said, 'That young lady there is a fine horse-woman.'

"I was married in 1858. The war, as you know, followed a couple of years later. Those were awful times. What a relief when it ended on the ninth of April, 1865!

"Immediately upon learning of Lee's surrender my husband planned a trip to Washington. The day after we arrived was Good Friday, April 14. I remember because we went to church. My husband was active in Trinity Church Sunday School, Newark. I was amazed when later in the day he said, 'We are going to the theatre this evening.' 'To the theatre on Good Friday?' I said. He explained that the President was to attend a benefit and last-night performance of Laura Keene in 'Our American Cousins' [sic] at the Ford Theatre, and it being a gala occasion and our only opportunity, probably, of seeing President Lincoln, we might waive our religious scruples.

"Theatres began earlier in those days. We were in our places on the centre aisle just a few rows back from the stage at 7.30, when the curtain rose. There was a flag-draped box on the left for the President, Mrs. Lincoln, Miss Harris, and Major Rathbone. They sat in the second box.

"The curtain had gone up on the second act when there was a shot. At the same instant I was amazed to see John Wilkes Booth, whom I had known so well, half jump and fall from the first box to the stage, twelve feet below. His spur had caught in the drapery on the box, so that his leap turned out to be a bad fall.

"For an instant no one realized what had happened. It struck me that John Wilkes Booth had committed suicide. It was not until some seconds later that Mrs. Lincoln screamed. The house turned from the stage, where all eyes had been on Booth, and saw the President, his head fallen on his chest, slumped down in the old-fashioned rocking chair in which he had been sitting. Then, of course, we knew the greater tragedy that had happened.

"Few people knew how badly Booth was hurt in his fall. I have read accounts and seen pictures of him hobbling off the stage to make his escape. This is as false as the story that he shouted 'Sic Semper Tyrannis!'

"Here is what did happen and I think I am the only person that knows how Booth made his escape. Knowing Booth, it was only natural my interest was keen enough to attract my attention back to him, even when I knew Lincoln was assassinated. When Booth's spur caught and threw him to the stage he broke his leg in a terrible way, so that the bone actually protruded through his trousers, and smeared the stage with blood. Naturally he couldn't move. Laura Keene leaned over and patted his head. Then, to my amazement, I saw a rope swing over, evidently thrown by some confederates, lasso him and whisk him into the wings. That was the last time I ever saw John Wilkes Booth.

"As we walked away from the theatre and the great tragedy, my husband said to me 'What next?' 'We must go home,' I said. And so we went to the hotel, packed our things and went immediately to the railroad station. The streets were seething with people. At the station the trainmen on a cattle train that was about to leave for New York had not heard the news so they let us ride in the caboose.

"We rode all night from Washington and arrived in New York in the early morning. Newark was just a way station in those days and the trains did not stop there. When we got in we learned that Lincoln was dead.

"Our family was surprised to see us back before we had planned. Being strict Episcopalians we did not tell them we had gone to the theatre on Good Friday, so we told no one of the thrilling scene of history we had seen enacted. Nor throughout my husband's life did we ever tell. It was only a few years ago that I let the truth out. I had gone to see a performance of 'The Birth of a Nation,' in which the assassination of Lincoln was shown. When I saw the scene I gasped out 'Why, it wasn't that way.' 'How do you know?' I was asked. Then I told that I was one of the few remaining witnesses of that great tragedy."

Mrs. Nelson Todd
Location: Unknown
Newspaper article, Louis A. Warren Lincoln Library
1935

Mrs. Nelson Todd, who witnessed Lincoln's assassination, died here last night after a three months illness, at the home of her grandson, Nelson

Todd. She would have been 98 years old on Aug. 17. Henry Clay and Daniel Webster were among notables she had met during her lifetime.

A participant in many civic events in Newark, Mrs. Todd was a guest of honor at the city's charter centennial celebration in the Mosque Theatre on April 15, 1936. She made her last public appearance on Feb. 4 as guest of honor at the New Jersey State Exposition in the L. Bamberger & Co. department store.

On Mrs. Todd's ninety-seventh birthday some one observed that she looked fit enough to reach the one-hundred mark.

"I don't want to be a hundred," Mrs. Todd said. "I have lived long enough."

Mrs. Todd was born in Albany, a daughter of Aaron and Elizabeth Garthwaite Rodwell. In infancy she was taken to Newark by her parents. She was married to Nelson Todd in 1858.

She often recalled the night she and her husband saw Lincoln shot at Ford's Theatre in Washington. She had often described how John Wilkes Booth jumped from the first box to the stage and how Mrs. Lincoln screamed as the President slumped down on his chair.

Also surviving, besides her grandson, Nelson, are five grandchildren, nine great-grandchildren and one great-great grandchild.

Thomas Sherman
Location: Unknown
Newspaper article, Louis A. Warren Lincoln Library
April 14, 1930

Thomas Sherman's account is inaccurate in stating that only polite applause greeted the president and that the audience came principally to see Grant. The audience gave Lincoln strong applause and many had come to see the president.

Seventy-one years ago today Thomas Sherman, a Maine youth who went to Washington because he had learned the new magic of the telegraph key, slipped into a balcony seat at Ford's Theater. The play sped on to the third act.

Suddenly a shot cracked through the theater. A scuffle broke out in a box from which the powder smoke lazily drifted. A man leaped from the box to the stage, and a cry rang out:

"Hang him! The President has been shot!"

Today white-haired, white-bearded 93-year-old Thomas Sherman quietly recounted the event when Abraham Lincoln was assassinated April 14, 1865.

Only a polite burst of applause greeted Lincoln when he entered his box, Sherman mused. "The crowd," he said, "had come principally to see General U. S. Grant, war hero of the day, who at the last minute was unable to come.

"The shot seemed like a trick of the play until someone issued from the President's box. Then a handsome young man of medium build, immaculately dressed in black, leaped from the box to the stage.

"He seemed a veritable fiend as he rose to his full height and brandished a dagger.

"The only actor on the stage, Harry Hawk, backed away, his hands held high; as John Wilkes Booth, the assassin, made a dive at him. Then both disappeared through the red curtained exit.

For a moment, Sherman related, it was said the murderer had been caught and there were cries "Kill him! Hang him!"

"I ran onto the stage," Sherman continued. "At the height of the confusion Laura Keene, an actress, came on. She seemed the only cool person there. 'For God's sake, gentlemen,' she begged, 'be quiet and keep cool.' She sent a pitcher of water to the President.

"Quiet was soon restored and the President, unconscious, was carried out by four men. Mrs. Lincoln followed, sobbing, and wringing her hands.

"Outside was pandemonium. No one knew what plot was afoot and the city was full of rumors until word of Booth's capture came hours later."

Charles L. Willis
Location: Orchestra level, seventh row
"Willis Revisits Site of Tragedy," *Washington Star*, Library of Congress
March 2, 1930

Charles L. Willis is 86 and has a keen sense of humor. He gets his "best laughs" he declares, from occasional death notices that assert "the deceased was the last person who was present at the theatre on the night of the assassination of President Abraham Lincoln."

Willis was sitting in the seventh row orchestra, directly below the presidential box in old Ford's Theatre in Tenth Street on that memorable night of April 14, 1865. He was 18 and he believes there were many, many more in the packed house his age and younger, thus discarding the belief that witnesses of the shooting can be counted within a dozen. He went to Ford's with a chum, John A. Downs, who died twenty years ago. "Our American Cousin" was the attraction.

"It was Good Friday and the Washington papers published President Lincoln and a party would attend the performance at Ford's that night," he said. "The theatre was well filled and the audience was appreciative and happy. Miss Laura Keene, popular as an actress at the time, was the leading lady. The first two acts passed pleasantly and we both left the theatre during the second intermission.

"Standing out front, we saw John Wilkes Booth come out of the theatre and enter a nearby restaurant. He was a handsome fellow with very white skin, black hair and piercing eyes. He was a favorite among the younger set. When we re-entered the theatre I saw Booth talking to John Buckingham, the doorman.

"The curtain rose for the third and last act, and hardly one word had been spoken when a sharp crack of a revolver was heard. We all knew it was not a part of the play, and for a few seconds everything was very still. A cry, 'the President is shot,' and the audience stood and looked toward the point from whence the sound came. I saw a man climbing over the rail in front of the presidential box, he leaped to the stage staggered; raising his right arm, he muttered a few words and quickly disappeared in the scenery on the left of the stage.

"A man sprang from the audience, climbed to the stage, and made pursuit. The audience was now all standing, and with little or no shouting or disorder, I suggested to my friend that we go out, and we did.

"As it appeared very few were coming out we re-entered the theatre and in my excited condition I went directly up on the stage where the actors and audience were mingled together. All were gazing up to the box where the wounded President lay. In all this excitement, to the best of my recollections there was not much noise, all were shocked, talking in subdued tones.

"The audience began to leave. On the outside the crowd was great, and I made for a place to avoid the crush. I took refuge on the porch of a house across the street and in a few moments four men, carrying the President, went up into the same house with him.

"In this house the President died the following morning, April 15, between 7 and 8 o'clock.

"The crowd by this time was great. Shouts of 'Lynch him,' and 'Hang him,' and 'They've got him,' were heard all around the crowd surged from side to side.

"When I reached home near midnight my mother hearing some tumult, asked what was the matter. I said 'nothing' I feared if I told her what had been done she and my father would sleep no more that night. The next morning I went to the government department where I was employed and after telling my experience, asked to be excused. I walked directly up F Street northwest, to the corner of Tenth Street and looked toward the hotel where President Lincoln lay. And what seems strange to me now, there were no crowds around the place. Later in the day all the government departments closed until after the funeral, which was held the following Thursday.

"When the body of the President was lying in stage in the rotunda of the Capitol thousands passed through to review the remains. Entering the west front, passing in double file, and leaving on the east side.

"I forced my way through the crowd, and for the last time I saw President Lincoln."

Jacob Soles
Location: Unknown
Source unknown, Louis A. Warren Lincoln Library
1930s

> *This account is the basis for the credit given to Jacob Soles and his fellow soldiers for carrying the stricken president from the theater, even though the account was first recorded more than six decades after the assassination. Daggett's, Leale's, and Taft's accounts, which were recorded within days of the assassination, are more reliable than Soles's. None of these mentions the assistance of any soldiers in carrying Lincoln. And finally, it is highly improbable that Lincoln could have spoken any words after being shot.*

Of the half dozen youthful blue-clad soldiers who carried the mortally wounded Lincoln from Ford's Theater to his death bed that fateful night of April 14, 1865, one still lives—the tragedy burned deeply into his memory.

A grayed and weather-beaten old soldier now is Jacob J. Soles. At 87, he lives with his memories in a little house in Turtle Creek, waiting "taps" good soldiers know they must answer.

A mine accident has cost him one eye; his other, he admits, "isn't as clear as it might be."

"But if I live to be 100," he exclaims, "I'll never forget that night. I don't need my eyes to look back on it!"

"Soles, three comrades of his company and two other young soldiers were seated together in Ford's Theater in Washington on the eventful night to see American Cousin." They were seated on the same side of the aisle, about 15 feet from the box where President Lincoln sat. "He was with a party," Soles relates. "From my seat I could see him clearly and noticed him laughing at one of the comical parts in the show.

"Then one of the actresses took the center of the stage—can't say I ever knew her name—but she was dressed in a long robe. I recall she kind of flirted with the audience.

"It was awfully still in the theater at that minute. Suddenly the sound of a shot cracked in the darkness.

"Mrs. Lincoln, I think it was, was the first to scream. 'The President is shot,' she cried.

"A man leaped from the box to the stage. It was John Wilkes Booth.

"We were at Lincoln's side in a second. We lifted him up. He felt limp, as if all the fight had gone out of him.

"Guards cleared the aisles and we walked to the door and then directed across the street—the six of us carrying him as gently as we could. Mr. Lincoln spoke only once and then in such a whisper that he could hardly make himself heard. I think I caught the words, 'where are they taking me?'

"We carried him across the street and up the steps of the house. Someone directed us to the room, where we put Lincoln on a bed.

"Back we went to the theater, but we weren't permitted to enter. But, even from the outside, we could hear the ram and jam behind the doors as guards tried to calm the people and prevent a stampede."

While an orderly, Soles frequently ran messages between his commanding officers at the barracks and the White House.

Mr. Lincoln, he likes to recall often would nod or smile at the brisk young messenger who was to carry him to his death.

Jacob J. Soles
Location: Unknown
"Four Men Who Bore Lincoln from Ford's Theatre Named," *New York Tribune*, Library of Congress
February 8, 1931

Every detail of the story of the assassination of Abraham Lincoln has been told except one. The identity of the men who carried the body of the stricken President from Ford's Theatre, the scene of the tragedy to the quiet chamber of death in the Peterson [sic] house, on the opposite side of Tenth Street, has never been established. Now, however, after an exhaustive investigation, it is possible to supply the one link which heretofore has been missing from the chain of that evening's events.

On Good Friday night, April 14, 1865, four comrades-in-arms, on leave from Camp Barry at Washington, sat in the dress-circle or first balcony of Ford's Theatre. They were near the State box, which President Lincoln and his party occupied that night. Hearing a pistol shot, then a woman's screams, the four soldiers rushed into the box, where they found their Commander-in-Chief wounded and unconscious.

Army officers who were at the theatre took charge of the situation and ordered the four soldiers who had so quickly appeared on the scene together, to lift the prostrate man and move him from the theatre. They carried him through the narrow corridor that led into the balcony, thence to the stairway leading to the street. Near the head of the stairs two other soldiers joined them and assisted in bearing the President across Tenth Street to the little brick residence of the Peterson family, where they laid him in the bed in which he died the next morning. Those four young soldiers, having done their simple duty, disappeared from the scene and hurried back to camp; their identity was lost, and it was only through a chance acquaintance who learned of my interest in Lincoln that I came upon the facts.

One of the soldiers who helped to carry the body of Lincoln from the theatre is still living. His name is Jacob J. Soles and he lives in North Versailles Township, Allegheny County, Pa., where he was born July 17, 1845. Three of his nine children are still living and he makes his home with one of them, Mrs. Laura Letter. He was a coal digger all his life until he got too old to do such work. Several years ago he lost an eye in a mine accident. He is not the emotional or imaginative type and could not have made up the simple, straightforward story he told in several conversations. His statement and my subsequent investigations in the War Department and elsewhere in Washington and in other places form the foundation for the following narrative.

During the last two years of the Civil War, Soles was a member of Thompson's Battery C, Independent Pennsylvania Light Artillery, which from the Fall of 1864 until the following June was stationed at Camp Barry, where it had been sent as a part of the defenses in and about Washington. The battery had been in many of the fiercest battles of the war, including Antietam, Chancellorsville, and Gettysburg, and had been shot to pieces. When Grant reorganized the Union forces in the Spring of 1864 many replacements were made to bring the battery up to its normal strength. At that time Soles and three of his friends Jabes Griffiths, John Corey, and William Sample—became members of the battery. These men, from Allegheny County, Pa., had enlisted at Pittsburgh in February, 1864, and were later assigned to Battery C for permanent service.

The individual records of the four soldiers, examined at the War Department by courtesy of L. A. Rosafy of the Adjutant General's office, show that they were all present with their company every day from March until the last of June, 1865, when they were honorably discharged.

On the night of April 14, they obtained leave of absence to attend the theatre. What occurred there, so far as they were concerned, may be told in the language of Mr. Soles, as he related it to me:

Bill Sample, Jabe Griffiths, and John Corey, and myself, all of Company C, Independent Artillery, went to Ford's Theatre at about 7:30 or 8 o'clock. Lincoln was shot some time later—I can't give the hour accurately; I know the play had gone on for some time after we came in.

We four were up in the balcony; we were on the same side of the balcony that Mr. Lincoln's box was on; we were back in toward the back of the theater, about fifteen feet from the box where he was shot.

We didn't know at first when we heard the pistol going off that it was in there, but they cried for help and we heard this woman crying and we four broke forward and rushed to the box, and we helped him down to the building where he was placed, in a little brick building standing across the street from Ford's Theatre.

We four fellows carried him to the stairway in the theatre, then two others fell in and helped carry him. As we carried him out of the theatre, he was carried out flat, with his feet foremost; I was down at his feet with one of the fellows, and two men at his head, and the middle of him was sagging until the two others took him in the middle and we six carried him out.

We carried Lincoln out of the theatre, and we had him out on the street about five minutes until we found a place to put him, and then they hollered out that is where he would be put. A young man directed us to the house, a young man that was not in soldiers' clothes; he told us to take him to the brick house. We put him in a room on the first floor; we went back through a long hallway to about the middle of the building. There was a bed in that room and we laid him on the bed.

When we took him into the room we had to get out. The guard put them all out. They wouldn't let anybody in without it was a doctor or something. The street was jammed. You had to push a road through whatever you wanted to get to. We waited around until the doctors came out and said it was fatal and then we pulled for camp.

The "Record of Events" of Thompson's Battery C, Independent Pennsylvania Light Artillery, and the individual records of the four men, as found in the files of the Adjutant General's office, verify those portions of Soles's story dealing with their military service. The records in the Pension Bureau confirm the details he related regarding the death of the three other men and their surviving families. An examination of the pension records disclosed the following facts: Jabes Griffiths died at McKeesport, Pa., Jan. 18, 1898, leaving a widow, Minerva Griffiths, and several children; John Corey was drowned in the Allegheny River near Pittsburgh in April, 1884, leaving a widow, Mary Corey, and several children, the widow having died April 29, 1898; William Sample died in the McKeesport Hospital Feb. 25, 1898, as the result of burns received in a steel mill; he left a widow, Lydia J. Sample, now dead, and several children.

Mrs. Griffiths lives with her daughter, Mrs. Leon Jeffers, on Third Street, Beaver, Pa. In a recent interview she related some of her husband's war experiences and soldiers who carried Lincoln from Ford's Theatre.

Dr. Samuel R. Ward
Location: Dress circle
Elgin Courier News, Ford's Theatre National Historic Site
April 14, 1931

> *Dr. Ward claims to have witnessed the Lincoln assassination, the Gettysburg address, and the Chicago fire.*

Sixty-six years ago today Abraham Lincoln was assassinated in Ford's theater at Washington. Few remain who saw the crime, but among them is Dr. Samuel R. Ward of Richmond, now retired, for many years a practicing physician in McHenry county.

Dr. Ward was a student at Georgetown university at the time. He had met the President, and had heard him speak at Gettysburg, but had never seen General U. S. Grant, and it was for that purpose that he attended the fatal performance. In an interview with Fred E. Holmes, Dr. Ward told of the tragic event.

"I was a student at Georgetown university in 1865," he said, "and was employed in the treasury department at Washington. I had seen President Lincoln several times, but had never seen General Grant. Therefore, when I read in the paper of the morning of April 14, that he and Mrs. Grant would accompany the President and Mrs. Lincoln and a party of friends to the theater that evening, I decided to go.

"My brother and his wife were living in Washington at the time and I purchased tickets for all of us. Being anxious to get a good view of General Grant, I was particular about the location of the seats and secured them in the dress circle, where we had an unobstructed view of the presidential box.

"The President and Mrs. Lincoln, accompanied by Major Rathbone of the regular army and Miss Harris, arrived very soon after we had been ushered to our seats. Major Rathbone was the father of Congressman Rathbone of Illinois, who represented this state at Washington and whose death occurred a few years ago.

"We learned that General Grant had been called to Philadelphia during the day, and could not be with the party as planned.

"The dress circle extended around the auditorium and was raised above the main floor. The boxes in which the President and his party sat were on the same level as our seat; consequently we had a clear view of the guests of honor. The box was draped with the stars and stripes.

"The play, 'The American Cousin,' [sic] was progressing smoothly, the large audience enjoying every moment, and rewarding the actors with frequent and well-deserved applause. Suddenly I heard a revolver shot.

"Not having seen the play, I imagined it was a part of the performance, but that idea was quickly dispelled when Mrs. Lincoln jumped to her feet, wringing her hands. Then we realized that the President had been shot, and there was great excitement.

"After the tragedy I was told that the assassin had a confederate stationed in a convenient place, his part being to turn off the lights. For some reason he did not and the assassin was forced to make his escape with all the lights burning brightly.

"Before he jumped from the box in which Mr. Lincoln was seated he stood in the front opening of the box making ready his jump for the stage. He had in his hand a bright, new dagger, perhaps fifteen inches long.

Mayor [sic] Rathbone reached for his arm to catch him, but the assassin struck back with the dagger and cut the major's arm badly.

"He then faced the audience and waving his dagger, shouted: 'Sic semper tyrannis' . . . With a friend I went up on the stage just in time to see them carrying the President out of the theater and to a house across the street.

"We spent 15 or 20 minutes in the theater talking to the actors and actresses, listening to the different versions of the tragedy. As I went down the stairs to the street, a man said to me: 'Do you know who that assassin is?' I answered 'no' and the man said 'That was J. Wilkes Booth, I have known him a long time and I know that is he.'

"I heard that shot every night for several weeks. Nothing ever left so deep an impression on my mind."

Kitty Brink
Location: Unknown
Newspaper article, Louis A. Warren Lincoln Library
February 12, 1935

> *Although this account is not entirely accurate, Kitty Brink does provide an excellent portrayal of John Wilkes Booth's likable personality. Unfortunately, she adds further erroneous myths to the assassination story by perpetuating the belief that Booth was not captured.*

As a young actress she was backstage in Ford's Theatre the night Booth's murderous pistol shots cut through the light comedy of the play to present a sudden and stark tragedy.

Mrs. Armstrong was then the child-wife of Edwin Brink, whom she had married at 15 shortly before the tragedy. Through her husband she was soon playing small parts with the troupe. She well remembers John Wilkes Booth, Lincoln's assassin, as a popular and light-hearted player.

"He was nothing like his terrible deed suggests," she recalls. "He was always ready for gaiety when with the company, and never struck anyone as particularly serious."

The play presented that fateful night of April 14 was "Our American Cousin"—a fill-in while Shakespeare's "A Midsummer Night's Dream" was being rehearsed for the Ford's Theatre company was at that time specializing in Shakespeare.

Kitty Brink did not have a role in "Our American Cousin," but her husband did. Kitty was relegated to the dressing-rooms to help make up the other actors.

"I recall something my husband told me during rehearsal that morning that puzzled me," Mrs. Armstrong says. "He had been talking to Booth, and said, 'Something will take place here tonight that will make the name of Booth live forever.'"

Here is the way the events of that night burned themselves into the brain of the child actress so that the little old lady still remembers them:

"Everything backstage was going along in routine fashion despite the fact that we were conscious of President Lincoln's presence. The knowledge circulated backstage just as he often arrived, soon after the curtain rose. We weren't too excited over that, as he often came to Ford's Theatre during the war, for relaxation.

"It was near the end of the second—or third—act, at about 10 o'clock when 'things happened.' In the dressing rooms we heard two indistinct noises. We thought nothing much about it until we heard shouts both from the stage and from the auditorium. Realizing that the shouts were foreign to the lines of the play, we stepped into a little hallway.

"Just at that moment we heard the clumping footsteps of someone running through the stage scenery down to the rear entrance out the door, and into the alley.

"That was Booth, though of course we didn't know it then.

"We rushed onto the stage. All was wild chaos. The first thing I saw was a number of men being lifted up from the stage into the President's box.

"And further back, I saw the picture that has never left me for a moment. Sitting in his chair, his great shaggy head slumped on his chest, was Mr. Lincoln!

"Mrs. Lincoln was screaming and crying unintelligibly. I heard her cry once, 'Mr. Lincoln has been shot!' By this time two actors of our company, Miss Keene and Mr. Ferguson, had worked their way through the panicky crowd and come up from the rear to the door of the box.

"I stood on the stage, glued to the spot, overwhelmed and terrified. I could see doctors working over Mr. Lincoln. Finally a group of men carried the chair with the President on it out of the theatre.

"The performance was hopelessly disrupted, of course. Patrons were leaving the theatre in a frenzy of excitement. No one was quite sure what had happened, and many had no idea that Mr. Lincoln had been shot.

"Miss Keene came back to the stage, and it was then that I learned that it was Booth, our fellow-player, who had done the slaying."

Mrs. Armstrong (she divorced Brink, married Nelson Armstrong, and is now a widow) is one of those who believe that John Wilkes Booth was not the man who was shot when cornered in a burning barn by pursuing troops.

"The man they got in that barn was not Booth," Mrs. Armstrong avers. "Of course I can't prove it definitely one way or another, but I, and a great number of other who knew him, have always been convinced that he got away and died under another name many years later."

William H. Fallon
Location: Unknown
Letter, Ford's Theatre National Historic Site
February 3, 1935

> *William Fallon's account has a few descrepancies. Lincoln was shot around 10:30 P.M. not 10:00 P.M., he died at 7:22 A.M., his wife was not with him and only two cabinet members were with him when he died, and Dr. Mudd was pardoned after four years in prison, not a few months.*

My Dear Darlene,

Now for the chief subject of your letter. It would take several pages to fully describe the tragic event of nearly seventy years ago, the assassination of our beloved President Abraham Lincoln, but I will endeavor to give you the facts as fully and as accurately as possible:

The President was shot and mortally wounded on Good Friday night, the 14th of April, 1865, while attending the performance of "Our American Cousin," put on by Laura Keene and her company, at Ford's Theatre, 10th street between E and F, Washington, D.C. The President had sent word to Mr. John T. Ford, the manager, that he would be there that night, accompanied by Mrs. Lincoln and General and Mrs. U. S. Grant. The war just about over, General Robert E. Lee and his troops had surrendered a few days previously, and there was much rejoicing by all at the ending of the civil strife. The manager of the theatre was especially pleased to know that he was going to have such prominent guests and made some changes in the private boxes they were to occupy by taking out a partition that separated the two upper boxes and by draping American flags on the audience front of the boxes. General Grant was called out of town on business the day before (Thursday) and he and wife could not attend, so President Lincoln invited two other friends to accompany them—Major J. H. Rathbone [sic] and Miss Harris, the daughter of Senator Harris of (Kentucky). The party was late in arriving and was escorted to the box, the orchestra playing "Hail to the Chief" and the audience standing until the President was seated. The theatre was packed—the play started. About the middle of the 3d act, shortly after 10 o'clock a shot rang out, but many of the people thought it was part of the play; The President was seen to slump over in his chair and there was a great rush toward the box by both audience and actors. A man was seen to jump from the railing in front of the box, but caught his spur in the flag and fell on the stage and shouted "Sic Semper Tyrannis," wielding a dagger, and made his escape out the back of the stage, badly cutting two of those who tried to stop him. He was then recognized as John Wilkes Booth, an actor, and the brother of Edwin Booth, the famous tragedian. The house was then in a turmoil. The curtain was rung down and the President was tenderly picked up and carried out of the theatre and across the street to a rooming house kept by a family named Peterson, [sic] put to bed and doctors called. The President never regained consciousness and died at 7:30 the next morning, in the presence of his wife, nearly all members of his cabinet, and other personal friends. Before the jumping from the box Booth also cut Major Rathbone who tried to stop the assassin. The theatre was quickly cleared of its audience many of them remained in the vicinity of the sick room until daylight. It was not long before news of the shooting became known over the city and the people became wild. Many a person was seen kneeling in prayer for the recovery of Lincoln. Steps were immediately taken to apprehend Booth and the others engaged in the plot to assassinate not only Lincoln, but also Secretary of State Seward, Vice President Johnson, General Grant, and others. . . .

The funeral service, or services, of our beloved President was undoubtedly the greatest ever accorded any human being. It lay in state at the White House for two days and was then taken to the Capitol for about three days, where immense throngs viewed the body with bowed heads. A special train was then used to convey the party to Illinois where the final obsequies were to take place. The car containing the body was heavily draped in black. The train left Washington towards the close of April (I can not remember the date) and stopped at all important cities enroute, where special services were held. Thousands of people, in addition to large bodies of troops and other officials, marched to the cemetery.

Joseph H. Hazelton
Location: Backstage
Newspaper article reprinted in *Lincolnian*, Ford's Theatre National
Historic Site
March-April 1986

> *Joseph Hazelton's account was recorded several decades before this
> article appeared, but it provides an image of Booth as his contempor-
> aries knew him. The Oldroyd museum in the Petersen house was op-
> erated by Osborn Oldroyd, who collected numerous items of Lincoln
> memorabilia.*

On the 14th of April, 1865, a little school boy, with his school books in a
strap thrown carelessly across his shoulder, romped down Tenth Street in
Washington, D.C., and as he approached old Ford's Theatre there stood
in front a tall, stately man, swarthy of complexion, raven black curly hair,
a drooping moustache, and a wondrous kind eye. That man was John
Wilkes Booth, who that night, by the act of a mad-man swayed the
destiny of our nation. The little school boy was myself.

It was a great thing for my little companion and myself to speak to Mr.
Booth, or to have him speak to us. We looked upon him as something
beyond the ordinary. As I started to pass him, I lifted my cap and said,
"how do you do, Mr. Booth." He beckoned me over to him, lifted my cap
from my head, ran his fingers through my hair and said, "Well, little man,
are you going to be an actor some day?" I was program boy and ran
errands around the Theatre at the time. I replied: "I don't know, Mr.
Booth, perhaps." Little did I dream at that time that I would spend fifty
years of my life in the theatrical profession. Booth took from his pocket a
little folder, which contained the coin of the day commonly known as
"shin plasters" of the denominations of five, ten, twenty-five and fifty
cents. Handing me a ten cent plaster, he pulled my hat playfully over my
eyes, patted me on the shoulders and bade me run buy myself something.
I have wondered, in the intervening years, whether that man had that
terrible crime on his mind at that time, when talking to an innocent little
school boy.

Well, I went around the Theatre that night, as was my custom, doing a
few chores for the actors, then went around in front of the house to
hand out programs. It was a gala night, the play was "Our American
Cousin" and Laura Keene was the star. Almost everyone knew that the
President would be there as the newspapers had made extensive note of

the fact. The house was packed, the gold lace of the Army and Navy predominating.

The President and his party came late, the second act was on, and as Mr. Lincoln entered the audience rose en masse and cheered, Mr. Lincoln came down to the front of the box which had been reserved for him, and with that sad, sweet smile, which he was wont to wear on such occasions, bowed his acknowledgements and took his seat and the play went on.

The third act was on and I was standing directly opposite the President's box, looking up at him and noting with childish delight to see how he was enjoying the play. I happened to turn my head toward the main entrance and saw Wilkes-Booth enter. He stopped a moment to say a word to Mr. Buckingham, the door-keeper, then started upstairs to the Dress Circle. As he passed along the side aisle toward the President's box, I noted the change in his dress. When he spoke to me in the afternoon he was dressed in the height of fashion, in the picturesque costume of the day, velvet collar and cuffs, now he was wearing heavy riding boots, spurs, a blue flannel shirt and an army slouch hat. I wondered in my boyish way what he was doing there on such a gala night dressed in such a garb.

I did not have long to wait, there was a flash, a report and President Lincoln had been assassinated. There are not words in the English language to describe the awful hush which fell over the house when the shot was fired. Everyone seemed to realize that something terrible had happened but no one seemed to take the initiative, until Laura Keene, rushing down to the footlights, cried, "Ladies and Gentlemen, the President has been shot." Then all was pandemonium.

When Booth fired the shot he dropped the weapon, a single barrelled affair, called a derringer, and drawing a Bowie knife ran to the edge of the box. Major Rathbone tried to stop him, and received an ugly wound on his arm. Booth leaped over the rail of the box to the stage, but his spur caught in the American flag which drapped the box and he fell to the stage. History says he broke his leg, such is not the case, had he done so he never could have gotten across the sixty feet of stage, however he did fracture the small bones in his ankle. To my dying day I shall never forget the look of anguish and despair on that man's face, as he half dragged himself to the center. Then brandishing the knife above his head and with a mania stare, cried out, "Sic Semper Tyrannis." He managed to get to the stage door where his horse was being held, mounted and rode rapidly away. Booth got across the Potomac River with young Dave Herold, who was in the conspiracy to kill Mr. Lincoln. They got to Chas. Garrett's farm in Rapahonoke [sic] county, where, history says, Booth was shot by Boston Corbett of Col. Baker's Secret Service Command.

But let's leave Booth and return to the theatre. They carefully lifted the President and carried him across the street to the home of Mr. Peterson, [sic] one of our merchants. The building is now being used as the Oldroyd Lincoln Museum. Mr. Peterson had a small house and a large family so the only vacant room was a small hall bedroom in the rear of the first floor. They took the President in, put him gently to bed and sent for the members of the Cabinet and his family, also Dr. Stone, his personal physician, and the vigil of the night began.

Gray dawn was streaking through the window on the morning of April 15th when Dr. Stone, holding the President's hand and feeling that his life was fast ebbing away, said to Secretary Stanton, who was Secretary of War, "Mr. Stanton what time is it?" secretary Stanton taking his watch out replied, "Twenty-two minutes past seven." Then Dr. Stone, placing the President's hand gently across his breast sighed out: "The President is dead." Then Secretary Stanton uttered that famous remark that will go thundering through the corridors of time: "Now he belongs to the ages."

And when the spirit of that mighty man soared its way to that bourne from which no traveler returns, it served to weld an unbreakable link of steel between the North and the South, making it one grand and beautiful nation that stood in 1865 as it stands today, with outstretched arms to welcome the oppressed of other nations to our shores; to build their homes here in America, and it still stands as it stood then when our martyred President met his doom, ready at all hazards, by force of arms, if necessary, to protect his honor, its integrity, and its flag—the flag of the greatest nation on earth—The United States of America.

Sincerely Yours,
Joseph H. Hazelton

David Dorn
Location: Orchestra level
Newspaper article by W. Emerson Reck, Louis A. Warren Lincoln Library
Date unknown

This is another account that perpetuates the idea that Booth limped across the stage.

A yellowed newspaper clipping found during spring cleaning at the Beatrice, Nebraska American Legion Club tells of a crippled soldier's conviction that being on crutches kept him from preventing the escape of Abraham Lincoln's murderer on April 14, 1865.

David Dorn, a member of the First United States Cavalry, was in a Washington hospital because of a wound received in a late battle of the war. On crutches, he went to Ford's Theatre on the night of April 14 and had a seat opposite the Presidential box.

"I . . . saw the whole tragedy," Dorn's story begins. "I was on crutches. The president's box was decorated with flags and the flag toward the stage partly obscured a full view of all those in the box. But I think Mr. Lincoln, Mrs. Lincoln, Major Rathbone, Tad Lincoln and possibly another man and woman were in the box. Mr. Lincoln sat pretty well toward the front. Laura Keene was on the stage at the moment playing 'Our American Cousin.'

"I noticed that Mr. Lincoln was laughing at something in the play. Just then I noticed the curtain in the rear of Mr. Lincoln's box pulled apart and I looked squarely at the man as he came in. At first I thought he was one of the theater attendants bringing in a glass of water and decanter, for something shone in each of his hands.

"Just then a shot rang out and Mr. Lincoln seemed partly to rise from his sitting posture and then sank back and his head lunged forward and I saw a little trickle of blood running down his cheek. Mrs. Lincoln screamed and Major Rathbone rose quickly and turned to seize the man, who struck at him with a dirk knife and, breaking loose from Major Rathbone, put one foot on the rail of the front of the box and sprang toward the stage. His spur caught in the flag and Booth partly fell on the stage. Laura Keene screamed as Booth rose to his feet, limping and waving the dagger, spoke out in deeply tragic voice, 'Sec [sic] Semper Tyrannis,' and then ran toward the rear of the stage.

"Some of the boys with me made an effort to get onto the stage and catch Booth, but they were held back and someone called out, 'Be calm, men, be calm; the president is only slightly hurt. The theater people have caught the assassin.'

"While I have suffered the tortures of the damned from my lost leg and have had to submit to partial amputations, I have never more regretted the loss of my leg than [at] that minute. I could have caught Booth when he started to fall on the stage, for I was an active lad in those days before my wound. But there I was, helpless. All I could do was cry.

"Necessarily I was one of the last persons to leave the theater. Mr. Lincoln had been taken some little time before. The curtain had been lowered in the meanwhile, though it was raised shortly afterward, when one of the theater people came to the front and said that Booth had escaped out the back window and had ridden away on a horse. Soldiers filed in immediately afterward and took possession of the theater."

Dorn's story, mounted on an 8-by-17 inch piece of cardboard, bears no date or any newspaper identification, but it is believed to have been published in a Beatrice newspaper many years ago. While it is basically accurate, some parts are incorrect, possibly the result of supposition or an overactive imagination. Tad Lincoln was not in the box, nor was Laura Keene on stage when Lincoln was shot. Dorn could not have seen John Wilkes Booth approach the President as clearly as stated, and there was no trickle of blood down the President's cheek after he was shot.

But for years to come the aged clipping, a gift of the American Legion Club, will be a treasured object in the Gage County Historical Society museum at Beatrice.

D. J. Richards
Location: Orchestra pit
Newspaper article, Louis A. Warren Lincoln Library
Date unknown

> *Despite the distance in time from the event, D. J. Richards's recollection is accurate. He was not, however, the last surviving eyewitness.*

D. J. Richards, or "Dad" Richards, as he is familiarly known, is, insofar as he is known, the only living person of those who made up the audience on the night of that tragic event when John Wilkes Booth fired that fatal shot in Ford's Theatre, April 14, 1865.

In his story, as told by him, the audience can almost see the tragedy reenacted before their mind's eye, so one of the prominent educators writes. He tells of the conditions, as they existed in 1865; the surrender of the Southern Army, the great rejoicing throughout the country, especially in the North; scenes witnessed while on the way to Washington the night of the 13th of April; his arrival with his father the morning of the 14th; the great joy of the people of that city, who for four years had lived in fear of each other because each thought the other was spying on their every movement. Then he tells of being in Ford's Theatre, where it had been announced the President and party would be present at the opening night of the play, "Our American Cousin"; the great disappointment of the audience when the party failed to make their appearance; the great ovation given when, while the orchestra was playing, "Hail to the Chief," the party entered and Lincoln made his appearance at the front of the box, bowing to the right, center, and the left; the progress of the play until the beginning of the last act, the pause, during which the President was shot— the assassin's leap to the stage; his appearance being applauded; when he made his presence known to the audience with an uplifted dagger in his hand and by the shout of "Sic Semper Tyrannis"—following this, another pause of several minutes—then the announcement which came like a thunderclap from a clear sky, "The President is shot." Following this, there is pictured the rush to the stage, the appearance of Mr. Ford stopping a stampede that would undoubtedly have injured many, perhaps killing many; Lincoln's removal to the house across the way, where at a little after seven the morning of the 15th he passed away to the Great Beyond. He died, but the spirit of Lincoln still lives and the statement of Secretary of War Stanton seems like a prophecy, which is being fulfilled from year to year. "He now belongs to the Ages."

This man is one of the very interesting persons in America today. On April 14, 1865, a fifteen-year-old boy sat in the pit in Ford's Theatre in Washington, D.C., absorbed in following the scenes of the play, "Our American Cousin," which was being enacted on the stage. There came a pause in the play, a pistol shot rang out, and in a few horrid seconds this fifteen-year-old boy learned that the President of his Republic had been murdered before his youthful eyes. That boy, hale and hearty in mind and body today, is "Dad" Richards, the last living witness of the assassination of the Great Emancipator. Out of the richness of his memory and the fullness of his devotion to the Great Martyr, "Dad" Richards offers this tribute.

His character was moulded and wrought in an environment of loneliness, sorrow, and privation. His heart bled from early youth until under the weeping skies of a sad April morning in " '65 " it was drained of its last crimson drop.

Looking back upon his strange career, it almost seems as if the man stalked across the stage of life with a crown of thorns upon his brow, bearing a cross to his calvary, beholding the world through a mist of tears. He loved his country, unselfishly, had he served it nobly and with unfaltering faith.

His spirit knew neither malice nor hatred; no impulse of vengeance ever sought refuge in his bosom. He was gentle of speech, sympathetic, charitable, compassionate, patient, tender, brave. Destiny made him the broken-hearted Commander-in-Chief of an embattled Nation; duty drove him through the tragic ordeal; and at the end, perfidy struck him down and left even his estranged kinsmen bowed and dumb above his prostrate form.

History reveals no counterpart of Abraham Lincoln. In body, heart, soul, mind, as well as in his fateful career, the world has had no other like him among all its sons—save One: the Man of Galilee.

The pyramids in time may sink beneath the desert sands, the temples of earth crumble in the dust of ages, the fame of Caesars vanish in the darkness of oblivion, but surely as long as the race endures, it will behold in the familiar figure of the martyred son—strange, gaunt, silent, colossal, with agony written in the lines of his kindly face, and love glowing in his wistful eyes—the saddest, gentlest, and most pathetic figure in all human history.

They said at his death-bed, "Now he belongs to the Ages"; to our present age, therefore, he is repeating to us his words first uttered when he took the Presidency: "You have no oath registered in Heaven to destroy the Government, while I have the most solemn one to preserve, protect, and defend it."

Gold is good in its place; but loving, brave, patriotic men are better than gold.

Samuel J. Seymour
Location: Dress circle
"I Saw Lincoln Shot," *American Weekly*, Library of Congress
February 7, 1954

Samuel J. Seymour was most likely the last surviving eyewitness of the Lincoln assassination.

The last known surviving witness of the assassination of President Lincoln is dead.

Samuel J. Seymour was 5 years old exactly 91 years ago today when he sat in the balcony at Ford's Theater in Washington. Lincoln sat in a box directly opposite.

During the play, actor John Wilkes Booth entered the President's box and shot Lincoln.

Seymour died Thursday at the home of his daughter, Mrs. Irene

Hendley, in Arlington, Va. He was 96. Burial services were scheduled to be held here today.

In an interview last year, Seymour said he was taken to Ford's Theater by his godmother, Mrs. George S. Goldsborough.

"When the intermission came Lincoln got up," he said. "Mrs. Goldsborough told me, 'Look he is about to say something.' I think he was standing, not sitting, when he was shot."

The accepted historical story is that Lincoln was sitting when Booth shot him.

"There was lots of excitement," Seymour said. "People were hollering and screaming and crying."

"I began to cry and Mrs. Goldsborough took me out of the theater."

NOTES

1. Carl Sandburg, *The War Years* (New York: Harcourt, Brace, 1939), 4:358, from a sermon by Reverend Justin Fulton in Boston, April 16, 1865.

2. The Conspiracy Trial Testimony is located in the National Archives, Washington, D.C. M-599. They were reprinted in Benn Pitman, *The Assassination of President Lincoln and the Trial of the Conspirators* (New York: Funk and Wagnalls, 1954), p. 100.

3. George S. Bryan, *The Great American Myth* (New York: Carrick and Evans, 1940), p. 166.

4. George J. Olszewski, *Restoration of Ford's Theatre* (Washington, D.C.: U.S. Government Printing Office, 1963) p. 17.

5. Daniel Veader's (1920) account is the only one that says the presidential party arrived on time *(Surratt Courier,* April 1989, p. 5).

6. Bryan, *Great American Myth*, p. 166; Jim Bishop, *The Day Lincoln Was Shot* (New York: Harper & Row, 1955), p. 193; W. Emerson Reck, *A. Lincoln: His Last Twenty-four Hours* (Jefferson, N.C.: McFarland, 1987), p. 84.

7. Jason Knox letter, April 15, 1865, Princeton University Archives, Princeton, N.J.; Spencer H. Bronson letter, April 16, 1865, Louis A. Warren Lincoln Library, Fort Wayne, Ind.

8. Joseph Hazelton, "The Assassination of President Lincoln," *Lincolnian*, March–April 1986.

9. John Buckingham's account in "Lincoln's Assassination," 1891, Louis A. Warren Lincoln Library, Fort Wayne, Ind.

10. Daniel D. Beekman, address in New York City, February 11, 1915; Bronson letter; E. R. Shaw, "The Assassination of Lincoln," *McClure's Magazine*, December 1908; Hazelton, "Assassination of Lincoln"; Knox letter; Dr. Charles Leale letter, July 20, 1867, War Department Records, National Archives, Washington, D.C.; Pitman, *Assassination*, p. 78; W. H. Roberts article; Charles A. Sanford letter, April 16, 1865, Clements Library, University of Michigan, Ann Arbor; W. H. Taylor, "A New Story of the Assassination of Lincoln," *Leslie's Weekly*, March 20, 1910; George B. Todd letter to his brother, Apr. 30, 1865, State Historical Society of Wisconsin, Madison; "The Pur-

suit of Booth," source unknown, 1889, Ford's Theatre National Historic Site, Washington, D.C.

11. Bronson letter; Pitman, *Assassination*, p. 78.

12. Pitman, *Assassination*, p. 78; Taylor, "New Story"; Beekman address.

13. Leale letter.

14. Shaw, "Assassination"; Hazelton account in "The Pursuit of Booth."

15. Leale letter.

16. Helen DuBarry, letter to her mother, April 16, 1865, Illinois State Historical Society, Springfield.

17. *Washington Evening Star*, April 14, 1903.

18. Pitman, *Assassination*, p. 78; Crawford's account in Thomas Turner, *While Lincoln Lay Dying* (Philadelphia, Union League of Philadelphia, 1968).

19. These calling cards were the 1865 equivalent of business cards today. Most likely, they would have been inscribed simply "John Wilkes Booth."

20. Todd letter; Ferguson's account in Turner, *While Lincoln Lay Dying*. In Todd's account, the manner in which the messenger allowed Booth to enter the box may seem puzzling. Yet Booth was a famous actor. His Southern sympathies were known to only a select few.

21. Pitman, *Assassination*, p. 78. In his diary entry, Booth claims that he was stopped outside the box but then "pushed on." The reliable eyewitness accounts clearly indicate that Booth entered the box with no hindrance.

22. Leale letter.

23. Pitman, *Assassination*, p. 76; *Sioux City* (Iowa) *Journal*, June 10, 1915; Shaw, "Assassination."

24. Bishop, *The Day Lincoln Was Shot*, p. 207; Bryan, *Great American Myth*, p. 179; Reck, *Lincoln*, p. 96.

25. Thomas F. Pendel, *Thirty-six Years in the White House* (Washington, D.C., Neale, 1902) p. 40; Metropolitan Police Records for John Parker, Washington, D.C.

26. Bryan, *Great American Myth*, p. 179; Reck, *Lincoln*, p. 96.

27. Pitman, *Assassination*, p. 78; Crawford in Turner, *While Lincoln Lay Dying*; Todd letter.

28. Pitman, *Assassination*, p. 78.

29. Ibid.; Fred W. Schwarz, newspaper article, February 20, 1916, source unknown, Louis A. Warren Lincoln Library, Fort Wayne, Ind.; Basset diary, April 15, 1865, Library of Congress; Beekman address.

30. Hawk statement in Turner, *While Lincoln Lay Dying*.

31. Harry Hawk, letter to his mother, April 25, 1865, Louis A. Warren Lincoln Library, Fort Wayne, Ind.

32. Hawk interview, *Boston Herald*, April 11, 1897.

33. Roeliff Brinkerhoff, "Tragedy of an Age: An Eyewitness Account of

Lincoln's Assassination," *Lincolnian*; William Fallon, letter, February 3, 1935, Ford's Theatre National Historic Site, Washington, D.C.; "The Night That Lincoln Was Shot," *Theatre Magazine*, June 1913; Ferguson statement in Turner, *While Lincoln Lay Dying*.

34. Knox letter; Crawford statement in Turner, *While Lincoln Lay Dying*; Julia Shepherd letter, April 14, 1865, Illinois State Historical Society, Springfield.

35. Pitman, *Assassination*, p. 82; Dr. George C. Maynard, "That Evening at Ford's," Louis A. Warren Lincoln Library, Fort Wayne, Ind.; "Remembers Lincoln Tragedy," February 12, 1935, Louis A. Warren Lincoln Library, Fort Wayne, Ind.; "Recalls Tragedy of Event," 1906, Louis A. Warren Lincoln Library, Fort Wayne, Ind.

36. Basset diary; Albert Daggett letter, April 15, 1865, Louis A. Warren Lincoln Library, Fort Wayne, Ind.; Knox letter.

37. Olszewski, *Restoration of Ford's Theatre*, p. 42.

38. *Washington Weekly Chronicle*, May 13, 1865, p. 5.

39. Knox letter; Bronson letter; Fallon letter; Ferguson statement in Turner, *While Lincoln Lay Dying*; Todd letter; Shaw "Assassination"; Henry Williams, source unknown, February 1905, Ford's Theatre National Historic Site, Washington, D.C.; Beekman address; *Sioux City* (Iowa) *Journal*, June 10, 1915; Taylor, "New Story"; "Veteran Recalls Assassination," source unknown, February 12, year unknown, Ford's Theatre National Historic Site, Washington, D.C.

40. Charles Sabin Taft, *Abraham Lincoln's Last Hours* (Chicago: Blackcat Press, 1934), p. 10; "An Eyewitness Account of Abraham Lincoln's Assassination," *Civil War History*, pp. 60–69; Edwin Bates diary, April 14, 1865, Library of Congress; Bronson letter.

41. William T. Kent affidavit to Justice Olin, April 15, 1865, Conspiracy Trial Testimony, National Archives; "A. C. Richards," *Washington Critic*, April 17, 1885; Hawk letter.

42. Shaw, "Assassination"; *Sioux City* (Iowa) *Journal*, June 10, 1915; "Mrs. Nelson Todd Saw Lincoln Shot," *New York Times*, June 29, year unknown, Library of Congress; "Actress who Played before Lincoln on Fateful Night Tells of Horror—Saw Lincoln Weep," source unknown, Louis A. Warren Lincoln Library, Fort Wayne, Ind.; Schwarz article; Williams article; David Dorn, source and date unknown, Louis A. Warren Lincoln Library, Fort Wayne, Ind.; Charles Byrne, *Evening Bulletin*, February 12, 1929.

43. Bishop, *Day Lincoln Was Shot*, p. 210; Reck, *Lincoln*, p. 107.

44. Booth diary; statements made by Dr. Mudd and David Herold before military authorities, National Archives, Washington, D.C.

45. Knox letter; "An Eyewitness Account of Abraham Lincoln's Assassination," *Civil War History*, pp. 60–69; Dr. Charles Sabin Taft, *Century Maga-*

zine, February 1893, p. 634; "First to Aid Lincoln," *Washington Post*, February 1928, Library of Congress; Bates diary.

46. Daggett letter; Ferguson and Hawk statements in Turner, *While Lincoln Lay Dying*.

47. Pitman, *Assassination*, p. 79; Jeannie Struthers Gourlay, letter, April 28, 1923, Louis A. Warren Lincoln Library, Fort Wayne, Ind.; "Recalls Vividly Details of Lincoln's Death," *New York Tribune*, 1915; Matthews interview in unknown newspaper, Louis A. Warren Lincoln Library, Fort Wayne, Ind.

48. Pitman, *Assassination*, pp. 79–80; "Recalls Vividly Details of Lincoln's Death"; Bates diary; Daggett letter; DuBarry letter; Hawk statement in Tanner testimony; Kent affidavit; "An Eyewitness Account of Abraham Lincoln's Assassination," *Civil War History*, pp. 60–69; Debra Bradley, "Soldier Saw Lincoln Shot," *Wassau-Herald Record*, March 12, 1976, Louis A. Warren Lincoln Library, Fort Wayne, Ind.; "A. C. Richards," *Washington Critic*, April 17, 1885, Louis A. Warren Lincoln Library, Fort Wayne, Ind.; Todd letter.

49. Pitman, *Assassination*, p. 79; "Recalls Vividly Details of Lincoln's Death."

50. Reck, *Lincoln*, p. 106; Bryan, *Great American Myth*, p. 181.

51. Hawk statement in Turner, *While Lincoln Lay Dying*.

52. Pitman, *Assassination*, p. 78; Hawk interview in *Boston Herald*, April 11, 1897; John Downing, Jr., letter, April 24, 1865, Louis A. Warren Lincoln Library, Fort Wayne, Ind.

53. Pitman, *Assassination*, p. 79; Booth diary.

54. Basset diary; Knox letter; Bronson letter; Ferguson statement in Turner, *While Lincoln Lay Dying*; Daggett letter; Bates diary; Taft article; "A. C. Richards"; Todd letter; Kent affidavit.

55. Bradley, "Soldier Saw Lincoln Shot"; Basset diary; Shepherd letter; Ferguson statement; Daggett letter; Maynard, "That Evening at Ford's"; "The Night That Lincoln Was Shot."

56. "The Night That Lincoln Was Shot."

57. "When Lincoln Was Shot," source and date unknown, Louis A. Warren Lincoln Library, Fort Wayne, Ind.

58. Sanford letter.

59. Knox letter; Bronson letter; Taylor, "New Story."

60. "Remembers Lincoln Tragedy"; Charles Greenwood, "I Saw Lincoln Shot," pp. 121–23.

61. Pitman, *Assassination*, p. 78.

62. "Recalls Vividly Details of Lincoln's Death."

63. Knox letter; Pitman, *Assassination*, p. 79.

64. Colonel Pren Metham, unpublished biography, Coshocton County, Ohio, Historical Society.

65. Basset diary; Hazelton, "Assassination"; J. E. Covel, June 16, 1893, Louis A. Warren Lincoln Library, Fort Wayne, Ind.

66. Beekman address; Gourlay letter; "Captain Greer Died Early Today," source unknown, December 1914; "Shot That Killed Lincoln Still Rings in Memory of Soldier Who Saw Him Die," *Washington Daily News*, February 11, 1933; *Surratt Courier*, April 1989, p. 5; "Maine Man Recalls Death of Lincoln 71 Years Ago," April 14, 1930.

67. Dr. Gatch's claim appears to be one of the easiest to refute. Both Dr. Leale's and Dr. Taft's accounts mention besides each other only Dr. King. Neither of their accounts, which were recorded within a few years of the assassination, mentions the presence of a fourth surgeon.

68. Taft article.

69. Shepherd letter; Bates diary; Bronson letter.

70. Greenwood, "I Saw Lincoln Shot"; Taylor, "New Story"; Maynard, "That Evening at Ford's."

71. Taft article.

72. Leale letter.

73. Greenwood, "I Saw Lincoln Shot"; "First to Aid Lincoln"; Shaw, "Assassination."

74. "Today's Anniversary," *Washington Evening Star*, April 14, 1903.

75. Knox letter.

76. Reck, *Lincoln*, p. 126; Bishop, *Day Lincoln Was Shot*, p. 216.

77. "Recalls Vividly Details of Lincoln's Death"; *Sioux City* (Iowa) *Journal*, June 10, 1915.

78. Greenwood, "I Saw Lincoln Shot"; Taylor, "New Story"; "Captain Greer Died Early Today."

79. Taft article; Leale letter.

80. "The Night That Lincoln Was Shot"; Bradley, "Soldier Saw Lincoln Shot."

81. Leale letter.

82. Bryan, *Great American Myth*, p. 186.

83. Soles in his questionable account also claims to have heard the mortally wounded Lincoln whisper, "Where are they taking me?" ("Shot That Killed Lincoln Still Rings in Memory of Soldier Who Saw Him Die").

84. Bishop, *Day Lincoln Was Shot*, p. 216; Reck, *Lincoln*, p. 124.

85. "Shot That Killed Lincoln Still Rings in the Memory of Soldier Who Saw Him Die."

86. Greenwood, "I Saw Lincoln Shot"; "Captain Greer Died Early Today"; "First to Aid Lincoln"; Hazelton, "Assassination."

87. Turner, Introduction to *While Lincoln Lay Dying*; *The Diary of Gideon Welles*, 2 vols. (Boston: Houghton Mifflin, 1911), 2:288.

88. John Nicolay and John Hay, *Abraham Lincoln*, 10 vols. (New York: Century, 1902), 10:302.

BIBLIOGRAPHY

Names in parentheses following bibliographical entries are those of the eye-witness whose account is in the source.

MANUSCRIPTS

Basset. Diary, Library of Congress, Washington, D.C.

Bates, Edwin. Diary entry for April 14, 1865. Library of Congress, Washington, D.C.

Bates, Edwin. Letter, April 15, 1865. Ford's Theatre National Historic Site, Washington, D.C.

Booth, John Wilkes. Diary entries for April 14–16, 1865. Ford's Theatre National Historic Site, Washington, D.C.

Bronson, Spencer H. Letter, April 16, 1865. Louis A. Warren Lincoln Library, Fort Wayne, Ind.

Daggett, Albert. Letter, April 15, 1865. Louis A. Warren Lincoln Library, Fort Wayne, Ind.

Downing, John, Jr. Letter to "My Dear Friend," April 26, 1865. Louis A. Warren Lincoln Library, Fort Wayne, Ind.

Downing, John, Jr. Letter, April 24, 1865. Louis A. Warren Lincoln Library and Museum, Fort Wayne, Ind.

DuBarry, Helen. Letter to her mother, April 16, 1865. Illinois State Historical Society, Springfield, Ill.

Dyott, John. Photograph inscription, date unknown. Louis A. Warren Lincoln Library and Museum, Fort Wayne, Ind.

Fallon, William. Letter, February 3, 1935. Ford's Theatre National Historic Site, Washington, D.C.

Forbes, Charles. Affidavit, September 17, 1892. Chicago Historical Society, Chicago, Ill.

Gourlay, Jeannie Struthers. April 28, 1923. Louis A. Warren Lincoln Library, Fort Wayne, Ind.

Knox, Jason. Letter, April 15, 1865. Princeton University Archives, Princeton, N.J.

Koontz, Samuel. Letter, April 24, 1865. Louis A. Warren Lincoln Library, Fort Wayne, Ind.

Leale, Dr. Charles. Letter, July 20, 1867. National Archives, Washington, D.C.

Metham, Pren. Unpublished biography. Coshocton County, Ohio, Historical Society.

Sanford, Charles A. Letter, April 16, 1865. Clements Library, University of Michigan, Ann Arbor, Mich.

Shepherd, Julia. Letter to her mother, April 14, 1865. Illinois State Historical Society, Springfield, Ill.

Stevens, John H. Letter, no date. Louis A. Warren Lincoln Library, Fort Wayne, Ind.

Todd, George B. Letter to brother, April 30, 1865. State Historical Society of Wisconsin, Madison, Wisc.

GOVERNMENT ARCHIVAL MATERIAL

Playbill for Ford's Theatre, April 14, 1865. Ford's Theatre National Historic Site, National Park Service.

Theatre company members listed:

Gourlay, Jeanie; Gourlay, M.; Gourlay, T. C.; Keene, Laura; Muzzy, H.; Parkhurst, G. A.; Ross, Jennie; Smith, Mary E.; Spear, G. G.

Conspiracy Trial Testimony, Microfilm 599, National Archives, Washington, D.C.

John Buckingham, May 15, 1865; J. L. Debonay, May 31, 1865; John Devenay, May 12, 1865; James P. Ferguson, May 15, 1865; H. Clay Ford, May 31, 1865; James R. Ford, May 30, 1865; David Herold, May 27, 1865; Isaac Jacquette, May 18, 1865; Henry M. James, May 31 1865; William T. Kent, May 15, 1865, and May 16, 1865; Captain Theodore McGowan, May 15, 1865; James L. Maddox, May 22, 1865; John Miles, May 15, 1865; Major Henry R. Rathbone, May 15, 1865; Jacob Ritterspaugh, May 19, 1865; Joseph S. Sessford, June 3, 1865; Joe Simms, May 15, 1865, and May 18, 1865; John F. Sleichmann, May 15, 1865; Joseph B. Stewart, May 20, 1865; William Withers, Jr., May 15, 1865, and May 31, 1865.

Metropolitan Police Blotter, April 14, 1865, National Archives, Washington, D.C.

Eyewitnesses interviewed:

Brown, William; Burch, W. S.; Cutter, James B.; Devenay, John; Fletcher, John; Gilbert, C. W.; Gratton, John; Hawk, Harry; Knox, J. S.; Larner, Jacob B.; Lully, Anthony; Maddox, James; Manwoning, Andrew C.; Shaw, Captain G. S.; Stewart, Joseph B.; Wray, E. D.

NEWSPAPER ARTICLES

Unless otherwise noted, newspaper articles are in the Louis A. Warren Lincoln Library in Fort Wayne, Indiana.

"A. C. Richards." *Washington Critic*, April 17, 1885.

"Actor Saw Lincoln Shot, Fled Stage." *Evening Bulletin*, February 12, 1929.

"Actress Who Played before Lincoln on Fateful Night Tells of Horror—Saw Lincoln Weep." Source and date unknown. (Helen Truman)

Article. Source unknown, 1908. (Edwin Bedee)

Article. Source unknown, February 5, 1909. (Oliver Gatch)

Boston Post, April 11, 1915. Ford's Theatre National Historic Site. (Charles Johnson)

Boston Sunday Globe, April 12, 1914. (James Mills)

Bradley, Debra. "Soldier Saw Lincoln Shot." *Wassau-Herald Record*, March 12, 1976. (Sheldon McIntyre)

"Brighton Widow of Civil War Veteran Recalls Details of Murder of President Lincoln." *Daily Times*, February 12, 1931. (Jabes Griffiths)

Buckingham, John. Source unknown, 1907. Ford's Theatre National Historic Site.

Byrne, Charles. *Evening Bulletin*, February 12, 1929.

"Captain Greer Died Early Today." Source unknown, December, 1, 1914.

"Chicagoan Tried to Catch Booth." *Chicago Daily News*, April 14, 1927. Ford's Theatre National Historic Site. (Edward Holy)

Cincinnati Commercial Gazette, 1894. (Harry Hawk)

Coyel, J. E. Source unknown, June 16, 1893.

"Describes Slaying of Lincoln as Seen by Actors from Stage." *Baltimore Sun*, February 12, 1926. (William Ferguson)

"An Exceedingly Interesting Incident." *Los Angeles Times*, February 12, year unknown. (Helen Truman)

"An Eyewitness Account of Lincoln's Assassination." *Minneapolis Sunday Tribune*, February 12, year unknown. (Jason Knox)

"Eyewitness to Lincoln's Assassination Lives Here." *Los Angeles Times*, February 14, 1923. (Helen Truman)

"Family Legend Spans History." *Washington Post*, February 11, 1968. (Joseph Stewart)

"Findlay Man Saw Lincoln Shot by Booth." Source unknown, February 11, 1917. (W. H. Roberts)

"First to Aid Lincoln." *Washington Post*, February, 15, 1911. Library of Congress, Washington, D.C. (William Flood)

"Former Actress, 91, Dies of Poisoning." Source unknown, December 29, 1924. (Helen Truman)

"Four Men Who Bore Lincoln from Ford's Theatre Named." *New York Tribune*, February 8, 1931. Library of Congress, Washington, D.C. (Jacob Soles)

"George C. Read's Story." *New York Sun*, September 1, 1914. Library of Congress, Washington, D.C.

Greenwood, Charles. "I Saw Lincoln Shot." Source and date unknown, pp. 121–23. (Edwin Bedee)

Hawk, Harry. *Boston Herald*, April 11, 1897.

"He Saw the Tragedy of April, 1865." Source unknown, January 27, 1923. Ford's Theatre National Historic Site. (Andrew Huntoon)

Interview. Source and date unknown. (John Matthews)

"James N. Mills." *New York Sun*, date unknown.

"Last Surviving Witness of Lincoln Shooting Is Dead." Source unknown, April 15, 1956. (Samuel Seymour)

"The Lincoln Assassination." *Washington Star*, 1885. (Harry Ford)

"Lincoln Death Is Recalled by Washingtonian." *Richmond Times-Dispatch*, May 19, 1929.

"Lincoln's Assassination." Source unknown, 1891. (John Buckingham)

"Lincoln's Last Days." *New York Independent*, June 20, 1889. (Clara Harris)

"Lincoln Shot 66 Years Ago." *Elgin Courier News*, April 14, 1931.

"Lincoln Shooting." *Harrisburg Telegraph*, November 26, 1910. (Herman Newgarten)

"Lincoln Shooting Witness Dead." Source unknown, April 22, year unknown. (Benjamin Judd)

"Maine Man Recalls Death of Lincoln 71 Years Ago." Source unknown, April 14, 1930. (Thomas Sherman)

"Major Maclay Dead." Source unknown, December 31, 1908.

"Man Now Living Here Saw Assassination of Lincoln." Source unknown, September 9, 1932. (Charles Quimby)

Maynard, Dr. George C. "That Evening at Ford's." Source and date unknown.

"Mrs. Nelson Todd Saw Lincoln Shot." *New York Times*, June 29, year unknown. Library of Congress, Washington, D.C.

"Newarker, 93, in Lincoln Talk." Source and date unknown. (Mrs. Nelson Todd)

O'Brien, Marie. "Woman Recalls Capital in Grip of Other Wars." *Washington Times-Herald*, August 2, 1942. (Henry Edward Riley)

Obendorfer, Emmanuel. Source unknown, March 31, year unknown.

Omaha World-Herald, 1916. Ford's Theatre National Historic Site. (John Reagan)

"Present When Lincoln Was Shot." *Elgin Courier News,* April 14, 1931. Ford's Theatre National Historic Site. (Samuel Ward)

"The Pursuit of Booth." Source unknown, 1889. (Captain William Williams)

"Recalls Tragedy of Event." Source unknown, 1906. (Isaac Hull)

"Recalls Vividly Details of Lincoln's Death." *New York Tribune*, April, 1915. (Katherine Evans)

Reck, Emerson. Source and date unknown. (David Dorn)

"Remembers Lincoln Tragedy." Source unknown, February 12, 1935. (Kitty Brink)

"Saw Abe Lincoln Shot 63 Years Ago." *Cleveland Plain Dealer*, April 15, 1928. Ford's Theatre National Historic Site. (Caleb Milligan)

"Saw Booth Shoot Lincoln." Source and date unknown. (Albert Boggs)

"Saw Lincoln Killed." *Philadelphia Bulletin*, January 5, 1931. (John Revord)

"Saw Lincoln Shot Says Ohio Veteran." *New York Times*, February 13, 1927. Ford's Theatre National Historic Site. (W. H. Roberts)

"Shot That Killed Lincoln Still Rings in Memory of Soldier Who Saw Him Die." *Washington Daily News*, February 11, 1933. (Jacob Soles)

Sioux City (Iowa) *Journal*, June 10, 1915. (J. F. Troutner)

Sunday Standard, April 13, 1919. (Henry Mason)

"Tell Original Lincoln Tales." *Chicago Daily Journal*, February 13, 1909. Library of Congress, Washington, D.C. (Earl Stirling)

"Today's Anniversary." *Washington Evening Star*, April 14, 1903. Library of Congress, Washington, D.C.

"Veteran Recalls Assassination." Source unknown, February 12, year unknown. Ford's Theatre, Washington, D.C. (W. H. Roberts)

Washington Star, February 13, 1908. (Laura Freudenthal)

"When Lincoln Was Shot." Source and date unknown. (William Ennis and Isaac Maclay)

"When the Tragic Story of Abraham Lincoln's Death Was News." *Sunday Star*, February 9, 1930. (W. J. Ferguson)

"William E. Widrick at Ford's Theatre When Lincoln Was Assassinated." Source and date unknown.

"William H. Flood Is Dead." *Washington Post*, February 15, 1911.

Williams, Henry. Source unknown, February 1900. Ford's Theatre, Washington, D.C.

"Willis Revisits Scene of Tragedy." *Washington Star*, March 2, 1930. Library of Congress, Washington, D.C.

Wiseman, C. M. L. "Several Are Living." Source unknown, March 14, 1900. (John Sears and John Busby)

"Witness of Lincoln Tragedy Dies." *New York Times*, February 26, 1930. (Henry C. Harris)

"Witness of Lincoln Tragedy Dies." *New York Times*, August 5, 1930. (Samuel Kirby Gleason)

"Woman Who Saw Booth Shoot Lincoln Is Dead." *New York Evening Sun*, December 1, 1932. (Levene C. B. Stewart)

"Woman Who Saw Lincoln Shot." Source unknown, January 23, year unknown. (Sarah Eastman)

"Woman Who Saw Lincoln Shot Dies." *New York Times*, April 8, 1924. Library of Congress, Washington, D.C. (Annie Wright)

MAGAZINE ARTICLES

"The Assassination of President Lincoln." *Lincolnian*, March–April 1986. (Joseph Hazelton)

Beekman, Daniel Dean. Address in New York City, February 11, 1915.

Bolton, Lt. John T. *Magazine of History*, 1914.

Brinkerhoff, Roeliff. "Tragedy of an Age: An Eyewitness Account of Lincoln's Assassination." *Lincolnian*.

"An Eyewitness Account of Abraham Lincoln's Assassination." *Civil War History*, pp. 60–69. (Frederick Sawyer)

Knickerbocker, February 20, 1916. (Fred Schwarz)

"Lincoln's Assassination." *Century Magazine*, pp. 917–18. (Julia Shepherd)

Morris, James R. *Ohio Archaeological and Historical Publications*, 1921, pp. 1–3.

National Republican, April 22, 1922. Ford's Theatre National Historic Site. (John Davenport)

"The Night That Lincoln Was Shot." *Theatre Magazine*, June 1913. Library of Congress, Washington, D.C. (E. A. Emerson and W. J. Ferguson)

"90, He Saw Lincoln Shot on Last Visit to Theatre." *Public Ledger Bureau*, February 11, 1931.

Pope, Katherine. "He Helped Carry Lincoln out of Ford's Theatre." *Farm and Fireside*, April 1922.

"Saw Lincoln Assassinated." *Madison County Record*, June 24, 1920. (Clara Harris)

Seymour, Samuel. "I Saw Lincoln Shot." *American Weekly*, February 7, 1954. Library of Congress, Washington, D.C.

Shaw, E. R. "The Assassination of Lincoln." *McClure's Magazine*, December 1908. (Dr. Gatch and Captain Gatch)

"Sun Life Annuitant Witnessed Assassination of Lincoln." *Monthly Agency Review*, May 1935. Library of Congress, Washington, D.C. (Mrs. Nelson Todd)

Surratt Courier, April 1989, pp. 4–5. (Andrew Huntoon)

Surratt Courier, April 1989, p. 5. (Daniel Veader)

Taft, Dr. Charles Sabin. *Century Magazine*, February 1893, p. 634. Library of Congress, Washington, D.C.

Taylor, W. H. "A New Story of the Assassination of Lincoln." *Leslie's Weekly*, March 20, 1910. Library of Congress, Washington, D.C.

Weik, Jesse W. *Century Magazine*, February 1913, pp. 559–62.

BOOKS

Balsiger, David. *The Lincoln Conspiracy*. Los Angeles: Schnik Sun Classic Books, 1977.

Bauer, Charles. *So I Killed Lincoln*. New York: Vantage Press, 1976.

Bishop, James. *The Day Lincoln Was Shot*. New York: Harper & Row, 1955.

Bryan, George S. *The Great American Myth*. New York: Carrick and Evans, 1940.

Chanlee, Roy. *Lincoln's Assassins*. New York: McFarland and Company, 1990.

Clark, Champ. *The Assassination*. Alexandria, Va.: Time-Life Books, 1987.

Crook, Colonel W. H. *Memories of the White House*. Boston: Little, Brown, 1911.

DeWitt, David Miller. *The Assassination of Abraham Lincoln and Its Expiation*. Freeport, N.Y.: Books for Libraries Press, 1909.

Eisenschiml, Otto. *Why Was Lincoln Murdered?* Boston: Little, Brown, 1937.

Ferguson, William. *I Saw Booth Shoot Lincoln*. Boston: Houghton Mifflin, 1930.

Forrester, Izola. *This One Mad Act*. Boston: Hale, Cushman, and Flint, 1937.

Hanchett, William. *The Lincoln Murder Conspiracies*. Urbana: University of Illinois Press, 1983.

Harris, T. M. *Assassination of Lincoln*. Boston: American Citizen Company, 1892.

Holmes, Torlief. *April Tragedy*. Poolesville, Md.: Old Soldier Books, 1986.

Kunhardt, Dorothy, and Philip Kunhardt. *Twenty Days*. North Hollywood, Calif.: Newcastle, 1985.

Laughlin, Clara. *The Death of Lincoln*. New York: Doubleday, 1909.

Loftus, Elizabeth. Eyewitness Testimony. Cambridge, Mass.: Harvard University Press, 1979.

————. Human Memory: The Processing of Information. Hillsdale, N.J.: Lawrence Erlbaum Associates, 1976.

————. Memory: Surprising New Insights into How We Remember and Why We Forget. Reading, Mass.: Addison-Wesley, 1980.

Nicolay, John, and John Hay. *Abraham Lincoln*. 10 vols. New York: Century, 1902.

Olszewski, George J. *Restoration of Ford's Theatre*. Washington, D.C.: U.S. Government Printing Office, 1963.

Pendel, Thomas F. *Thirty-six Years in the White House*. Washington, D.C.: Neale, 1902.

Pitman, Benn. *The Assassination of President Lincoln and the Trial of the Conspirators*. New York: Funk and Wagnalls, 1954.

Ray, Jo. *American Assassins*. Minneapolis: Lerner Publications, 1974.

Raymond, Henry. *The Life and Public Services of Abraham Lincoln*. New York: Derby and Miller, 1865.

Reck, W. Emerson. *A. Lincoln: His Last Twenty-four Hours*. Jefferson, N.C.: McFarland, 1987.

Starr, John, Jr. *Lincoln's Last Day*. New York: Frederick A. Stoles, 1922.

Stern, Philip Van Doren. *The Man Who Killed Lincoln*. New York: Literary Guild of America, 1939.

Taft, Charles Sabin. *Abraham Lincoln's Last Hours*. Chicago: Blackcat Press, 1934.

Taylor, Tom. *Our American Cousin*. Washington, D.C.: Beacham, 1990.

Turner, Justin C., and Linda Levitt. *Mary Todd Lincoln: Her Life and Letters.* New York: Knopf, 1972.

Turner, Thomas. *Beware the People Weeping.* Baton Rouge: Louisiana State University Press, 1982.

———. *While Lincoln Lay Dying.* Philadelphia: Union League of Philadelphia, 1968.

Weichmann, Louis. *A True History of the Assassination of Abraham Lincoln and of the Conspiracy of 1865.* New York: Vintage Books, 1977.

INDEX